Virginia Kelley

LEADING
WITH MY
HEART

WITH JAMES MORGAN

SIMON & SCHUSTER
New York London Toronto Sydney Tokyo Singapore

For my family, the reason I've run the race.

To grow up female in the South is to inherit a set of directives that stay with you for life. This is true for high-born ladies as well as farm women.

I grew up believing that at heart a woman was a steely, silent creature, with secrets no man could ever know, and she was always—always—stronger than any man. ("Now you don't have to let on about it," my mother would advise.)

—from *Womenfolks,* by
Hot Springs native Shirley Abbott

Foreword

INAUGURAL DAY, JANUARY 20, 1993. I woke up early, like I always do, but never in my life had I seen a morning like this.

Back in Hot Springs I get up around 4:30, because I like to have those peaceful predawn hours to myself. I'm a firm believer in the soothing power of a routine, and mine never wavers. After finishing in the bathroom, I go to the front door and send Champ, my German shepherd, out to the driveway to fetch the paper. While he's going for it, I stand at the door and pray—not that he'll find the paper, as a friend of mine thought when I told him about this regimen; Champ seems to have a pretty good nose for news. My prayer is a simple and very personal one: Thank you, God, for letting me see another morning. Then I ask a blessing for my sons and my husband and my friends, and after that, as the sun begins to come up across Lake Hamilton, I turn on the coffeepot and open the paper and settle in to see what craziness the world has gotten into since last I checked.

But on that January morning in Washington I was at loose ends. We—my husband, Dick; his brother, Al; and Al's wife, Nancy—were staying at the Mayflower Hotel. It was a lovely suite, with the Presidential Seal in the ceiling and baskets of fruit everywhere. I ordered up some coffee and tried to read the paper, but it was no use. I couldn't get past the headline of The Washington Post: "An Oath at Noon Opens Clinton Era." I may've pulled back the drapes and peeked out the window, I don't remember. Or maybe I saw it later on TV. But I know that even at this early hour, on this bitterly cold, clear winter day, thousands of people were already making their way toward the Mall to be there when my son became President of the United States.

We were due at the church for an early prayer service, so I fell back on another of my morning rituals—putting on my makeup. Actually, I sleep in my makeup, a habit I got into when I was working— I sure didn't want to scare a patient to death if I got called to the hospital in the middle of the night. I change paint only once a day; when you wear as much as I do, you don't want to repeat the process. I've gotten it down to about forty-five minutes, but back when I smoked, it took an hour and a half. That's one reason I quit smoking—that and the little wrinkles I got around my lips from puffing on a cigarette. I hate wrinkles, even in my clothes. I have friends who've asked the doctor about getting face-lifts, and he tells them not to even talk to him till they're ready to stop smoking.

I used to take a cosmetic case with me when I traveled, but it got so heavy I started wanting to stay home. Then somebody told me about carrying makeup in clear Ziploc bags, which is what I do now. I match my lipstick and other makeup to the clothes I'm going to be wearing, and that's all I take with me.

At home, though, it's different. In every house I've ever lived in, I've had a dressing table with my paraphernalia in exactly the same place. One of Bill's high school friends came over the other day and sat on the tub while I put on my face, and she said, "Virginia, I could walk in this bathroom blindfolded and put my hands on anything on that table. That's the same arrangement you had at 1011 Park Avenue and the same one you had at 213 Scully Street." Those were the houses in Hot Springs where Bill and Roger grew up. And she's right. I keep my radio over by my right hand, and my little palette with all my eyebrow pencils on the left. In the center is my tray with all my perfumes, and next to it are all my lipsticks.

The first thing I do when I sit down is put on my hair net; I pay too much at the hairdresser's every week to ruin it all by getting makeup in my hair. Then I put in my contacts. I don't have eyebrows so I have to draw them on, and I've found that contacts make putting on my eyebrows a lot easier. After the contacts, I wash my face. Fortunately, I have oily skin, so I don't have to waste time with cream. I've saved a million dollars by having oily skin. Speaking of money, I use the cheapest astringent I can find—it's called O.J.'s Beauty Lotion, and it costs about a dollar and eighty cents. So I clean my face with that, and then I open my drawer and get my bases: Max Factor, as cheap as you can buy. But it does the job, so I put that on and go over it with a wet sponge that has some pancake makeup on it.

While my face dries, I go into the bedroom and make up the bed. I don't just make up the bed, though: I flip on the TV to catch CNN, hoping I can see Bill. Sometimes when I watch him, I can separate the man from my son. In those moments I see him as the world leader he is, the eloquent speaker and erudite thinker and earnest consensus builder. Other times, especially when he's hurting, he's just a big old gray-headed version of my little boy. Speaking of Bill hurting, I also tune in so I can see what awful thing Bob Dole has said about my son since yesterday. Bill's above this sort of thing, but I'm keeping a list.

After the bed's made, I switch off the TV and go back to my dressing table and put on my eyeliner and my eyelashes. There's a benefit to using so much makeup—besides the obvious, which is that it enables me to go out in public. Sitting there looking at yourself for so long eye to eye gives you a chance to think out your problems, to remember who you are underneath the paint.

During the campaign, a lot was written about my life, and much of it was made out to be a real-life soap opera. I'll admit I've been dealt my share of tough hands, and in fact there's an Elvis song I particularly love because I identify with it so much: "This Time You Gave Me a Mountain." I've been given many hills to climb, and even a few mountains. But you know what? I wouldn't change a thing. I had a mother who met every day with anger and took it out on me and my father. My firstborn son never knew his father, because a blowout on a Missouri highway took him from us when I was six months pregnant. My second-born son grew to hate his father, for his alcoholism and the way he treated me. My third husband, a good, good man, was never the same after he made a mistake and had to go to prison. I had lost all three of those husbands—to accident, cancer, and diabetes—by the time I was fifty-one.

At the same time, various forces in Hot Springs tried for thirty years to destroy my career as a nurse anesthetist, because I was a woman who wouldn't fall into line with the way they wanted to do business. My career was vital to me, not just financially but emotionally, because when you've lost three husbands, you have to have something to cling to. Besides my children, work was it for me. Work was where my life was okay. But they finally succeeded in forcing me out. Then my precious son Roger, for God only knows what reasons, turned to drugs and alcohol, and I had to watch while he was handcuffed and taken off to the penitentiary. Then I discovered I had breast cancer, and two years after that was first treated, I found out it had spread to my back. I'm climbing that mountain now.

&

Some people have said I look like a spider with these eyelashes, but I like them. I've worn false eyelashes since they first came out, I guess. If they're put on properly, I think they're pretty. And they're good protection. Now when I have to go to the eye doctor without them, I feel like everything in this world is flying into my eyes. Oftentimes I'll take them with me to the doctor's office so when he's through I can put them back on immediately.

While all that glue dries, I start drawing on my eyebrows. I've lost twenty-five years of sleep because I have to jump up and start drawing on my face every morning. No telling what I could've accomplished in this world if I had been born with eyebrows. These days you can have them tattooed on if you want. Eyeliner, too. But that's just never appealed to me. As much as I complain about it, maybe there's something therapeutic in the process itself.

Children, especially, are fascinated by my eyebrows. One time years ago when I took my son Roger to kindergarten, one of the kids started pointing at my eyebrows and saying, "Mickey Mouse! Mickey Mouse!" Oh, the honesty of children. Chelsea used to inspect them really closely, and she would sometimes say, "Ginger, you've got one higher than the other." There was even a brief moment when I decided to heck with it, I'm not going to all that trouble—who needs eyebrows, anyway? So I went out without any. Do you know how bald you look from your chin to your hairline if you don't have any eyebrows? They're put there for a reason—to hold your face together.

Speaking of holding together, I think I've done pretty darn well, considering all that's been thrown my way. In fact, I would say that I've led a charmed life in which the good has far, far outweighed the bad. I've loved and I've been loved, and I've had the joy of raising the two kindest, dearest sons a mother could ask for. I have wonderful friends, whom I see or talk with every day, and who have stood by me through all the crises. I had a career that fulfilled me, despite the battles; heck, maybe even the battles fulfilled a little part of me, if the truth were known.

One friend of mine, when we were discussing my writing this book, said to me, "Virginia, the thing about you is, you lead with your heart." I had never thought about it that way, but it's absolutely true. I'm so softhearted it hurts. I love people. I trust people. I will take you at face value, and until you do something that can be proven to be detrimental to me, I'll defend you with everything I have. I don't care how many people tell me otherwise, because I don't listen to hearsay. And I'm not judgmental. The only way I judge you is by how you treat me. I would walk through hellfire for a friend, and I would never betray anybody in this world. I believe deeply in the principles of trust and loyalty. That's the way I was brought up: "There's going to be a day when you don't have anything but your word; please keep it."

Of course, there's another side to this leading-with-my-heart business. At times in my life I've consulted my heart when others might've thought I ought to consult my head. I took Roger Clinton back—remarried this man who had abused me and my children for twelve years—because I felt sorry for him. Because he was in pain. And I don't regret it. I fought tooth and nail against the men who, because they were MDs and I was a lowly nurse anesthetist, expected to just waltz into town and have me suddenly work for them. Ask them today and I'll bet they'll tell you it was a long, long waltz.

The way I've gotten through life is by living in the present. Bill Clinton laughs at me because, unlike him, for most of my life I had no concern for history—no interest in antiques, no sense of historical events, no real curiosity about my own ancestors. You know what they say about people who don't pay attention to history: They're doomed to repeat the mistakes of the past. I've done that a time or two. But I've always maintained that whatever's in someone's past is past, and I don't need to know about it. That's my heart talking, not my head. I've trained myself not to worry about what-ifs, either, because nine times out of ten, what-ifs never happen. And when bad things do happen, I brainwash myself to put them out of my mind.

I call it brainwashing, a term my sons have some problems with, and in fact the process is more elaborate than that. Inside my head I construct an airtight box. I keep inside it what I want to think about, and everything else stays beyond the walls. Inside is white, outside is black: The only gray I trust is the streak in my hair. Inside is love and friends and optimism. Outside is negativity, can't-doism, and any criticism of me and mine. Most of the time this box is strong as steel. I just tell myself I'm going to be okay—I am going to be okay. And I get up every day and I push ahead, and I never quit.

This is not the same as denial; this is choosing how you want to live your life, no matter what kind of life is thrown at you. You have to focus—like a laser, as Bill would say—on the good things. That's where your strength comes from, and God knows, you need every ounce of strength you can muster in order to get up and face each and every day.

So I'm a shameless reveler in my sons' careers and accomplishments. I've sat in smoky clubs to hear Roger sing, and I've worn funny hats and worked in Bill's campaigns. I cherish my friends; there's a group of us called The Birthday Club—twelve of the craziest, most fun-loving women you ever saw—and we get together for lunch at least once a month to celebrate one another's birthdays. But we don't need birthdays as an excuse: A handful of us meet for lunch every day. And when we do, we sip a glass of wine or maybe have a Bloody Mary, and we cut up like schoolgirls. Every day during racing season I go to Oaklawn Park, where I sit in a box with one of my oldest, dearest friends, and I almost always win a few bucks betting on the horses. Even if I don't win, I don't lose much, because I'm a die-hard two-dollar bettor.

And at the end of the day Dick pours me a Scotch and water or two, and I sit on the couch and watch the news (a friend of mine says that since Bill's been President, CNN is my home movies). While I'm doing that, Dick sips his vodka and fixes supper. I used to cook when my boys were growing up, but I don't do it anymore—and I mean never. I'll admit it took me a long time to get over the guilt of not cooking, but I think I've finally got it licked.

&

After my eyebrows, I do my rouge, and then my lipstick. When it comes to lipsticks, I say the brighter the better. I have every color in the rainbow, and I match my lipstick color to my clothes. If I'm going to wear bright yellow or orange or something like that, then I like a lipstick that's not deep burgundy or some other color that'll clash. I read someplace not long ago that that's not necessary, but it's my taste. It's just me.

You used to be able to buy lipstick that would last all day, but lipstick just hasn't been the same since the Food and Drug Administration got involved in it. Today they put in all this moisturizer that makes it run. Of course, you can blot it and that'll help some, but not completely. I looked and looked and finally found a brand that's a little drier than most, but I still have to freshen up my lipstick during the day. I'm also a firm believer that if you put it on the right way, it'll last. I have a pencil that I use to line my lips with, and then I fill in slowly. I also use a brush to really smooth the color in, and I let it set a long time before I blot it.

After the makeup is done I take the net off my hair and perk it up with my comb. Then I get dressed and I'm ready to go. On inauguration day, I wore a black suit. As much as I love bright colors, black is really my color. My third husband, Jeff Dwire, taught me that. He was a hairdresser and was an absolute artist with hair. It was Jeff—long before he was my husband—who persuaded me to leave the gray streak in my hair. That streak had first started to gray back when I was in high school, and I had always colored it. When Jeff saw it, he said, "If you want to color it, go someplace else to get your hair done. I'm not going to hide that streak."

That's sort of the way I feel about this book. To most of the country I'm known—besides for being Bill and Roger's mother—for my weird hair, my heavy makeup, my loud colors, and my penchant for playing the horses. I'm a character, a cut-up, a kook. That's me, all right, but it's not all of me. When I sat down to write this book, I decided it was time to take off the makeup. Time to let people see beneath the surface. Time to stop coloring all streaks, no matter how wild or how gray. Even though I'm far from perfect, I'm proud of the life I've lived.

And, as a betting woman, I bet you my hat you'll find it colorful enough without the rouge.

Hot Springs
December 1993

One

BODCAW, ARKANSAS, is a little town in the southwestern part of the state, the area where pine trees grow straight and tall right up to the edge of winding two-lane highways. If you take a shady drive on any one of the roads leading into Bodcaw, you'll most likely encounter a logging truck, since timber is big business around here. Also oil, especially a little further to the south and east, toward Smackover and El Dorado. When you grow up in this part of Arkansas, as I did in the 1920s and '30s, there's a dimension beyond the usual horizonless rural life: Texas lies a few miles to the west, and Louisiana about the same distance to the south. It may not be Europe, but at least you know something else is out there.

I was born in Bodcaw, population about one hundred, but right away my mother declared that she wasn't raising any child of hers in the country. Actually, I wasn't even born in Bodcaw proper; the true site was a four-room, tin-roofed board house across a dirt road from my grandfather's cotton farm, in a tiny settlement known as the Ebenezer Community. The house is still standing, shaded now by a huge cottonwood tree that I don't even remember being there when I was a child, but I guess it was. Please don't tell me I'm older than that massive tree. My birthdate was June 6, 1923. I was named Virginia Dell Cassidy, Dell being just a name my mother found pleasing. My mother, Edith Valeria Grisham Cassidy, was twenty-two when I was born, and my father, James Eldridge Cassidy, turned twenty-three a couple of months later. In fact, his birthday is August 19, the same as my son Bill's.

Like so many rural areas, the Ebenezer Community was made up of just a few families—in this case, the Grishams, the Cassidys, and the Russells. The Russells and the Cassidys had come to Arkansas from Alabama in the 1800s, already intertwined by marriage. The Grishams—my mother's family—seem to have been here forever. When I was growing up, we had more to do with them than with the Cassidys—probably out of sheer force of my mother's will, and the fact that she didn't like anybody else very much.

My mother was the oldest child in her family, which also included her sister, Opal, whom I came to call Otie, and who has since died. The baby of the family, Oren, whom everybody calls Buddy, is now in his eighties, and he's turned into a kind of philosopher in his old age. In 1980, when Bill was defeated for his second term as governor of Arkansas, one of the first people he went to see was his great-uncle Buddy. Bill asked him what he should do, and Buddy said, "You go back to the people and you tell them you're sorry, that you made mistakes, and that you've learned your lesson." That's exactly what Bill did, and he was reelected. In 1992, just after he was voted in as President, he went to see Buddy again, and Buddy gave him some advice Bill will never forget: "Washington is like a big old greased pig, and you've got to hold tight to its tail, the closer in the better, because the tail gets smaller and slipperier the farther out you get."

There's a wisdom that comes from being close to the land, and my family—on both sides—had been about as close to the land as you can get. Both the Cassidys and the Grishams had farms, and all the children were expected to work in the fields. Uncle Buddy only finished the fourth grade, and my mother quit after the eleventh. I don't know why she quit, but I do know it wasn't because she didn't have ambition. I've never seen anybody burn with intensity the way she did. She had coal black eyes that came from some long-ago strain of Indian blood in her family, and those eyes could bore in on you and almost disintegrate you with their heat. She was a beautiful woman—a little heavy, but she took meticulous care of herself. Not so incidentally, she also wore a good bit of makeup.

Her worst trait was her temper, which was uncontrollable. She was angry somewhere deep inside her, and she took it out on anybody who happened to be around. For years I've tried to figure out where her anger came from, what it was about. Maybe she just resented her circumstances—the cruel trick of fate that caused her to be born to an impoverished farm family in south Arkansas, and not to some refined and wealthy parents who were lucky enough to live someplace else. She grew up in the fields, working shoulder to shoulder with her brother and sister, and when she married, she naturally married someone whose life had been just like hers. You position yourself to have opportunities, and there weren't many opportunities in Bodcaw in the early 1920s. Your life became like the land itself—the same cycles over and over, but never really changing much for the better.

So when Edith Grisham married Eldridge Cassidy in early January 1922, all they did was cross the little dirt road in front of her parents' house and move a hundred yards or so away. It wasn't much of a leap, but at least it got Mother out from under her parents' thumb so she could maybe do something better. Looking back, I believe her ambition mainly took the form of wanting to improve herself financially. She was very concerned with that. Somebody once asked me if her anger came from wishing she had married a rich man, and maybe that was part of it later. But there weren't all that many rich men to be found in Arkansas in the twenties, and certainly not in Bodcaw. My father may not've been her ideal mate, but he was high on the local list of available men. And besides, she could control him.

I loved my father as much as it's possible for a daughter to love her dad, but the truth is, he was too good for his own good. He was kind and gentle, and he loved laughing and fishing and storytelling and people—especially me. He called me Ginger, and he was the only person in the world to call me that until Chelsea Clinton came along. Now she calls me Ginger, and every time she does, it reminds me of my father.

He was the second oldest of the four Cassidy children, three boys and one girl. Daddy's older brother was named Oscar, and then came Daddy, and after him there were Minnie and Colonel. I don't know where my grandparents got that name, but at least it showed they had faith that their son would amount to something. They could've named him Private.

As I said, I wasn't as close to my father's family as I was to my mother's. For one thing, my paternal grandfather had died back in 1908, so I never knew him at all. And the only thing I remember about my father's mother was hearing my own mother say, "I just can't please her, I just can't please her." So it sounds like the sparks flew between them.

Not that I'm at all surprised. My mother created sparks wherever she went. Which means that my father and I were the ones who got burned the most.

&a.

But I'm getting ahead of my story. When I was born, my mother announced that she wasn't about to bring up her child in the country. I don't know what Daddy thought about that—maybe he was ready for a change, though he wasn't exactly prepared for any career but farming. But Mother didn't give him any choice: Five months later we moved to the big city of Hope, twelve miles away.

It seemed like a big city, anyway. By this time, Hope—with a population of around five thousand—had been incorporated for some fifty years, and it had grown and prospered, mainly because it was on the Cairo & Fulton railroad line, someday to become the powerful Missouri Pacific. One of the town's early historians even said that Hope was the most important point between St. Louis and Texas, if you didn't count Little Rock. Hope was a place where things *happened*.

The sounds of train whistles echo through my memories of childhood, because it seems we always lived near the tracks. The train depot was the very first building put up in Hope, and the town naturally took shape around it. Elegant strangers would step off the train and put up at the plush Capitol Hotel, just across Division Street from the depot, or at the ritzy Barlow Hotel around the corner on Elm. Some of the downtown buildings were very ornate, and the sidewalks were covered with canopies so people could stroll through the shopping area without worrying about rain or sun. The downtown and main residential streets had been paved in 1920, and cars were becoming pretty commonplace. After all, in the twenties cotton was king, and Hope was the marketplace for all of Hempstead County. One downtown street was even known as Cotton Row because that's where all the buying and selling took place—and where quite a few people became very, very wealthy.

Hope was also big enough to have entertainment. Traveling tent shows would set up in a vacant lot near downtown, and entire families would come out on balmy evenings to catch the show, which might be anything from a carnival to a minstrel to vaudeville. The Barnum & Bailey Circus even came one time. Hope had several theaters as well, including the Queen, the Saenger, and the Grand— which also had a stage for traveling road shows. On summer evenings, young men played minor league baseball in a park on North Elm, and of course the high school teams brought the fans out in droves.

So it's no wonder my mother wanted to move from the monotonous country to the aptly called Hope (named, by the way, for the daughter of one of the town's founders). In Hope, at least, there were possibilities. My daddy found work right away, getting on with the Bruner-Ivory Handle Company, which made walking canes, ladder rungs, shepherd crooks, ax handles, and probably a lot of products I don't even know about. I have a photograph of him standing in that factory, which must've been a huge change from the kind of work he had been used to.

At first we lived in a rental house, but the first house I really remember was the house on Foster Avenue, two blocks south of the train line and a few blocks east of downtown. It was a small house, maybe four or five rooms, but I have wonderful memories of that place because somehow my father had saved up enough money to *buy* it. He was so happy and proud.

After a time he left the handle factory to take a job delivering ice. Of all the jobs my father had or was to have, I believe this one was his favorite. There were five or six routes around town, and Daddy had one of them. He would wear a black leather apron that hooked at his throat and went down his back to keep the ice from dripping on him. I can see it as clearly as if he were standing in the room with me. It had pockets at the bottom to catch the water as the ice melted. Daddy wasn't a big man, but he could take those ice tongs and hook a hundred-pound block of ice and throw it over his shoulder like it was nothing. And he could cut the ice exactly, so that if you wanted just twelve pounds, he knew right where to score it.

The icehouse was on Walker Avenue just past the tracks, which was about three blocks from where we lived. In the early days of the job, my father drove a horse-drawn wagon. He and his helper, Dick Moore, who was about twelve at the time, would get over to the icehouse at around three A.M. and load the wagon. Then they would start their route, Daddy driving and both of them delivering. From time to time when the ice was running low, Daddy would call the icehouse and the ice truck would come and replenish his supply. I remember he used to come by our house every day about midmorning, and he would always stop the horse and shout for me to come give him a hug. That was the highlight of my morning. I must've been four or five at the time.

As I've said before, my father loved to be with people. He had an infectious smile, which not only lit up the room but accentuated his long chin—the one I obviously inherited from him. He was kind, too. His route was residential, not commercial, which meant that the ice blocks he delivered were smaller and so he could use young boys as his helpers. Dick Moore worked for him for years, but one summer Sheriff Wilson asked Daddy if he would hire the sheriff's eleven-year-old son, John. Daddy said he couldn't afford the twenty-five cents a day to pay John, but Sheriff Wilson said he would pay Daddy so he could pay John. Young John worked for Daddy for two summers, and he felt very proud of himself for having a real job. It wasn't until years later that he found out his father had concocted this scheme to keep him out of trouble.

John Wilson and Dick Moore still live in Hope, and they love to tell about the days they worked the ice route with my father. John recalls he once asked Daddy to pay him in two dimes and a nickel—"so I can feel the change." During the Depression, the sensation of money jingling in your pocket was rare indeed. Of course, John being eleven, he lost one of the dimes on the way home from work. He says he *still* looks for that dime whenever he's on that street.

John and Dick called my father Cass. Another story they tell is how they used to kid him because he liked to stop off and have coffee with various customers—usually, John says, the prettiest ones. The boys would drive on and keep delivering, and Daddy would catch up with them a few houses down.

❧

Maybe my mother had heard that last story, because it was in Hope that she began her nightly screaming fits.

I remember lying awake in the dark in that little house on Foster Avenue, listening to my mother shrieking at my father in their bedroom next door. Just pacing the floor and screaming. Sometimes this would go on all night.

And he would say, "Please, please, the baby." He always referred to me as the baby, even after I was older. But he would say, "Please, the baby has to go to school tomorrow. Please."

But she would keep on. What it was, she was accusing him of things involving other women. She was insanely jealous, though as I grew older, I began to doubt that the jealousy was real. She was just using it, I decided, as an excuse to express her anger.

But these fits went on for years, and I didn't really know what to think. I couldn't believe that my daddy, as devoted as he was to both of us, would do anything with another woman. And I adored my mother, really loved her, but I couldn't understand her behavior. It hurt me very much to lie there listening, hearing my sweet daddy pleading with her to calm down. I don't remember her naming any names; these accusations were just in general. But she would keep shrieking, and sometimes she would lunge at him and try to hurt him physically. He protected himself, but he never took the offensive. I thought at the time, *Why don't you stand up to her, maybe even strike her once? Maybe, just maybe, that might teach her a lesson.* But he didn't. These days we hear mostly about wife abuse, but believe me, there's another side to that story.

My mother was one of those people with a vindictive, manipulative mind. She would go out of her way to help people—until they crossed her. Then she would stop at nothing to undermine them, to hurt them in terrible ways. Later on in Hot Springs, I saw a nurse trying to cost another nurse her job, and I thought, *That's so like my mother.*

With Daddy, she knew exactly where to hit him. After the stock market crash of 1929 and the onset of the Depression, money became extremely tight. In fact, Daddy lost the Foster Avenue house—just couldn't keep up the payments. I thought he was going to die, it hurt him so much. And not for his sake, but for Mother's and mine. I remember, he used to always make sure I had a new Easter dress. He would save his pennies and I would look like a million dollars. Then one day, he stopped by the house on his route and said he had something to tell me. "I just can't buy you a new dress this year," he said, and the tears welled up in his eyes.

"That's all right, Daddy," I said, and I put my arms around him and hugged him tight. Never again did I care anything about having a new Easter dress every year.

But on occasions like that, Mother inevitably blamed my father for failing us. When we lost the Foster Avenue house, it was all his fault—never mind that people were going broke left and right. The poor man just couldn't win.

After we left Foster Avenue, we rented a house on Elm Street, just south of town. I must've been twelve or so by then. In those days, you could pick up the phone and order your groceries, and they would be delivered. But doing it that way cost money, of course, and we were almost totally without money at this time. So we weren't ordering a lot of groceries; we were shopping carefully, making sure we bought only what we absolutely needed.

One day on Elm Street I heard Mother standing in the kitchen ordering groceries. And as young as I was, I knew she shouldn't be doing that. Later, when Daddy got home from work, he walked in and saw the bags of groceries all over the table and his face sank. He slumped like a man defeated, and he cried, and Mother acted like nothing was wrong—except she had that edge to her demeanor, like she knew exactly what she had done. What she had done was to willfully plunge him even deeper in debt as payback for something that had displeased her. It was one of the cruelest acts I've ever witnessed.

❧

A friend recently sent me a picture of me taken at about this time. I'm standing, posed before an elaborate backdrop that shows a massive staircase rising toward a huge fairy-tale castle. I'm wearing a raincoat, with the buttons fastened all the way to the collar. The friend who sent it says the picture was taken on my way home from school one day when it was raining and I ducked into a store where they had those photo booths.

I've been studying this photograph a lot lately, trying to remember who I was when it was made. The look on my face isn't exactly dreamy, the way you might think someone posed before a fairy-tale scene would be. My head is cocked to the side, and there's the hint of a smile on my face. But my eyes are hooded, not revealing much that's going on behind them. By this time, I guess, I had already learned to keep my dark secrets to myself.

I was not a dreamer, not ever. If anything, I was a planner, someone who looked for a plausible—not a magic—way to get from point A to point B. At that age I was probably mainly concerned with getting ten cents to go to the picture show; later on, there would be high school clubs and boyfriends; and still later, what to do with myself after high school was over.

As a young girl, I spent a lot of time with my mother. During the Depression we had a car, a Pontiac, that we usually drove only on Saturdays. We couldn't afford to drive it the rest of the week. The car was black or navy blue, I don't remember exactly. But I do recall that Daddy had bought it used, and that he was so proud of that car. Every Saturday Mother and I would drive downtown and park on Main Street, near the grocery store, and we would get out and watch the people and visit with them, too. Saturday was the day everybody came to town to do their trading—country people, town people, everybody all together. And Mother and I would browse in the window of the Ladies Specialty Shop—I was already attracted to bright-colored clothes—and we would look around at Mooreland's Drugstore, and maybe, if I was lucky, we would get something at Louis's Confectionery or the Checkered Cafe. As poor as everybody was during those years, I remember Saturday as a wonderful day.

Occasionally, on Sundays, Daddy, Mother, and I would drive out to Bodcaw to visit my grandparents. I remember that Mother would get furious if Daddy had to stop and buy gasoline. She would just throw a fit, as though he had had time to buy gas during the week, when he worked from before dawn until late in the afternoon. *Why hadn't* she *bought gasoline?* I wondered.

Incidentally, that Pontiac of my father's came to a sad end. While we were living on Elm Street, we woke up one night and the car was ablaze. We were never exactly sure what happened, but Daddy smoked, and we figured he must've let a hot ash fall down in the seat or something. Fortunately, he had insurance, so the car was paid for. But of course there was no insurance to be had against my mother's anger.

During the week I spent as much time as possible with my friends. The girls I ran around with were all from families with more money and higher social standing than mine. One was the banker's daughter, another the postmaster's daughter, and so on, and yet for some reason I just fit in. I guess it was a matter of attitude. I've never felt inferior to anybody. Once, in grade school, a girl told me she couldn't play with me because I was from the country. "That's all right," I said. "I have lots of friends." The only hint of our relative situations was that occasionally, when some big movie like *Gone With the Wind* would come to town for a couple of weeks, some of the girls would see it two or three times. I couldn't afford that.

So I played a lot of bridge, even though I was never wild about cards, and I listened to the radio—I remember my freshman year in high school I fell in love with the Andrews Sisters, whose song "Bei Mir Bist du Schön" nobody could pronounce, but it sounded great. During the school year, we girls would all walk to town together after class and go get refreshments at Louis's. We would stay there awhile, and then we might go over to one of the girls' houses—except mine, of course. My mother didn't like for me to bring my friends over, and considering her temperament, that was fine by me. In later life, though, I made sure that my sons' house was the center of activity for them and their friends, because I know firsthand how important it is to a child for his friends to want to come to *his* home.

Part of Mother's problem with my having friends over was undoubtedly that she was busy studying. One day she was reading the paper and she saw an ad for a course in nursing that you could take by correspondence. Right then and there she announced that she was going to become a nurse. The course was out of Chicago, as I recall—the Chicago School of Nursing. Daddy and I were surprised, but she meant it. For something like eighteen months she received her lessons and pored over them at the kitchen table and then shipped them back as quickly as she could. Her energy was amazing, because while she was doing this, she was also keeping house and fixing meals and taking care of me.

Finally, at the end of all that work, she received her degree as a practical nurse. It seemed to make a tremendous difference in her attitude. A doctor friend of mine in Hope recalls the day she got her nurse's cap and cloak and how angry the other nurses were, because they had gone to regular nurses schools and Mother had gotten her degree by correspondence. But Mother didn't care: a degree was a degree, and a cloak was a cloak. After that, even though she was still intense, still vindictive, and her gaze could still sear you, she obviously felt better about herself, because the night shrieking seemed to fall off a little. Not completely, but a little.

Of course, maybe she was just too tired to fight. After she got her diploma, Mother was gone a lot, working long hours as a private-duty nurse. This was a break for me. Mother had always been very strict, very protective, which I had grown to think of as her trying to control my life. She wouldn't let me learn to swim, for example; *she* was afraid of the water, so she wanted me to be. I learned to swim later, enduring the humiliation of taking lessons along with four-year-old Bill.

Whenever I did something wrong, Mother would whip me furiously. Mostly she used her hand, but sometimes she would step outside and choose a special kind of switch she favored—one that inevitably drew blood from my legs. In general, I thought I was a perfect child and that she was overreacting. But to this day, I still remember the sting of one particular whipping that was entirely justified.

I was probably three years old. One day *I* was playing in the dirt in front of the Foster Avenue house when an old Negro woman walked by. "Hi, nigger," I said. Those were not enlightened times racially, and that awful word was one you were likely to hear quite frequently around town.

But not much in my house. Not in that tone of voice, anyway. My mother happened to be in the living room and heard me say that. Judas priest, she tore out of that house and wore me out. Didn't even take time to snap off a switch. Don't try to tell me a spanking doesn't stay with you. But in that instance, the whipping left a more lasting impression than even my mother's palm print: Bill and Roger's enlightened views on race started long before they were born, with that furious spanking in Hope in 1926.

৯৯

With Mother gone, I had some blessed breathing room—time to decide some things for myself, to start becoming who *I* wanted to be.

Maybe because I was an only child—and one whose home life left
something to be desired—I had already begun keeping my own coun-
sel on important matters, and some of them I wasn't too happy about.
For example, I knew I was developing a temper like my mother's: I
would sound off at people sometimes for no reason, although I tried
my best to keep from letting it show. Even as a girl I was learning to
brainwash myself. I had also inherited some of my mother's will-
fulness—which could be good or bad, depending on how I used it—
as well as her energy and ambition.

Today my son Roger describes me as "street smart," and to some
extent that's true: I've learned to get along in the world as it is. But
street smart conveys an image of ruthlessness, which is not me at
all. I'm tough when I have to be, but never ruthless. I had also inherited my father's outgoing personality and his love for people. If
my mother saw the bad in people, my father saw the good, and so
did I. Some people have called this trait naïveté, but I prefer to think
of it as hopefulness. I love people, and I dearly want them to be good
and loyal and trustworthy and true. Maybe the key is that I like myself—did even as a girl (except, of course, for thinking I was fat and
having no eyebrows)—and so I'm able to like and trust others. Bill
and Roger have inherited this trait, and we've all been burned by it
at times. But better that than negative and cynical and suspicious,
like my mother. To the extent that I was like her, I compensated by
calling attention to my cheerfulness, my flamboyance, my optimism,
my upbeat outspokenness. I kept the darker feelings inside, deep
down and out of sight.

About the time I got to high school, I also decided I wasn't going
to cater to my mother's bullying anymore. This wasn't something I
announced with great fanfare, mind you—I was gutsy, but not crazy.
It was, however, a decision I made and was determined to stick with.
Because I had her ambition, I knew I'd never be able to do what I
wanted in life if I succumbed to her tyranny all the time. I remember once in about my junior year, after we had left Elm Street and
moved to a new house over on Hervey Street, I was sitting upstairs
in the bathroom smoking. I had decided I was fat, and somebody

told me that if you smoked, you could lose weight. So I was puffing away like mad—and suddenly the door swung open. There was my mother, looking aghast, and she said to me, "Virginia, are you smoking?" The room was positively blue with smoke.

I looked up at her, then I held the cigarette out and gave it a couple of dramatic flicks, scattering the ash. "Why, no, Mother," I said. "Whatever gave you that idea?"

Being a teenager, I was hormonally prone to such a stance, of course. But I also feel, even today, that I *was* capable of looking after myself by then. There's another picture of me from that time that amazes some people when they look at it today. It was taken during my senior year, and that group of girls I ran with had posed in bathing suits for the local paper, the *Hope Star*. We were positioned around the diving platform, and I was standing at the very top. I had a nice figure, but the thing that people comment on is my facial expression: the camera had caught a look of supreme self-confidence that makes me appear more mature than my years. As one friend says, "This was before people talked about 'attitude,' but you had it even then."

I guess I did. I had reached puberty early, at age eleven; I started menstruating at school one day, and I ran home in a panic, blood coursing down my legs. My mother had told me nothing about such things. Later our housekeeper, France—a black girl only about a year older than I, and so short that Mother had to pull up a chair for her to wash the dishes—told me she had seen a spot of blood on my underwear and had urged Mother to sit me down and explain what was happening. But Mother hadn't been able to bring herself to do it.

So I developed early and alone. I discovered boys early, too, and I began to date. You can imagine how hawkeyed my mother was about the boys who came to our house. But it was in my relationships with boys that I struck a major, and lifelong, blow against my mother's way of doing things.

Some young girls—women, too, for that matter—find jealousy a game. In other words, they like to make their boyfriends jealous just to make themselves feel more desirable. They're flattered when a boy flies into a rage and accuses them of looking at someone else. Well, I had seen what jealousy could do to people. I had heard it screeching in the night. I think I knew, even then, that jealousy isn't a game, it's a disease. It's as bad as alcoholism or temper. Nine times out of ten, it's totally unfounded, because most of us, when we're committed to someone, have integrity. And false accusations can make home life miserable. Much later, when Bill's friends would be over at our house in Hot Springs, I would advise them, especially the girls: Do not be flattered by jealousy.

I can truthfully say that I have never felt one pang of jealousy toward anybody in my life, and that attitude started when I was a girl. There was a song out when I was young called "Don't Fence Me In." I liked that song, and I liked the ideas it conveyed. I dated several boys during my first couple of years in high school; I wasn't jealous of them, and if any of them got jealous because I was going out with others, I crossed him off my list.

But my favorite boyfriend was Richard Fenwick. He now lives in Camden, Arkansas, and Dick Kelley and I see him and his wife from time to time. Richard was a year older than I was, and his family didn't have any more money than mine did—maybe they had less. But Richard worked at the movie theater, which was a plum job for a high school student in those days. He started out selling popcorn, as I recall, and then he worked himself up to some job where he was always in a coat and tie. It was *very* impressive to go to the movies with your girlfriends and have your boyfriend be the man in charge. Plus, I probably got a little extra popcorn in my bag.

Mother and Daddy both approved of Richard, but I loved him anyway. I should say that my mother approved of him providing we didn't become too serious, but by my junior year, he and I were a couple. Maybe we still occasionally went out with other people, but mostly it was just us. We didn't have a lot of money to do things—as Richard says, "If you had fifteen cents, you could have a date. You went down to the Checkered Cafe and a cherry Coke was a nickel. Then you'd buy five Lucky Strike cigarettes for a penny apiece, and you'd sit there and smoke up those five cigarettes and sip that Coke and then you'd walk home." Whenever I think of Dentyne chewing gum, I think of Richard, because he would always have a stick of Dentyne in his mouth. Richard's brother had a car, which he borrowed as much as possible, though there weren't really a lot of places to go. Of course, the object of having a car wasn't necessarily transportation in those days; it was to have a place where you could be alone.

Sometimes there would be dances at the school, and dancing is one of my favorite things to do, though Richard wasn't wild about it. Anyway, he was a musician, a trombonist—like Tommy Dorsey, I thought—and he was often up on the bandstand playing. I remember those wonderful songs from that time, like "One O'Clock Jump," "Stardust," and "Sentimental Journey." One time Richard was performing at a school dance and I went up to him afterwards and said, "Oh, Richard, you were wonderful," or some such girlish nonsense.

"Shows how much you know," he said, obviously unhappy with his performance. Maybe that's why I was so attracted to Richard—he didn't care what others said, he just had to please himself.

❧

My high school years stretched from 1937 to 1941, and it was a strange time to be young. The Depression made the present difficult, since nobody had any money; and then, over in Europe, Adolf Hitler was wreaking havoc, putting the future up for grabs. I've always been a newspaper reader, even in high school, and I used to read about Hitler's doings with my mouth wide open. Everybody said it was just a matter of time before we would be in a war. Already, boys in our high school were quitting to join the service, and we would see trainloads of soldiers passing through town.

In our house on Hervey Street I had the big bedroom facing the street, and I would sit at my dressing table putting on my makeup (my mother didn't approve of my wearing all that much in high school, and, oddly, I didn't fight it) and inspecting the gray streak that was already showing in my hair, and I would try to figure out what I wanted to do with my life. High school was fun—I was in the Press Club and the Dramatic Club and the Science and Music and Library and Art clubs; I had been in class plays and worked on the school newspaper; I was chosen class secretary and a member of the National Honor Society; in our class will, I see now that I bequeathed to Mary Jo Monroe, a junior, my "magnetic attraction for boys. (Help us, please, if she turns it on full force.)" I had had a good time in high school—and yet I was anxious to get on with the real thing.

College never even occurred to me. I was too practical, too eager to be independent and self-sufficient. The plan I came up with was to enroll in nursing school, but not because I wanted to be a nurse. For some strange reason—maybe I had seen it in a movie or something—I had my sights set on becoming a nurse anesthetist, and nurse's training was a prerequisite for that. In those days, general-practice physicians basically did their own anesthesia using that old drip-ether method. I thought nurse anesthetists, who weren't doctors but knew a heck of a lot more about modern anesthesia than any general practitioner, were the wave of the future. This was an exciting, even romantic, idea to me. I could just *see* myself wearing those crisp, important-looking whites.

The house on Hervey Street had a front porch with a swing, and Richard and I would sit out there for hours on end, talking and swinging, ruminating about the future—and *our* future. Despite my mother's disapproval, most people in town expected us to get married someday, and I guess we did, too. Of course, I still had a year of high school to go after Richard graduated, and Richard had the draft to think about. He hadn't registered yet, but he would have to eventually. There was a government program through which they were looking for people to do all kinds of jobs, and they had an opening in Seattle working at the shipyards. Richard was talking about doing that for a year or so before joining the service. I had decided to apply for nurse's training at Tri-State Hospital in Shreveport, Louisiana, which was fifty miles away. Geography aside, we at least had sense enough to know that neither of us could support the other right now.

It looked like this was the end of the road, at least for a while. But before we parted, Richard gave me a ring. It wasn't an engagement ring exactly—more like an engaged-to-be-engaged ring. Richard says now that it probably came from a Cracker Jack box, because he sure didn't have the money to buy fine jewelry.

But it didn't matter, I loved it. The ring was the thing, its circle tying the future to the past. We kissed for the last time in my front-porch swing, two kids about to discover firsthand that there are no guarantees in this old world.

Two

SHREVEPORT WAS ACTUALLY the second big city I had ever
been to. The first was Hot Springs, Arkansas—population then
33,000—where we high school grads-to-be had gone on our senior
trip. We spent one whirlwind day in Hot Springs, and during that
day we went to Oaklawn racetrack. I was awed. I found the horses
beautiful, the people glamorous, the action exhilarating. I had never
placed a bet in my life, but on that day I put down two crisp dollar
bills on the daily double, and I won $84. I've often wondered what
my life would've been like if I had lost that bet.

But I didn't. I cleaned up.

So when I got to Shreveport, I had already had some experience
at conquering the wider world, and I was ready for more. Nurse's
training wasn't at all like winning the daily double, however. It was
more like running the races themselves.

The owners of Tri-State Hospital were two doctors named Willis
and Knighton. Dr. Knighton was the sweetest man you could ever
hope to meet; Dr. Willis was mean as a snake. How they ever became partners I'll never know. Dr. Willis was the doctor who first
made me think Playing God 101 is the introductory course in medical school. He treated everybody like dirt, especially the graduate nurses; we students usually weren't around him enough to bear
the brunt of his rudeness. But I remember being in the room one

day when he was berating some poor nurse, and I thought to my-self: *I could never put up with that.* So I said something, I don't even remember what. It didn't matter—this was a time when you just didn't question authority, a rule I must admit I've always had some difficulty following.

Dr. Willis gave me the evil eye. After that, whenever he happened to spot me on rounds, he would say to the graduate supervisor of the floor, who always accompanied him, "Remind me, we don't accept any more students from Arkansas."

If Dr. Willis was God, then his archangel in charge of nursing students was Nurse Frye. She was strict and she was stern. Before the three-year course was over, fully 25 percent of our class would drop away, many of them because they couldn't meet Nurse Frye's exacting standards. Not that she was unreasonable: Where we trained, you took care of the patients or you were gone. That sounds easy, but it's not. And back then—gosh, I had hoped I would never get to the age to say, "We didn't do it like this back then," but here I go—back then, we didn't have all this paperwork to divert our attention from the care of the patient. One night during my first six months we lost a young mother. It was just one of those things—complications from a delivery. But I didn't think I could stand it, and Nurse Frye saw me crying. She came over and looked me straight in the eye and said, "If I ever catch you crying again, you won't finish nurse's training here."

The hospital also had a rule that students had to be there six months before they could go home for a visit. I waited exactly six months, then I called my father and had him come get me. I didn't get permission. I didn't fill out any paperwork or anything. When I got back after a couple of days, there was a note in my room telling me to report to Nurse Frye's office. I'll never forget her words as long as I live: "You know, I just didn't realize how important it was for you to go home. Now you can go home and stay." She let me twist in Hope for thirty excruciating days, and then she called and asked if I was ready to come back.

The only thing that saved me was that I worked hard and I was good at my work, because I was also seen as being a bit mischievous for Nurse Frye's and Dr. Willis's taste. The student nurses lived in dormitories, one for the day nurses and one for those on the night shift. At first we stayed in huge multibed spaces, and then, as we gained more seniority, we moved to smaller four-bed rooms. Downstairs was a reception area with couches and chairs where we could meet visitors. My steady bunkmate and, later, my perennial roommate was a girl named Norma Truitt from Shreveport; she's now Norma Howell and lives in Omaha. Norma was a wonderful person, and that's not just a gratuitous compliment. I once let my temper get away from me and found myself hurling a running electric fan at her. The moment it happened I said to myself: *You are your mother! You are your mother! You will destroy yourself if you don't get hold of this!* More than fifty years later, I've forgotten why I did it, but that scene has stuck in my head and scared me to death ever since. As far as I know, that's the last temper tantrum I've ever thrown in my life. I saw Norma recently and thanked her for helping me get my temper in check. She doesn't even remember the incident.

What she does remember, however, is the time she and I smuggled a bottle of whiskey into the dorm. It was a small bottle—probably a pint or so—and we downed it pretty handily. Then we realized we had to hide the evidence—the bottle itself. Nurse's training was part school and part military life, and we often had inspections of our quarters, so we couldn't just leave an empty whiskey bottle around. Finally, I—according to Norma—got the bright idea of dropping it down the laundry chute. It made a hellacious racket, but we got away with that one.

I wasn't so lucky on other occasions. That first fall the hospital had installed new carpeting in the reception area of the nurses' quarters, and somebody had promptly dropped a hot cigarette ash and burned a hole in it. Nobody would own up to it, of course, so Nurse Frye grounded the entire dorm for thirty days.

For the life of me I couldn't see how they were justified in punishing all of us for something one or two people had done. Maybe my indignation also had to do with the fact that New Year's Eve fell smack within that thirty-day period, and I *love* New Year's Eve. I had been dating some that fall, and I sure didn't want to be stuck in the dorm with a bunch of girls in white when I could be out having fun on the biggest party night of the year. After mulling over our options awhile, a friend—I've forgotten who now, but it could've been anybody in the dorm—came up with what we thought was the perfect crime: We would sneak out New Year's Eve, and then, instead of coming back to our dorm where we might be seen, we would sneak into the night nurses' dorm, which would be empty because everybody who lived there would be working. Then we would get up early in the morning and go to work directly from the night nurses' dorm. We would essentially be two places at the same time, and nobody would ever know.

Except that in the wee hours of that morning one of the night nurses' feet started bothering her, and she got permission from her supervisor to go back to the dorm and change shoes. When she got there, she saw us in bed sleeping and it scared her to death—she thought maybe some bums had sneaked in for a few hours of shelter.

The next thing we knew, a policeman was standing over us with a flashlight. The night nurse supervisor was right behind him, along with the nurse with the sore feet. We were caught, and you can be sure that we suffered the inimitable wrath of Nurse Frye.

It's not even far-fetched to say that Nurse Frye didn't like my looks. She didn't like the lace handkerchief that I thought looked so stylish protruding from my pocket; that was being "out of uniform." And she surely didn't like my makeup, which she considered excessive. It's a funny thing—when I was young, I went through a period of being embarrassed by my mother's makeup, which *I* considered excessive. And then, here I came following in her footsteps, doing exactly the same thing or worse. Truth is, I like bright colors and I like people to notice me. In fact, I hate for them *not* to notice me. I think Bill and Roger and I are all alike in that way: When we walk into a room, we want to win that room over. Some would even say we *need* to win that room over, and maybe that's true. And maybe that makes us vulnerable to other people. Roger says the three of us, if there are one hundred people in a room and ninety-nine of them love us and one doesn't, we'll spend all night trying to figure out why that one hasn't been enlightened. Nurse Frye was usually the one in any given room who wasn't won over by my particular charms.

Just like in the military, we nursing students had to line up for daily inspection, and upperclassmen would often do the inspecting. One of Nurse Frye's minions was a girl who happened to be president of the senior class when I was a freshman. I had never understood why Nurse Frye favored this particular girl so—her shoes and stockings were always dirty, and I couldn't for the life of me figure out how she got away with it. I, personally, was always scrupulously clean. My uniform was spotless and pressed to perfection. However, I did like a little color in my nail polish.

So we were lined up for inspection and there she came in her dirty shoes. I confess that I had really been laying for her. You've seen people who've never had any authority in their lives and will never have it again and they're going to make the most of it: that's this girl. Thank God I've forgotten her name, or I would gladly publish it. But when she got to where I was standing, she stopped and scrutinized me. The only thing she could find wrong was the little bit of color I had in my nail polish.

"Take that off immediately," she said.

I answered, loud enough so everybody could hear: "I want to make a deal with you. If you'll take a bath, wash your hose, and polish your shoes, I'll be delighted to take this fingernail polish off."

That's not only a true story, it's the story of my life.

&

The Japanese bombed Pearl Harbor during my first semester at nursing school, and the war we had all been waiting for was suddenly upon us.

I had a date on the night of December 7, 1941, with a young man who happened to be a captain at Barksdale Field, the Air Force base in Shreveport. We had been seeing each other for a while that fall, and he would always come to pick me up wearing civilian clothes.

As a girl brought up in a small town, I had been taught not to have anything to do with military men. I don't know why they carried such a stigma—maybe it was because they moved around so much and you didn't know anything about their backgrounds. But it was a disgrace to be seen with a military man. It just wasn't done.

So on the afternoon of December 7, he called. "I'm free to keep our date," he said, "but I have to wear my uniform." For a second I didn't know what to do. But my parents, especially my father, had taught me to think for myself, and I just decided that this would be okay.

That night we talked for the longest time about the horrors of Pearl Harbor and what it would mean for the country. He, for one, would be sent overseas soon. And though I didn't know it at the time, we would start losing nurses—some joined the service and others moved with their servicemen husbands—causing a serious shortage.

My world seemed to be changing everywhere. Back home in Hope, my father had started coughing a lot and was having trouble breathing. He went to the doctor, who told him he had to give up the ice job. His condition was called bronchiectasis, which is a severe form of bronchitis. It was too late to cure him, the doctor said, but he had to stop going in and out of the cold. Oh, Daddy hated hearing that; he loved that ice-delivery job more than anything. But if he wanted to live, he had no choice.

Fortunately, a man named Jett Williams, a wealthy cotton broker in Hope, owned a liquor store that he needed somebody to run. My daddy said he would give it a try. So, after nearly fifteen years of delivering ice, he began a new career standing behind a counter selling liquor. Ironically, it was behind this very counter that he would meet, and introduce to me, the man who would become my second husband.

But marriage—at least to anyone besides Richard—was the farthest thing from my mind those first couple of years in nursing school.

And then Bill Blythe walked into my life.

It was a hot night in July of 1943, and I was working the three-to-eleven shift at Tri-State. At about ten P.M. a couple rushed into the

emergency room, and the man said the woman was having excruciating pains in her side. Immediately the emergency room staff hoisted
her onto the table and went into action.

Because it was after hours, the regular business offices were
closed, and it was up to the nurses to get all the information they
could from the patients. We already had the woman's name, so I
picked up a clipboard and walked into the examination room to see
what else the man could tell me about her.

I want you to know something: There *is* such a thing as love at first
sight. When I stepped into that room and saw him standing there, I
was stunned. It's been more than fifty years since that night, but I
remember it as though it were yesterday. I looked at that tall, handsome man holding that woman's hand, and he turned and his eyes
met mine. He smiled, and the only way I can describe it is that he
had a glow about him. I was weak-kneed—and also embarrassed,
because I was afraid everybody in the room could see what I felt.

And he was being so nice to her, so considerate. She was obviously in terrible pain, and he would squeeze her hand and lightly
rub her brow and lean over and talk to her and smile. And all I could
think was, *I've got to know if they're married or not.*

So I decided I would try calling him by her last name. "I beg your
pardon," he said. "We're not married. We're friends." I was never
so relieved in all my life.

The woman had appendicitis, and they had to operate on her right
away. He went with her as far as the operating room, and I was shameless—any excuse I could think of, I used it to get into the area where
he was waiting. When the surgery was over, I was standing behind
the desk at the nurse's station and he walked by on his way out of
the hospital. He looked at me and said, "Good night," and then continued on. He started walking down the steps at the end of the hall,
and I thought, *I will die if he leaves without saying another word.*

He must've been halfway down the steps, and then I heard him
stop and begin coming back up again. I busied myself with the charts
and tried to act like I wasn't paying attention, and I heard him walking over to the desk and stopping. I looked up. He looked me in the

eye, and then he reached over and touched the ring that Richard had given me, and he said, "What does that mean?"

And just like that I said, "Nothing." After four years of going with sweet, wonderful Richard, I told this total stranger that my ring didn't mean a thing.

Bill looked like he was as relieved as I was. "What time do you get off?" he asked.

"Eleven o'clock," I said, "but I only have thirty minutes to get from here to the nurses' home." Of course, our dorm adjoined the hospital, so I knew I could make it in five minutes; that gave us twenty-five minutes to get to know each other.

"Well," he said, "that's time enough for a Coke."

"Yes, it is," I said.

There was a little drive-in restaurant not far from the hospital, and we drove over there in Bill's car. I never talked and drank as fast in my life: We literally had fifteen, maybe twenty minutes. And I remember that we kissed that night, which was something you just didn't do in those days—kiss on the first date. But I knew the moment I laid eyes on Bill Blythe that all the rules were out the window.

The next day he called me, and the next night we saw each other again—and every day and night after that. He had only been passing through Shreveport on his way back to his hometown of Sherman, Texas, where he was planning to join the Army. His job was selling heavy equipment for a company out of Chicago—wheel-balancing machines, things like that. I remember the Bear Equipment Company was their top competitor. His boss in Chicago was a good friend—I only remember his first name, Joe—and he had told Bill his job would be waiting for him when he got back from the service. Once Bill met me, though, he postponed his plans for a while. He took an apartment in Shreveport and got a job selling cars at Rountree Olds Cadillac.

Of course, I had to tell Richard what had happened. He and I had been writing letters during the past three years, and we had even seen each other once. When he had left the Seattle shipyard job to go back home and join the service, I caught a ride up to Hope to visit him. We talked about our situation and whether or not we should get married, but it still didn't make any sense. So we parted again—he for Camp Robinson in Little Rock and I for Shreveport.

I dreaded telling Richard about Bill, but was determined that, if possible, I would tell him face-to-face. I wrote him a letter and said I had something to tell him, and that it was better told in person. I asked him to come to Shreveport as soon as he could get leave.

He couldn't make it in time. He was about to ship out for two and a half more years and wouldn't get even a weekend leave before Bill had to go into the service. Months later, Richard and I met briefly in New Orleans before he left for overseas. By then I was married. Our meeting was short and sweet, with tears over what might have been.

The next time I would see him after that would be on a day that was at once one of the happiest and saddest of my life.

સ

But that was all in the far and unknowable future, and Bill and I were too occupied with the magic of the present to be worried about anything else.

What we had was the textbook definition of "whirlwind romance." It was wartime, and you had to talk fast. He was in Shreveport six weeks, two months—something like that. We talked fast, played fast, fell in love fast. Bill was charming and funny, and totally disarming. My roommate Norma remembers one time when she had to get in touch with me, and she called Bill's apartment and asked if I was there. "Yes," he said, laughing, "she's lying right here beside me." If he were alive today, I would smack him for that indiscretion, but that was Bill. He had a way about him that let him get away with saying things others couldn't.

We found we had a lot in common. We both loved movies. My favorite was *Gone With the Wind,* and I also saw a lot of what they call B movies, the kind Ronald Reagan starred in. (I want to make it clear, though, that I was *not* a Ronald Reagan fan.) Bill just plain liked movies—westerns, comedies, romances, thrillers. I remember we went to see *Casablanca* together, and I cried and cried. I'm the most sentimental slob you could ever find. And I still cry when I see *Casablanca,* because it was the last movie Bill and I went to together.

We were both music lovers, too, and we loved to dance. Frank Sinatra was driving half the nursing class crazy, but he was too skinny for my taste. I was still an Andrews Sisters fan, and Bill was wild about Glenn Miller's music. We would go to clubs and he would dip me to songs like "String of Pearls." Or we would drive out to Cross Lake and park and kiss and listen to the radio. If you could get past the silliness of "Mairzy Doats," there were some wonderful songs out then. This was the year of "I'll Be Seeing You" ("in all the old familiar places") and "You'll Never Know" ("how much I love you"). But our favorite, the one we considered "our song," was "I've Heard That Song Before." I thought I had a pretty good voice myself, and I would sing along and Bill would just look at me and laugh. He could see that I was crazy in love, and I could tell he was, too.

I was so in love, in fact, that I was willing to sacrifice the career that I had spent the past two years pursuing. Tri-State didn't allow married students, and I wanted us to get married. Bill tried to talk me out of it. Just like Richard, Bill reasoned that he was getting ready to be away for who knew how long, and he thought it unfair to tie me down to a husband who wouldn't be back for years—if he made it back at all. He said I would probably get lonesome for male companionship since I was so young—only twenty. He was twenty-five, and clearly had more experience in the ways of the world than I did.

But I argued and argued with him. It wasn't that I was afraid of losing him, and he certainly wasn't afraid of losing me. It was that I was in love like I had never been in my life, and love was simply all that mattered. I wanted to prove my love for him by becoming his wife and waiting out the war for him. The truth is, I really didn't have to twist his arm a lot. Practicality aside, deep down he wanted me every bit as much as I wanted him.

When I called my parents and told them I was getting married, Mother said to hold everything, she was on her way to Shreveport. She still didn't think I was old enough to get married, of course. I thought I was nearly an old maid—people just got married much younger then than they do now. Daddy probably felt a little wistful at the idea of his "baby" leaving the nest, but if he did, he didn't say so. To him, my happiness was his happiness.

We met them at the little reception area in the nurses' dorm. Mother was very cool to Bill at first, but eventually even she couldn't resist his charm—the ultimate test, as far as I was concerned. His looks and his comfortable way of meeting people gave him a strength to match her own, and the truth is, she liked that. People like my mother respect anyone who stands on his own two feet. After the meeting, you would've thought the marriage was her idea.

So with my parents' blessing, Bill and I headed his Buick for Texarkana—me riding as close to him as I could possibly squeeze— where we were married by a justice of the peace. The date was September 3, 1943. I don't remember why we selected Texarkana, though in hindsight it was a perfectly fine choice: Being on the border of Texas and Arkansas, it represented the joining of our home states.

Then, of course, the moment I'd been dreading was upon us. We drove back to Shreveport and I got out, and Bill essentially turned around and headed for Sherman to join the Army. I watched until his car was out of sight. I had known this man just two months, and now, suddenly, we were married. In the world's eyes we were supposed to meet all of life's joys and obstacles together, as a team— and yet what did I really know about him? I hadn't met his family, and all I knew of his life was what he had chosen to reveal to me.

For many people that wouldn't have been enough. But for me, the important part wasn't the past or even the future. If the truth were known, I hadn't told Bill all that much about Richard, either. For whatever reason, during my twenty years I had come to believe that relationships started from the moment two people met, and that the only acceptable way to judge people wasn't by what they had or hadn't done in the past or would or wouldn't do in the future; you judged them by the way they treated you in the present. It's a measurement taken as much by the heart as by the head, and according to that measurement, I didn't have a doubt in the world that William Jefferson Blythe II—my *husband*—was every bit the man I knew him to be.

&

Tri-State made an exception to their marriage rule for me, which eventually meant that I was the first married graduate in the history of the school. When Bill left, I had about a year to go, and I applied myself with a diligence and responsibility befitting my new station as a mature married woman. Often I volunteered to take double duty, handling the late shift so one of the other girls could go on a date. Or I would fill in for somebody for a couple of hours in the afternoon so she could run errands. The funny thing was, they all thought I was doing it for them, but I was really doing it for myself. I wanted to keep busy so the time would pass faster.

Soon after Bill was in the service, I received a letter from his mother inviting me to come to Sherman for a visit. I was a nervous wreck at the prospect of meeting this big family that I was now technically a part of but which I had never laid eyes on. I wanted them to like me, and I didn't know if they would. But I gave it everything I had: I got my best clothes together and had my hair and nails done. On the appointed day I boarded the train, which left Shreveport in the morning and soon crossed the border into Texas, and from then on it was just more and more Texas. I remember looking out the window at the passing flatland and wondering what lay in store. I also checked my makeup about every fifteen minutes.

Finally the train chugged into Sherman, and to be honest I don't remember a thing about stepping off that platform and being greeted by my new relatives: I guess I was in shock. But Bill's ten-year-old niece, Ann Blythe—now Ann Grigsby—says she remembers it as clearly as if it were yesterday. And I like her description—I couldn't have come off better if I'd hired my own PR person. "When you stepped off that train, you were absolutely striking," Ann tells me today. "I remember how long and dark your hair was. Your nails and makeup were stunning, and you were dressed fit to kill." If she'd only known how nervous I was inside.

Since the Blythe family home was so small, I stayed with Bill's brother Earnest and his wife, Ola Mae, Ann's parents. I was only there a few days, but during that time I got a deeper sense of who my husband was. They called him W.J. He had grown up on the family farm near the Red River, the very same river that runs east nearly to Hope before it turns southward into Louisiana; it was almost as if we had been connected by that river all our lives without knowing it. Bill was the sixth of nine children, and even though they didn't have much money, they remembered happy childhoods swinging on grapevines, riding horses, going to church picnics, playing in the creek.

Their circumstances changed drastically during the early 1930s. First the Depression hit, and then Bill's father, also called W.J., developed cancer. Bill was barely in his teens at the time, but he was the oldest family member who didn't have his own spouse and children to take care of, so he essentially became the man of the house, taking responsibility for his mother, father, and younger sisters. He was going to school at a little two-room schoolhouse, and he would leave school early every day and walk to his job at a nearby dairy. After that, he would walk home, do his chores and homework, get a few hours' sleep, and then get up at three A.M. and walk to the dairy to put in a few hours before school started.

After Bill's father died in 1935, the family sold the farm and moved to town. Bill had dropped out of school after the eighth grade and, at seventeen, was working full-time as a salesman for an auto-parts company. Eventually that job led to his traveling job, in which he covered Arkansas, Louisiana, and part of Texas. He was a natural salesman, of course. As his sister Vera Ramey says, Bill never met a stranger.

And I didn't either on that visit to Sherman. His family was so good to me, taking me in like I had always been one of their own. They told me wonderful stories about Bill and explained that he had always been the family's linchpin. I laughed and cried hearing those stories. They made me feel closer to him, and I missed him more than ever.

Back in Shreveport, I plugged away at my nursing. In our last year, the class embarked on the adventure we had all been looking forward to—six months of advanced study affiliating in pediatrics and obstetrics at Charity Hospital in New Orleans. Nursing classes from schools all over the country would be there. Wartime, New Orleans, and a bunch of twenty-one-year-old nurses-to-be let loose in the big city for six months: It had all the makings of a great party.

Or a great disaster, if you happened to think in such terms. Nurse Frye certainly thought that way—especially when she got word that I had been elected president of the affiliates. Many, many schools affiliated with Charity Hospital, so this was a great honor for me and for Tri-State. Nurse Frye fully recognized that fact, but she was afraid that I might not—so she caught the next airplane and flew down to New Orleans to meet with me. The conversation generally went along these lines: "Tri-State Hospital has always had a wonderful reputation at Charity, and please don't do anything to change that."

I promised her faithfully that I wouldn't disgrace her, and I was as good as my word.

Not that we didn't have fun in New Orleans, a town that—when combined with copious quantities of alcohol—brought out the showoff in me. When we had time off we would go to the French Quarter and hear Dixieland jazz or big-band music, and I would embarrass my friends by getting up and singing with whoever was up there. I wasn't obnoxious or anything, I was just convinced I had more talent than most of the singers we heard, and I didn't want to deprive anybody of the chance to hear me.

When I wasn't hogging the spotlight, we might drive out to Lake Pontchartrain and become bathing beauties, or load up on *beignets* and coffee at the Morning Call cafe. I remember Norma kicking off her shoes and going wading in a fish pond late one night on Canal Street after we'd had way too much to drink. I thought they'd have to take us to the emergency room, we were laughing so hard.

In spite of such shenanigans, during those six months in New Orleans it began to dawn on me that I felt pretty grown-up. I was the only married one in the crowd, of course, and my colleagues had thrust a great deal of responsibility on me. But also just being that far away from home for the first time made me understand that I had shed some of the protective layers of childhood. Not all, but some.

Finally it was graduation day. Three years of study, and *what* an education. I'll never forget the moment Nurse Frye presented me with my nurse's pin and my graduating cap. As I walked up to shake her hand, there was a twinkle in her eye. It was as if she was thinking, *I hope you do good, but I just don't know.*

Three

AT FOUR-THIRTY IN THE MORNING I felt somebody shaking my arm. "*Baby,*" a man's voice whispered. "*Baby.*" I rolled over and squinted into the face of my father, who was smiling. "Come go with me," he said.

This had started when I was in nursing school and would come home for a weekend visit: Daddy would wake me up early and want me to go have coffee with him at the little all-night café down the street. But of course this would make Mother mad. "You let her sleep," she would tell him. "She needs her rest."

The truth is, I didn't mind at all. I loved those early-morning times with my father. So when I graduated from nursing school and went back home to work while I waited for Bill, Daddy and I would often—on the nights I wasn't working—get up early and go have coffee together. Between us there were no secrets, and these predawn hours were the times we talked most.

He was still going through a transitional phase in his life—I say that as though *all* of life isn't a transition, but I didn't know that then. Hempstead County had voted dry in 1944, so Daddy, at age forty-four, had quit the liquor store and opened a small grocery up on North Hazel Street across from the cemetery. It was the kind of neighborhood grocery that you used to see all over the place, before there were supermarkets and convenience stores. I have a picture of Daddy standing behind the counter, looking natty in a dark shirt and bright tie. All those years he delivered ice he generally wore khaki pants and shirts, but after he stopped delivering ice he began dressing up to go to work.

Actually, Daddy's store had two checkout counters. On one—which I always thought of as the grown-up counter—there was a case full of cough drops, Luden's and Vicks and Smith Brothers. On top of that case were boxes of cigars, and men would stop off in the morning on their way to work and pick up a few smokes to get them through the day. While the men were at work, housewives would come in and do their shopping—Daddy carried a pretty complete line for such a small store. And after school, kids would come in and get their afternoon snacks. Those were found at the other checkout counter, the one I always thought was Daddy's favorite.

That's the one he's standing behind in my picture. In front of the counter, on a low table so the children could reach, Daddy had lined up several large plastic canisters of Lance products—Nabs, cookies, Fig Newtons, and things like that. But maybe the favorite target for children was the Made-Rite ice cream box next to the cash register. You lifted up one of the lids and reached down into it, and it was cool and had that unmistakable smell of frozen dairy desserts.

I don't know how my father got the money to open the grocery store, but there was a rich man in town who used to lend him money when times were tough, and maybe that's who helped him get set up in the business. Daddy never had to sign a thing to borrow money because the man knew he was good for it. Years later, this man died owing my father $40 on account, and Daddy told me he wouldn't even think of trying to collect. He was just so happy that he could finally do something for the man who had helped him for so many years. I doubt that Daddy ever told anybody but me about that: He wasn't being generous for the effect, he was doing it because that's who he was.

Daddy loved the grocery store because he loved people—but, once again, maybe he loved them too much for his own good. I remember he used to tell me he was worried because he had allowed some customers too much credit. Then when they had cash in their pockets, instead of coming and paying my father, they went and bought from other grocery stores that wouldn't let them charge. I never could understand how people could do that: If somebody trusted me enough to let me buy on credit, there's no way I would ever go shop anywhere else.

Those early-morning conversations were as therapeutic for me as they were for my father. I missed Bill terribly. By now he had been gone more than a year. He had been sent to Fort Hood, Texas, and from there to Germany. I scanned the newspapers every day, wondering if the battle I was reading about was one that he was in. From the moment he left I had been writing to him daily. While I was still in nursing school—I especially remember it during those months in New Orleans—I would go to the mailbox with my fingers crossed, and nine times out of ten I'd have a letter from my mother or my father, or maybe from Bill's relatives, but nothing from Bill. Then, suddenly, my mailbox would be stuffed full of letters from him. I would arrange them by date and read them in order. Mostly he told me how much he loved and missed me; he wasn't permitted to say much about what he was doing, but the love letters were enough for me. Sometimes the letters would contain money. All the soldiers were given so many packs of cigarettes a month, and because Bill didn't smoke, he would sell his, at enormous profit, and send me the cash. That money helped me tremendously.

Back in Hope, most of the people I had known in high school were gone—off to college or to war or to some future they had found in another place. If you were to ask me today if I had ever been lonely, I would probably laugh my most confident laugh and tell you I've never experienced a lonely day in my life. And generally that's true. But that year and a half wait in Hope was when I came the closest. I made sure to keep myself busy during the days—helping Mother, visiting relatives, things like that—and I worked as much as possible. Work has always been my salvation.

But in Hope most of the nursing jobs I got were private-duty jobs, and they didn't do much to help keep my mind off Bill. I often worked at night, all night, sitting beside a sleeping patient. I confess that when I got out of nursing school I was as guilty as some of the doctors I had seen—I thought I knew it all. But it doesn't take long out in the real world to discover just how little you really know. When you do private-duty nursing, you spend a lot more time with the same patient than you do as a hospital nurse, or than I had done in nurse training. I found right away that familiarity breeds—well, annoyance, at least. But of course I wouldn't let the patient know that for anything.

One of the things I learned during this time was that I had a tough act to follow. By then Mother had been working as a nurse for almost ten years, and the amazing thing to me was that this woman who had been so strict and domineering at home absolutely spoiled her patients rotten. Anytime I would have to care for someone she had nursed, I was in for a long and humiliating night. Apparently a patient's every wish had been my mother's command. I soon decided that private-duty nursing was too monotonous for someone with my disposition, but this period taught me as much about patience as patients.

Not that I knew exactly what I was going to do with this eye-opening experience I was getting. I had consciously put my goal of anesthesia aside, the way I had been willing to put my nursing career aside when Bill and I married. This was an era when women went unquestioningly wherever their husbands went, no matter what the sacrifice. For all my spunk and outspokenness, I was still a traditionalist in such matters, and I guess I thought that when Bill came home, we would go wherever he wanted and I would get a job as a nurse—that is, if I wasn't home raising babies. It was years later before my cumulative experience taught me that a woman had better be able to support herself *and* her children—no matter what her husband, if any, does with his life.

So I would sit there beside my patients through the long nights, and I would write to Bill, telling him how much I loved and missed him. Inevitably a train whistle would sound in the distance, expressing my feelings exactly. It was during that time that I started doing cutwork, which is a kind of handwork involving iron-on patterns that you apply to a linen towel, say, so that you can cut an intricate design into the towel. I must've done a thousand of them. I found I could get lost in this kind of handwork, which is exactly what I was looking for.

And then, suddenly, on the little radio they'd play "I've Heard That Song Before." My heart would leap into my throat and I would just sit there looking into space.

❧

Bill came home in November 1945. I didn't have much notice as I recall—a few days or a week: just long enough to glue on my eyelashes, paint on my eyebrows, and get a new coat of paint on my nails.

He had already been home to Texas to get his car and his clothes, but instead of his coming on to Hope, for sentimental reasons we decided to meet in Shreveport. On second thought, maybe the reasons were as much practical as sentimental—after all, I was living at home in the room next door to my parents', and Bill and I had a lot of catching up to do.

I saw him from the train window and he looked wonderful, grinning ear to ear. All over the country couples were coming back together after years apart. Some wouldn't survive the test of time and distance, but I had no doubt that Bill and I would. I flew into his arms and he held me tight. I could feel him tingling, he was so excited. He just couldn't wait to get on with his life. He had the job waiting for him in Chicago, and he wanted to go there right away. And he wanted to get started on a family. Ann Grigsby remembers Bill kidding her father, whose wife was pregnant again after years of Ann's being an only child. Bill was laughing and saying *he* wasn't going to dawdle around like Earnest had; he was going to start working on becoming a father immediately.

We spent just the one wonderful night in Shreveport and then drove on to Hope. On the way home I nuzzled close to him the way I had when we went to Texarkana to get married, and he talked about all he wanted us to do. He had saved some money, and he planned to buy us a house when we got to Chicago. He had already called his old buddy Joe and told him we would be up there soon.

He never talked much about what he had done in the war, and I didn't ask. The only thing I remember is that he was so proud of what he had been able to do with the Army's heavy equipment. Because of all his knowledge in that area, he was able to fix tanks and other equipment that would've ordinarily been junked, and he saved the government hundreds of thousands of dollars that way. He had received a citation for his service to his country. Of course I was incredibly impressed, and I'm sure I spent most of the next week or so looking up at him moony-eyed, blinking my false eyelashes, and smiling. It was good to have my husband home again.

Mother and Daddy seemed as ecstatic to have Bill back as I was. We stayed in Hope about a week, during which Mother cooked all her best dishes. Daddy and Bill would sit in the living room talking while Mother and I worked in the kitchen. During the day Daddy showed Bill the store, and of course we drove around so Bill could meet all the friends and relatives. Bill charmed everybody—even my uncle Buddy, who doesn't charm easily. Buddy still talks about a day when Bill was driving in the area and came upon a family trying to move a big piano. He stopped his car and helped them get it on their truck—then he followed them to where they were moving it and helped them unload it. That kind of spirit, the kind that farm families from the likes of Bodcaw count on in their neighbors, impressed Buddy mightily.

When it was time to leave for Chicago, I had a hard time deciding what clothes to take, and I remember how Bill kidded me about all my luggage. But mostly what I remember about that time was how hopeful it all felt—not just with us, but with everybody. The Depression was a memory, and now so was the war. Finally we were ready to get on with our lives.

We packed Bill's dark maroon Buick and started driving northeast on Highway 67 toward Little Rock, then up to Searcy and Corning and on into Missouri. At Poplar Bluff we turned onto Highway

60, a narrow strip of highway built on a continuous man-made mound that ran through low, flat farmland, with deep ditches dropping off on either side. We took this road east through the little town of Sikeston, then jogged north. Before long we crossed the Mississippi River into Illinois.

૭ઽ

Many years later, when I encountered Hillary Rodham for the first time, I would feel some consternation about how different her Chicago background had been from my Arkansas upbringing. Some of that may've been my own lingering memory of how different Chicago had felt to me in the winter of 1945–46. It was as alien a place as I had ever visited.

We lived in a hotel down in the Loop. The Sherman Hotel, I think the name was. It was a nice place, and I remember it had a balcony from which I would gaze down at the city. Once I watched President Harry Truman come through in a parade. There he was, his motorcade snaking through the biggest crowd of people I had ever seen in my life. It felt so odd for me to be perched on this little piece of concrete so high above the ground, and I'll never forget how my stomach rolled when I dared to look straight down. This city was much different from New Orleans—noisier, more people crowded closer together, taller buildings, cold.

We thought we would only be in the hotel a short time, until we could find a house. We didn't figure on the fact that thousands of other servicemen were in the same boat, meaning that houses were extremely hard to find. Bill was working during the day and also trying to find us a place to live. His new territory sometimes took him as far as two hundred miles outside Chicago, but he would always turn around and drive back to be with me at night.

Fortunately, I make friends easily. I've always enjoyed talking with strangers—the more different they are, the better I like them. One day, as I walked past a grocery store in the Loop, I happened to see a pile of turnip greens lying out by the Dumpster. I love turnip greens, and I couldn't believe my eyes. So I went inside and I asked the produce man, "What are all those turnip greens doing out in the garbage?" I noticed he had a bin of turnips for sale.

He thought I was crazy. "What do you mean?" he said. "Nobody eats that." He held up a turnip for me to inspect. "*This* is the part you eat."

"Well, where I come from," I told him, "we eat it all." He laughed, and soon several other grocery people were over there talking with me. I never could convince them to save the greens, but I did get to know them and would stop in and talk with them almost every day.

I also spent many, many hours wandering around Marshall Field's department store. For a country girl like me, this was truly amazing. The store was gigantic, with high, high ceilings and chandeliers, and I remember how smartly my heels would click on the marble floors. I was especially astonished at the makeup counters, which seemed to take up the entire first floor. There was every name, every brand, you could think of, and somebody behind each counter to help you try the makeup on. When I die, if I open my eyes and I'm standing in the middle of Marshall Field's makeup department, I'll know I made it to heaven.

Of course there were things I didn't like about Chicago. I'm an outdoor person—I hate being cooped up in the house—so in spite of the bitter cold I made myself get outside and explore the city. That was uncomfortable enough, but then, whenever I would get home, I'd discover my blouses were covered with soot. I guess all those furnaces and chimneys were just pumping it out in an effort to keep the city warm, and most of the people I talked with about it didn't really notice it. But I'm meticulous about my clothes—not to mention my personal cleanliness—and this seemed a mighty big drawback to Chicago for me.

Just before Christmas of 1945 I began feeling a little queasy in the mornings; being a nurse, I knew exactly what it meant. A doctor confirmed my suspicions, and one night when Bill got home from work, I told him he was going to be a father. He was ecstatic—and was on the phone to his brother Earnest immediately. After that we talked to my parents and everybody else we could think of to call.

It was a wonderful Christmas present for us, and we promptly went out to celebrate.

Bill and I loved the clubs in Chicago, the places where we could have a couple of drinks and supper and hear some live music. Of course, that winter you couldn't go to any of the local clubs without hearing some moody saxophone playing "Laura" or "For Sentimental Reasons." Even when we couldn't go out, we would sometimes dance to the radio. It was so romantic up there in our room with the lights low and the city spread out and sparkling outside our window. I'll say this for Chicago: It's a wonderland during the Christmas season, with all the snow and the bright lights and the people scurrying from store to store to do their last-minute shopping. There were times that holiday season when I felt like life had become a movie, and I was the star.

❧

We found a house in a western suburb called Forest Park. It was red brick, and though it wasn't big, it was beautiful to me. The problem was, the people weren't ready to move out yet. They had to find a place, and then they had to close on their deal, and then after they moved, we would have to get in and clean up the house before we could move in. It was going to take weeks.

In mid-February, Bill's fifty-three-year-old mother had a stroke in Texas, and we had to go down to see her. Bill planned to drive, but because I was pregnant, he didn't want me to have to sit in the car that long. Instead, he bought me an airplane ticket. I had never been on an airplane in my life, and Bill laughed at me later because he said I strode onto that plane with so much confidence I looked like I had flown for years. Sometimes, I've found, you have to *pretend* you have confidence before you actually get it.

I sat with Bill's mother—Lou was her name—for a day and part of a night, and she died before Bill got home to see her. It was Valentine's Day. I felt so bad for Bill and wished he had flown.

Back in Chicago, we found that the house deal was going to take even longer than we had expected, and that, coupled with my increasing morning sickness, prompted me to suggest that maybe I ought to just go back to Hope and wait until the house was ready. I thought this might also be easier on Bill, because he was killing himself driving all over Illinois by day and then coming back to be with me at night. Maybe with me gone, he could get a little rest.

Reluctantly, he agreed. But before I left, we went out for a special evening on the town. An Army buddy of Bill's named Max Williams had gotten married, and he and his bride, Rosalie, were coming from Little Rock to Chicago for their honeymoon. Seems to me it was in March. They were there for three days, and we showed them the sights—it felt funny for me to be showing newcomers around Chicago, but by then I had been there more than four months, and I had had plenty of time to get to know a certain slice of the city. I remember Bill was so happy to see Max, and I liked Rosalie fine. One night we all dressed up and went to the Palmer House. The lobby in that hotel looked like something out of a fairy tale—it had ornate carvings and a painted ceiling and gold everywhere. It was my kind of place.

This night produced yet another memorable photograph in my life: the picture of Bill and me that has appeared in the press so much since my son ran for President. The actual photograph includes all four of us—Max and Rosalie and me and Bill—but most of the publications have used just the section with us in it. I love that photograph because it was the last one Bill and I had made together. In it I'm wearing a corsage, and there's a story about that, too. I remember we went into the Palmer House's fancy supper club and the maître d' seated us, and I noticed Bill was glancing around the room with a look of concern on his face. In a minute he excused himself and was gone for a while. When he got back, he was carrying this beautiful corsage, which he pinned to my dress. He had noticed that all the other women in the room were wearing corsages, and he wanted me to have one, too.

I never saw Max again after those three days were over, but years later, I met up with Rosalie once more. Her name is now Rosalie Brown, and ironically, she's moved to Hot Springs Village, Arkansas, just twenty minutes from where I live. When Bill Clinton ran for

President and she saw Bill Blythe's name in a magazine, she contacted me and we reminisced about that brief time we shared in Chicago. She says that through all these years two things have stuck in her mind about that evening at the Palmer House. One, she thought I looked so "exotic" and imagined me to be "well traveled" because she had never seen anyone wearing false eyelashes before; and two, she remembers how thrilled Bill and I were about having a baby, and how we couldn't seem to keep our hands off each other. They were the honeymooners, but she says she'll never forget how much in love we were.

Bill was killed late at night on May 17. He died alone, lying in a flooded ditch along Highway 60, three miles west of Sikeston, Missouri.

He had called me that day to say he was coming for me. The people had finally moved out of the house, and Bill had gotten in there and cleaned it up and moved all the furniture in. That was such a sweet surprise, because I had thought I was going to have to do all that myself.

Bill had planned to drive straight through without stopping. Early in the morning of May 18, Mother and I had just gotten back from the grocery store and were planning to fix a big breakfast to welcome him home. As we were carrying in the bags of groceries, the phone rang. I answered it, and on the other end of the line I heard Joe, Bill's friend and boss, telling the operator, "No, I don't want to speak to Mrs. Blythe, I want to talk to one of her parents, Mr. or Mrs. Cassidy." I handed the phone to Mother, and I stood there watching her as she turned pale and the tears began to come.

Daddy left for Sikeston that morning. They had taken Bill to a funeral home there and dressed him in a dark suit. Daddy claimed the body and tried to make sure that all Bill's papers and belongings were accounted for. Bill had told us he was bringing a case of bourbon as a gift for my father, but of course that was somehow missing. Also, some of his papers may've gotten lost, since his briefcase had been thrown from the car with him. But Daddy found what he could, and then he turned around and led the hearse carrying Bill's body on the long trip home.

Nearly thirty years later I was sitting in a hotel coffee shop in Hot Springs talking with a lawyer friend of mine. It was early in the morning, and I was having my breakfast there as I always did before going on to work at the hospital. Another one of the breakfast regulars, a man named Elmer Greenlee, was sitting at the next table. I knew Elmer to say hello to because I was in a service club with his wife, but as long as I had been coming to that coffee shop, we had never really had a conversation.

On this particular morning, however, I happened to be telling my lawyer friend about Bill Blythe's death. Suddenly I felt someone else's presence, and I looked up and Elmer Greenlee was standing there at the table. "Pardon me, Virginia," he said, "but I couldn't help overhearing your conversation. I was there. I was the first one at the wreck that night."

He sat down and began to tell the story. Elmer, then twenty-four, had grown up in Sikeston and ran a skating rink there. On the night of the accident, Elmer had closed the skating rink at around ten-thirty P.M. and, with his father, had started driving west on Highway 60 toward home. It was a clear night, and the stars were out. Elmer explained that Sikeston is situated high up on what they call a prairie bank; on both sides of town, going west and east, the land drops off and gets flat, and drainage ditches run parallel to the highway. At about eleven o'clock, the Greenlees were passed by a dark-colored Buick going at a high rate of speed. They didn't think much about it, and the taillights quickly disappeared ahead of them. But a minute or two later, as they got to the first bridge west of town, they saw the Buick off the road to the right, lying upside down in a cornfield.

Elmer and his dad pulled over and Elmer got his flashlight. They went down the bank to the car and saw that the driver's door was open—but there was no sign of the driver. They walked around the car, flashing their light inside. Elmer recalls seeing the case of bourbon in the backseat, still intact and with all the bottles sealed. They flashed the light on the ground immediately around the car, but still there was no driver to be found. By this time, other people with other flashlights were beginning to arrive at the scene. The Greenlees organized the group into a large circle around the car, and they all walked slowly, flashing farther out into the field. No driver.

Then it occurred to them that the driver must be pinned underneath the car, so they all lent a hand and started rocking it, and soon they had the car righted. It was amazing, Elmer said—as though the driver had vanished.

Elmer was curious, so the next day he went down to the funeral home and asked if they had ever found anybody out at that wreck the night before. Yes, said the mortician, the victim was a young man, twenty-eight years old. He had a blowout. And it was the darnedest thing, he only had one small bruise on the back of his head, which certainly wasn't enough to kill him. But when he was thrown from the car, he had landed in the drainage ditch; the shock must've kept him from getting up, so he lay there and drowned. But they knew he did try his hardest to avoid dying. At four A.M. one of the searchers spotted his arm sticking out of the water, with his hand clutched tightly around a bush that he had grabbed in an attempt to pull himself up.

I thanked Elmer for telling me the story. Then I went outside to my car and cried.

Four

I'M NOT BIG on funerals. Maybe it's because I've had to plan so many.

Somebody has to be awfully close to me for me to go to their funeral. And when it comes to going to the cemetery, I've got to believe that not another soul will be there before I'll even consider doing that. Sometimes that's the case, especially with older people who've outlived all their friends and relatives. I hate the thought of anybody being buried with no one there to bear witness, but some people go a little overboard—they get all dolled up and make every funeral in town. I sometimes think they're there trying to catch widowers. A funeral, to me, is a private thing—a family's last few minutes with their loved one.

We buried Bill in Hope. Even though we had been together only a relatively short time, his family knew he had been happy and wanted him to be with us. Rose Hill Cemetery is the oldest cemetery in town, and there the graves are shaded by massive magnolias and evergreens and oaks. Coincidentally, the cemetery is just across the street from where my father's grocery store was. You could stand in the store and look out the window, and if you knew what you were looking for, you could see the marble stone at Bill's feet. My mother and father had bought a plot large enough for them, me, and my husband, and that's where Bill was laid to rest. Today he's buried to my mother's left, and my father is buried to her right. The marker at their feet is actually two stones, with BLYTHE on one and CASSIDY on the other; linking them, there's a slab with an urn that looks like it might've come from classical Greece.

By 1946 the country had passed the era of burying young men with such numbing regularity, so maybe this death shocked people more than some others had. Also, I was a twenty-two-year-old widow who was six months pregnant. The funeral home was packed, and I've never seen so many flowers in my life. And letters. One in particular has stuck with me through all these years; I've forgotten who sent it, but its message has comforted me time and time again: "Please always remember that you must endure some of this or die young yourself."

Within days I began building that airtight box in my head. Outside was death and all those unknowable things you couldn't control; inside was family, friends, and especially the memory of my husband through the baby I was carrying. I've said many times that my children have held me together, and it started in May 1946, before either one of them was even born.

ও

Many years later, my memory of Bill Blythe would be jolted by revelations made after his son had become President. I say *jolted*, but not shaken. Not shattered.

And, probably surprisingly to many, not betrayed, either.

It appears that Bill had indeed been married before he met me. He never told me that, nor did anyone in his family. So as the news accounts of his alleged three previous marriages came out, I admit I was hurt and confused; I just couldn't understand why I hadn't been told.

Bill Blythe's niece, Ann Grigsby, says that at the time we were married, Bill was so happy they didn't see any point in meddling. They thought he had finally found the right one—that I was the love of his life. Then he died, and there was no point in telling me after the fact. Who knew that forty-five years later our son would become

President, bringing onto all of us the scrutiny that comes with that office?

As Ann tells it, Bill's first marriage, in 1935, wasn't of his own choosing. The Blythes suspected that the girl, Adele Gash, was pregnant and that the father was another relative who was separated—but not divorced—from his wife. Anyway, Bill married Adele, perhaps to protect the relative. In press reports, Adele has denied that version of the story, and in fact either she wasn't pregnant or she had a miscarriage, because her son wasn't born for two more years—after Adele and Bill were divorced, but while, as Adele tells it, they were still seeing each other. As for Bill's other alleged marriages, Ann says the Blythes did hear, later, that he was briefly married to Adele's sister Minnie Faye, but they never saw any proof. They knew nothing at all of the third one.

It's hard enough for me to reconstruct what happened in my own life last year, much less what happened in other people's lives sixty years ago. But I told Bill Clinton when the first supposed half brother emerged, "You can expect twenty or thirty more before this is over. You hide and watch." Ultimately, this is the way I feel about it: You can put anybody's name on a birth certificate. Specifically, I don't believe Bill was married that third time before me, and no birth certificate is going to convince me otherwise.

As for why he never told me about his previous marriage or marriages, when did he have time? Even though we were married for two years and eight months, we were actually physically together for only seven months. The rest of it, he was off in the Army or in Chicago waiting for our house to become available. And think about it: Was he going to break the spell of that whirlwind romance? Was he going to drop that bombshell just as he was leaving for war? Was he going to lay it all out in writing from overseas? Was he going to spoil our reunion with such news? Was he going to risk shocking his young, pregnant wife?

There was never a good time—and then he died.

I'm convinced that had Bill lived, he would've eventually found the moment to tell me about his past, even though I've always felt the past is irrelevant. So in memory I judge Bill Blythe the way I judged him then—by how he treated me. And no matter what happened to him before he met me, I'll go to my grave knowing I *was* the love of his life.

❦

The telephone that had given us the news about Bill's death sat on a table at the foot of the stairs. If you took those stairs up and made a sharp right turn at the top, and then a left at the first door off the hall, you would be in the bedroom we prepared for the birth of Bill Blythe's child.

I was in that room recently, for the first time in probably forty years. It's a small room with a wall paneled in narrow, horizontal boards. Sometime along the way somebody has painted the walls a kind of baby-girl pink, and the faded remnants of that color persist to this day. I hope this means it's been used for other babies since we used it that way; it was a wonderful first bedroom for my son to come home to.

Mother and Daddy were alternately excited and concerned that summer as we fixed up the room and got ready for Bill's arrival. Of course, back then we didn't know whether the baby was going to be a girl or a boy; I just knew that whatever it was, it was sure getting heavy. Also, whatever it was, Mother couldn't wait to get her hands on it; maybe she hoped to do better with it than she had with me. The weather was awfully hot, I remember, and that caused me discomfort and added to Mother and Daddy's concern. But of course their concern went deeper than the heat: They watched for the slightest change in my spirits. I tried to keep myself up around them; when I needed to cry, I would sit in my bedroom and shed my tears privately, the way I had always done. Then I would look at that bulge in my stomach and vow to be strong for my baby.

Out of necessity, we had also started dealing with the paperwork that inevitably follows death. Bill had had life insurance, one of those $10,000 policies the government made available to all servicemen for a nominal monthly premium. And he was diligent about making those payments—about paying *all* his bills, in fact. I used to kid him that he was worse than I was about paying bills: Mine got paid the minute they came inside, but he didn't even let them in the door. By the tenth of every month, everything we owed was paid. And I remember that in Chicago there were all these places where you could go cash checks and get money orders and cashier's checks and things like that; I had never seen such places before, and they were really handy. I went with Bill several times when he got the money order or whatever it was he needed to pay that insurance policy. When he died, I had every receipt but one—the April receipt. We found May, but April was missing. It was probably in his briefcase, which had been thrown from the car with him, and that receipt had probably been blown by the wind to Kansas or washed down some river to the Gulf of Mexico.

But that one receipt turned out to be vital, because the U.S. Army had no record of Bill's having the insurance at all. I couldn't believe it when they told me. Finally, we found out that the department where such records were kept had moved—from St. Louis to Washington, D.C., or vice versa. And in that move many of their records were lost. I was heartsick: I had a baby on the way; I *needed* that money.

But I never collected a penny of it. Attorneys worked on it. Senators worked on it. Nobody ever charged me, and friends would say, "Oh, just think how much you'll get when you collect and they add the interest to it." But I never collected at all. This of course added to my parents' concern and affected my attitude considerably, no matter how hard I tried to block it out. Now, instead of just being heartbroken, I was also scared to death.

I had kept in touch with my old roommate Norma, and she invited me to come visit her at her parents' home in Shreveport. It was a nice break from my troubles in Hope, though there were way too many memories of Bill lurking in that town for me to lose myself entirely. I remember Norma and I just talked and talked and talked, and we made each other laugh like we always had. We slept in the same double bed, and forty-seven years later she told me, "If I'd known you were carrying the future President of the United States, I'd have given you the whole bed."

The weather was awful on the day before Bill was born. It was Sunday, August 18, and the temperature hit 101 degrees, then dipped to 71. It was later to be deemed the hottest day of 1946. That night there was a violent electrical storm—thundering and lightning like I had never experienced before. I lay awake in my bed and listened for the crash of thunder and counted the seconds till the lightning slashed through the sky; usually I didn't have to count long. *Dear Lord,* I prayed, *please don't let it hit this house.* By dawn the storm was over, and Daddy brought the car around and he and Mother helped me in. At 8:51 A.M., I first laid eyes on my son. The announcement appeared that very afternoon in the *Hope Star*:

B I R T H S
Mrs. William Jefferson Blythe, II, announces the birth
of a son, William Jefferson Blythe, III, on Monday, August 19,
at the Julia Chester Hospital.
Mrs. Blythe will be remembered as the former
Miss Virginia Cassidy.

Richard Fenwick remembers that he had come home from the war in January 1946, while Bill and I were in Chicago. He and some of the other local vets had received what Richard calls the "52/20" deal, which meant the government would pay them $20 a week for fifty-two weeks—until, as Richard says, "we either went to school or calmed down or got shot or whatever happened to us." So for seven months he and his buddies had been "hell-raising" around Hope. I hadn't seen or heard from Richard since I had been back.

But on the night of the day I brought Bill home from the hospital, a bunch of the guys were sitting around the Checkered Cafe listening to the jukebox and shooting the breeze, and one of them said, "Hey, Virginia went home from the hospital today." One thing led to another, and pretty soon it was decided that they would all come to see me.

They showed up on the front porch that Richard and I had sat on together so many times, but this time it was all so different. I can imagine that some of the boys may've suddenly wished they could retreat to the café, but it was too late—they had already knocked on the door. Probably it was Daddy who went to answer it. When they stepped inside, they were quiet, polite, reverent almost. Because for all the experiences we had all had since leaving high school— and *they* had been to war—I was the first girl they knew, Richard says, who had gotten married and had a baby. It was a big step toward real life, and it wasn't lost on anyone that there was no husband standing beside me on what should've been a joyous day for a married couple.

These boys—young men now, actually, the dear, sweet friends I had known in what increasingly seemed like a lifetime ago—trooped up the stairs and took a quick peek at Bill lying in his crib. There were smiles and whispers and maybe a nervous joke or two. I loved seeing them and tried my best to make them comfortable, but I don't remember much real conversation, even from Richard. I understood: It was hard for *anybody* to know what to say in a situation like that.

֍

Daddy propped a picture of his grandson, naked and pink and plump, on the shelf behind his checkout counter. I'll bet my hat there wasn't a soul, big or little, young or old, who darkened the door of that grocery store who didn't receive the proud-grandpa routine before being allowed to escape. My father was truly Bill Clinton's first advance man.

Mother, meanwhile, was totally involved in showing me how mothering was done. She meant well, but I felt like a lowly student nurse again, running around practically taking notes while old Dr. Willis, now having assumed the form of my mother, played God. She had Bill on an unrelenting schedule—he ate his breakfast at the same exact hour every day, had his bowel movement on schedule—napped, played, ate, burped, slept, in an unwavering cycle. Most mothers are happy for their babies to sleep, but I remember wanting so much for him to wake up and *play* with me. I guess I felt about him like my father had always felt about me.

But Bill was out, oblivious to the conscious world. Maybe he was just exhausted from all the scheduling, but I would go up into that little corner room and watch ever so carefully just to make *sure* his little chest or back was still rising and falling. On one of his early checkups I told the doctor, "I'm so worried about this child. If I leave him alone, he'll sleep for sixteen hours." Back then, doctors in small towns like Hope seldom had any specialized training, and I'm sure this one had done no advance work in pediatrics; he just confined his practice to children. But he was the best I had. "My goodness," he said, "don't worry about that. That's wonderful." He explained that it was because he had taught me not to bother the baby when he was wet, but to let him sleep. "If he gets uncomfortable, he'll wake up," the doctor said.

I accepted his word, though reluctantly. Today I think the reason Bill Clinton doesn't sleep much is because he got in a lifetime's worth the first couple years of his life. This period also probably explains his inability to follow a schedule: After being bound to my mother's strict regimen for so long, I don't doubt that the man sometimes feels a need to dawdle.

The plan I had settled on was to eventually go back to working as a nurse in Hope, but the first week I had that baby everything changed. I was looking at him one day and I thought, *You deserve the best I can give you, and nursing isn't going to get it.* I had abandoned my old goal of becoming a nurse anesthetist because I knew I couldn't take my baby with me for the year of additional training, and I couldn't bear the thought of leaving him behind. But I decided it was in his best interest that I go, so I called Charity Hospital in New Orleans and asked what I needed to do. I had no idea that they required a couple of years nursing experience, but, fortunately, I had already gotten that while Bill was away. I've always thought that if you just leave God alone and don't nose around too much, He'll take care of things. You'll see that, for me, that happened time and time again. In this case, the only snag—and again, it was a godsend—was that Charity had an eight-month backlog in admissions, so I would have to wait in Hope for almost a year. I was ecstatic: It gave me more time before I would have to leave my baby.

So from the fall of 1946 through the spring of 1947, I had a wonderful time getting to know my son. When Mother wasn't monopolizing him, I would take him out for a spin in his carriage. A good friend of mine from high school had a baby about Bill's age, and she and I would often stroll through the streets of Hope together, showing off our babies. I remember loving that time so much. The summer had started giving way to fall, and there was sometimes a crispness in the air. We had to watch to make sure leaves didn't fall into the carriages and cover up our babies' precious faces.

Other times, Mother would take care of Bill and I would go downtown to a movie. I saw a lot of movies during the fall and winter of 1946; that was the year *The Best Years of Our Lives* came out, and Alfred Hitchcock's *Notorious,* and *The Postman Always Rings Twice.* It was nice getting away from everyone and everything and losing myself for a couple of hours in a dark theater. Many times, of course, I wanted to talk with someone—I mean *talk,* not just be polite or funny or social. My mother's sister, whom I called Otie, was the baby of her family and was really closer to my age than my mother's. She was a nurse, too, and I could talk with her about things Mother and I couldn't have discussed in a million years. I don't even remember what those things were, other than, probably, Mother herself—and, of course, my present and my future, whatever *that* was going to be.

In the spring of 1947 that future was cast—though I didn't know it yet—when I met a new man. Actually, it was a remeeting. Years earlier, during one of my visits home from nursing school, my father had introduced me to a friend he had made back when he ran the liquor store. This hadn't been intended as an introduction for a date or anything like that; I just happened to be somewhere with Daddy one day and we ran into this man who happened to own a Buick dealership in Hope. When I met him again, he was thirty-six, and I remember thinking he was attractive, and a lot more dashing, in a dangerous sort of way, than most of the men in Hope. His name was Roger Clinton, but a lot of people called him Dude.

I could see why. He dressed fit to kill, with sharp-creased trousers and fine-tailored sport coats and two-toned shoes. He was tall, though not as tall as Bill Blythe had been; I guess Roger stood about five feet eleven inches. Tall enough. His hair was dark and curly, and his eyes twinkled when he talked because he was always about to say something funny. Wherever he was, he kept everybody laughing. He was the life of the party, and he partied a lot. There was also something else about him that it didn't take you long to find out: He absolutely loved to gamble.

People fell under Roger Clinton's spell. Men seemed to like being around him because he was in a man's business and he talked men's talk and he liked things men liked—speed and money and risk. Women liked him because he was charming. When he asked me out, I said yes.

I didn't know much about his background, and of course I didn't pry. Some things were obvious, however. He was from Hot Springs, that wild gambling town to the northeast of us, and he felt somewhat adrift in dull old Hope. To understand Roger Clinton, you need to know a little about this town he had come from. For twenty years Hot Springs had been run single-handedly by its mayor, a dapper, ruthless political boss named Leo P. McLaughlin, who had rigged the town so that its prime industry was gambling. Gambling was flat-out illegal in Arkansas, you understand, but every week McLaughlin's people paid off a number of state officials up to and including the governor. A lady in my Birthday Club was the person who actually carried the brown bag full of money to the governor's office.

With this gambling came tourists—some of them pretty notorious. As the story goes, Al Capone and his archenemy Bugs Moran, who had been trying to murder each other in Chicago, would declare a truce every now and then and go to Hot Springs for a vacation. McLaughlin told these killers they could stay as long as they behaved themselves *that's* the kind of power the man had. And behave they would, because there was so much to enjoy in Hot

Springs—the gambling, the mineral baths, the nightclubs, the prostitution. Every name entertainer in the business played there. So for all of Roger Clinton's life Hot Springs had been one of the premier playgrounds in America. It had also been a place where gangsters were cool, and rules were made to be bent, and money and power—however you got them—were the total measure of a man.

Roger talked all the time about going back, but his older brother, Raymond, owned the Buick dealership in Hot Springs. When the war was getting started and the Army established the Southwestern Proving Grounds in Hope—where they stored bombs—the potential for car sales in Hope suddenly looked promising, so Roger, as he told it, came to Hope to build *his* successful dealership. I don't suppose the words were actually spoken, but Hot Springs didn't seem big enough for both Raymond and Roger.

Some things about Roger Clinton were not so obvious. For one, I knew he had been married, but we never really talked about his wife. I assumed they were divorced. For another, it was his brother Raymond who had sent him to Hope to open the dealership. Still another was that when Roger was drinking, which was often, he was prone to get into fights. A close friend of mine in Hot Springs, who knew Roger and Raymond well in their early years, says that Roger once bashed a Puerto Rican boy in the head with a cue stick, and Raymond had to come get Roger out of trouble. Raymond also had to intercede when Roger rigged a craps table in Hope and then had the audacity to lure a city official of Hope into the game. The relationship between successful Raymond and his somewhat reckless baby brother was also not immediately obvious, but I guess if you paid attention to events like these, a certain pattern might begin to emerge.

As usual, I didn't pay a lot of attention to such things; I accepted Roger at face value. One thing I certainly didn't know—in fact, didn't know it until I started writing this book—is that Roger had probably started a little business venture with my father. When Hope went dry in 1944, the closest place to buy a bottle of whiskey was in Texarkana, thirty-five miles away. Apparently, as a service to the doctors and lawyers and other "right people" who wanted a toddy and were willing to pay to avoid driving all that distance, my father maintained a supply of selected beverages at the grocery store—under the apples, or so I've been told. Roger was the supplier and Daddy handled sales, and it seems that everybody in town but me knew about the arrangement.

My initial attraction to Roger Clinton was nothing like the fireball of feeling I had when I saw Bill Blythe for the first time. For Bill, the All-American Boy, I had felt instant love, instant desire to be with him for the rest of my life. When I met Roger, the Gambler, I had no idea that we would someday get married, nor would I have believed it if anybody had told me it was going to happen; he just seemed like someone fun to pass the time with, and right about then I needed a little fun in my life.

So we began going out. Because most of the things Roger liked to do were illegal in Hope—I'm talking about drinking and gambling—we sometimes drove to Texarkana for dinner and nightclubbing. More often, though, we'd go to Roger's apartment and lots of his friends would come over. Everything revolved around Roger there, and he would keep the party lively. His trademark phrase was "God dang it!" I remember he used to say, "God dang it, let's all get drunk and talk about the chances we had to marry!" He was hilarious. Those evenings also served as my introduction to a cast of characters you couldn't have made up if you were a novelist. Little did I know that they would become part of my life for decades.

Many of them were local would-be Guys and Dolls, but Roger's closest running buddies were imported from Hot Springs. Probably his best friend was Van Hampton Lyell, whose family owned the Coca-Cola bottling plant in Hot Springs. Roger always called him Van Hampton, using both names. Whatever you called him, he was a wild man and a daredevil, and to make matters worse he had a pilot's license. There are scores of stories about how Van Hampton would take people up in a rented plane and they would be floating peacefully above Hot Springs when suddenly Van Hampton would decide to fly *under* the Highway 70 bridge that spanned Lake Hamilton. His passengers would scream and plead, but that only delighted Van more. He must have been a good pilot, because nobody ever got killed. The biggest danger in flying with Van Hampton Lyell was a heart attack.

I'll never forget an incident that happened early on in my relationship with Roger. Van Hampton and Roger were always fabricating excuses to go somewhere. "I've got car-dealership business and Van Hampton and I have to go to Memphis," Roger would say—you fill in the name of the town. On this particular evening it was Coca-Cola business, and Texarkana was the place they had to go. While they were away, I had a girlfriend—I've forgotten who—in town to visit, and we decided to take a drive. We headed out in a leisurely pace on Highway 67, which was the road to Texarkana. Suddenly I saw Van Hampton's car pass us going fast in the opposite direction behind a big semitrailer truck, and I promise you the hood of that car was underneath the trailer of that eighteen-wheeler—that's how close to the truck Van Hampton was driving.

I whipped my car around and tried to catch them. Dumb me, I thought I might be able to get their attention and make them stop. They beat us home, of course, and when we walked in, I said, "For God's sake, do you realize how you were driving?" And they both just died laughing. "We thought we were parking in the garage," they said, each thinking the other was the funniest thing he had ever seen. And you know, my friend and I were just so happy nobody was killed that we laughed along with them. Back then—especially in Hot Springs—getting drunk and crazy was considered cute, and though I hate to admit it, for a time I thought it was, too.

Roger's other close friend was Gabe Crawford, who owned several drugstores in Hot Springs and one in Hope. Gabe was married to Roger's niece, also named Virginia, who happened to be about my age. She was a beautiful girl—a dazzling blond—and had been the very first Miss Hot Springs. If you thought I was a live wire, you obviously hadn't laid eyes on Virginia Crawford. She called Roger "Uncle Baby Boy" because his mother still referred to him as her baby. On weekends Virginia and Gabe would breeze into Hope astride Gabe's big motorcycle, fueled by Coca-Cola and a half pint of whiskey. I remember the first time I met them, Roger had told them how cute Bill was, so they made me go back home and get him. Many years later, Gabe Crawford would play an important role in Bill Clinton's political career.

Like Raymond Clinton, Gabe had also seen the business possibilities in Hope when the Proving Grounds was put in, and he jumped at the opportunity to expand his drugstore operation. But with Gabe and Roger being such good friends, and Roger missing the action of Hot Springs so much, it was probably inevitable that Gabe's drugstore would deal in more than Q-Tips and prescriptions. Hot Springs had several bookie joints, and at Gabe and Roger's invitation two or three of the bookies moved to Hope to set up a bookie operation in the back of Gabe's drugstore. They even brought in a few slot machines. In Hope, "running down to the drugstore" took on a whole new meaning.

But Roger Clinton didn't have to leave his apartment to gamble if the mood struck him, which it did with predictable regularity. I remember an evening soon after we had begun dating. Roger had some people over, as he usually did, and they were sitting around the living room drinking and decided to get up a game of craps. So Roger turned the coffee table upside down to use as the craps table—the edge of the table kept the dice from rolling off onto the floor. I was watching, not playing, and I don't think I've ever seen so much money in my life. And Roger was getting drunker and drunker and drunker.

But I just thought, golly, he's sure winning, so he must be all right. In a little while, though, I noticed that the other people were beginning to cheat him. So whenever Roger would win a big pot, I would slip most of the money in my purse—I'd leave him just enough to stay in the game. He no more knew what I was doing than anything.

The next day he took me to lunch and said, "You know, it's a funny thing. I was in a craps game last night." I don't think he even realized I had been there. "It seemed like I was winning all night long," he said, "and today I don't have any money." I said something like,

"No kidding," and then I opened my purse. "*Here's* your money, Roger." He was as happy as a baby.

&.

When the time came to leave for New Orleans, I almost couldn't do it. On my own I wasn't going to be able to afford the cost of flying back to Hope at all, and I hated the thought of not seeing my baby for a whole year.

But if Roger Clinton ever loved anybody in this world, it was my son Bill. He also loved me, of course—I don't doubt that. But his love for Bill wasn't complicated by all the things that get in the way between a man and a woman. Roger promised me he would pay for me to come home to see Bill, and I loved Roger for that. For that kind of kindness you could overlook a whole lot of shortcomings, and I surely did. I have to admit that his money and apparent success had also turned my head a little bit. I still had no thought of marrying him, but in the short time I had been seeing him he had certainly become a force to be reckoned with inside our family.

Predictably, my mother was less enthralled with him than Daddy and I were, but I don't think it all had to do with me. She was very, very protective of Bill, and she probably resented—and maybe even feared—Roger Clinton's attentions toward my son. So she had *two* reasons to be glad I was leaving: It would remove me from daily contact with Roger, and it would give her total control of Bill.

That was the situation I left as I boarded the train and headed south.

Five

IT ALMOST KILLED me to be away from Bill, and yet I'm convinced that my second stint in New Orleans ultimately saved my life.

Nurse-anesthetist work is all-consuming. You don't do it halfway. You don't daydream, you don't let your emotions wander. You're the person responsible for putting another human being into a state of unconsciousness—a state somewhere between life and death. For thirty years, from the minute that I would walk into that operating room and start talking to the patient and begin putting him to sleep until I got him safely back to the recovery room, nothing in this world could have crossed my mind. I don't care what problems were on the outside, I don't care what problems I might've been having at home. I never thought of my life beyond the moment.

I loved nurse-anesthetist school. We learned all about cyclopropane, nitrous oxide, oxygen, sodium pentothal. We learned to operate a gas machine. It was a heady time for us students, because in a year we would all be out in the real world in business for ourselves. This appealed to my independent spirit. A nurse works for a doctor or a hospital, but, back then anyway, a nurse anesthetist only worked for the patient. And a nurse anesthetist has so much more earning power than a regular nurse. I was proud of myself, proud of my courage in leaving my baby and coming to a distant city to prepare myself. But my pride wasn't just personal: It occurred to me that Hope had never had a trained anesthetist. At that time, the doctors just sort of did a lot of everything, including putting the patients to sleep. If you're over forty, you may remember ether. Doctors would put that mask over your nose and turn on the drip themselves. But now I was going to be trained in more advanced methods. How wonderful, I told myself, to be able to take this expertise back to my old hometown.

Of course, in the quieter moments I was as homesick as I could be. Roger did pay for me to fly home at least twice, and those were wonderful visits. I remember I had an awful time making myself climb the steps to that airplane on Sunday night. When I got back to New Orleans, I would hurt inside for half of the next week, missing Bill so. I thought I couldn't possibly wait until the next trip home. Then one day Mother called and said she and Bill were going to come see *me* for a visit—Daddy had somehow gotten the money to send them on the train. Now I wonder if it was Roger who helped him. I'll never know, but I do know this: It was an extraordinary gift to me. Mother and Bill came down twice during that year, and we would spend the weekend taking long, lazy walks and pushing Bill in his stroller. New Orleans is a fascinating city, and even without money or transportation we were enthralled—especially watching Bill discover this wider world. He loved it when we would buy popcorn and feed the pigeons. By Saturday night, though, I would start getting that sad old Sunday feeling. The next day when Mother took Bill from my arms and boarded the train north, I literally dropped to my knees by the tracks, I was aching so.

Roger flew down to see me several times himself. He and I hadn't had any kind of "understanding," so I was dating other people—a few med students, a few doctors, nothing terribly serious. Roger, I'm sure, was cutting his usual swath through Hope. But when he would come to New Orleans, he wouldn't question me and I wouldn't question him; we would simply pick up where we had left off. He loved New Orleans, which was almost as lively a town as Hot Springs.

But Roger was a little surprised to see the effect New Orleans had on me. I particularly remember a night at the Roosevelt Hotel when the performer was Georgia Gibbs, later to become famous for her hit song "Tweedle Dee." I knew all the words to the song she was singing, and I couldn't contain myself. So I simply excused myself from the table, and I guess Roger thought I was going to powder my nose. Next thing he knew, I was standing onstage and singing along with Her Nibs, Miss Georgia Gibbs. Roger had to have an extra drink just to settle his nerves.

Those weekends weren't all wildness, though. Roger and I would talk a lot, especially about Bill. It was nice to be with someone who understood that emptiness I felt inside. Roger, it occurred to me, was becoming very special in my life, and part of it was because he cared for my son so. That's a very attractive trait in a mother's eyes—almost irresistible, in fact.

One of my trips home came in December 1947, when Roger insisted that I be in Hope for his annual Christmas eggnog party. For someone studying anesthesia, I should've gotten school credit for being there: The stuff Roger was serving would put you out faster than the stuff I was studying. Roger called it moonshine, and it was something like 150 proof. I asked him where he got it, and his eyes began to take on that bad-boy twinkle.

"The police save it for me," he said. He loved that, of course. It was *so* Hot Springs—except, of course, liquor was legal up there. Hempstead County was dry, which meant that moonshiners could do exceptionally well, if they didn't get caught. Whenever the police would raid a still, however, they would confiscate the moonshine and take it back to the station. And there they would keep it safe and sound for Roger's party.

I had never been to one of these events, but of course I had heard about them. The Eggnog Party, held every year at the Buick dealership, was on its way to becoming a major holiday tradition—Roger Clinton's repayment to the local citizenry for their loyal trade throughout the year. And yet Roger derived more pleasure from it than anyone. He loved being the center of attention, the big man, the chief frog in the Hope pond. I mean that in a good way: It was fun to be around him, and to watch him operate. Even his vast vanity was charming. I like a man who likes himself, and Roger Clinton certainly seemed to approve of Roger Clinton. He was always trying to catch his reflection in a mirror or a window. And when he was playing host, you've never seen such strutting in all your life.

But the thing was, he made you feel like strutting, too.

I didn't have much opportunity for strutting once I got back to Hope packing my new diploma. I thought I was bringing the future home, but I soon learned another lesson of life: When you start thinking you're the answer to everyone's needs, you better go back and rephrase the question.

When I got out of nurse-anesthetist training, I invested in a gas machine. I don't remember how much it was, but it was enough so that I had had to start paying it off on time. Oh, I was bushy-tailed. I was ready to jump into my career full force. But my professional arrival in Hope was met with a resounding yawn.

The doctors simply didn't want to change. They had "girls" they could tell to drip a perfectly suitable can of ether, so what was the point of paying me for what I said was a better way? There's such a thing as getting ahead of your times, but it wasn't only that. Doctors don't like to be told there's a better way—especially by someone who doesn't have an MD after his name. Or maybe I should go ahead and say *her* name, because I'm convinced that sexism played a part in my career, from start to finish. I was always friends with the doctors at the places I worked—I would go have coffee with them in the mornings, would sit and laugh and talk and tell stories with them. They would kid me, and I would kid them right back. Most of the time I was the only female. I began to feel that I was "one of the boys," but that was my mistake. If you're a female, you can never be one of the boys, and thinking so only heightens your disappointment.

Ultimately, the doctors in Hope probably thought of me as just another of the "girls," and I suppose my personality worked against me some, too: I'm friendly, I'm outgoing, and I like men. Always have, always will. Men like me, too. Back then there wasn't an open war between the sexes, and there was a lot of flirting back and forth between the doctors—most of whom were men—and the nurses, who were virtually all women. It didn't mean anything, but, in hindsight, it probably did create an atmosphere that allowed most of the men in power to dismiss, or at least disregard, any professional aspirations that happened to be held by a woman.

In other words, this was a period when I was getting *my* consciousness raised.

I landed a few anesthetist jobs, but mostly my gas machine sat around gathering dust. To pay the bills I had to take private-duty work at the various hospitals. One night I was sitting with a patient at Josephine Hospital and Dr. Jim McKenzie, the owner, happened to be there. It was a quiet time for both of us. I had known Jim since my last nursing stint, and I had always liked him. I think he thought I was funny; forty-five years later, he still remembers me saying to somebody who had done something kind of boneheaded, "Were your mama and daddy cousins?" So I made my pitch to go to work for him at Josephine Hospital, doing anesthesia when possible and filling in on the floor as needed. The man showed brilliant judgment: He hired me on the spot.

It was a relief to have a regular job to go to. Dr. McKenzie was a jokester and I was, too, so we got along fine. I remember once he came in carrying this huge box, and he was straining, it was so heavy. When he handed it to me, I was ready for something weighing a ton, but it was so light I banged my chin with it. The box was filled with cotton balls. Dr. McKenzie got a huge kick out of that, because it was one of the few times that he got me instead of the other way around.

Once again, as a working nurse I found that my mother's track record was hard to live up to. The private-duty nurse's job is to make the patient as comfortable as possible, and boy, she did her job. If I was on hospital duty and had to look after a whole floor of people she'd been nursing one-on-one, I found myself cursing Mother under my breath. Darn it, I didn't have *time* to go around and rub all those people's backs with alcohol or lotion every thirty minutes the way she had.

But for all her light touch with patients, at home Mother increasingly rubbed me the wrong way. I was twenty-five, twenty-six, even twenty-seven and still living with my parents. It was a blessing, of course, that I had somebody to take care of Bill during the day. But there's always a price to be paid for such a service. Mother had already grown incredibly attached to Bill while I was in anesthetist school, and now, with me working, she still held sway over him. She would dress him and feed him and walk him and buy him things. Nothing was too fine or too expensive for her beloved grandson: I've got a picture of him at about age three, and he's wearing an outfit Mother had bought him, a little pin-striped suit and a little navy overcoat.

She had begun to focus her ambition on him, as well. I can still see them sitting at that kitchen table by the window on Hervey Street, Bill age three or four and Mother in her late forties by then, her dark eyes intense as could be while she drilled him with homemade flash cards. Actually, they were playing cards that she would arrange in the crossbars of the window, and she would quiz Bill on his numbers, one through ten. He loved learning even then, but of course he didn't dare not learn, if that's what his Mammaw wanted him to do. You didn't cross her. Bill jokes that he can attribute his weight problem to the fact that he'd still be sitting in his high chair on Hervey Street if he hadn't cleaned his plate.

Mother remained amazingly immune to Roger Clinton's charms, and I still couldn't understand it. I pointed out to her how good, for example, he was with children. My cousin Dale Drake, then Dale Hefner, remembers a year when it snowed in Hope and Roger pulled her kids, who were older than Bill, in makeshift sleds behind his Jeep. And Roger had a big German shepherd named Susie, which is where I got my love for German shepherds. Bill loved Susie, and Roger would bring her over to our house and let Bill play with her out in the backyard. This was during the time that Vince Foster's family lived in the house behind us, and Vince used to play with Susie, too. Roger would watch them bounding around in the yard after Susie, and he would get the biggest kick out of the kids' having so much fun. Daddy would be out there, but Mother wouldn't have anything to do with Roger when he would come over. Roger, incidentally, didn't care much for Mother, either, and though he was always polite, he didn't go out of his way to play up to her.

Her disapproval of him wasn't always passive. Once, for some occasion, Roger gave me a beautiful white leather jacket. It was buckskin, I guess you'd call it, and it was the softest and best-smelling garment I'd ever had on my back. The coat had fringe, and when I would do the shimmy, the whole thing would shake. I loved that coat.

One night I was getting ready to go out and I couldn't find my buckskin jacket anywhere. I'm one of those compulsive people who puts things back where I found them, so I knew I hadn't misplaced it. Mother knew I was looking, but she hadn't uttered a word. Finally, I said, "Mother, do you know where my white leather jacket is?"

She looked at me the same way she had looked at my father when he had come home and discovered the groceries she had ordered. "I burned it," she said.

&

At times, when Mother got to be too overbearing, I would take Bill and go stay the night at a girlfriend's house. And I would spend as much time as possible at Roger's apartment, which was on Elm Street.

Even when I got home from anesthetist training, Roger and I weren't dating each other exclusively. I was seeing a drug salesman for a while, and I also dated a doctor or two. But as time passed, the other people started falling by the wayside. Roger and I were spending most of our weekends together, with Gabe and Virginia coming from Hot Springs or us going there. We were heavy, heavy partyers in those days. Virginia Heath insists on reminding me of the times when we would visit them and I would climb up on the counter, obviously under the influence of something like Roger's moonshine, and sing this absurd song I had made up "I'm the Hempstead County idiot," it went. Which I obviously was.

By this time I had my own key to Roger's apartment, and I guess I had the expectations that come with being given your own key. So one weekend, when Roger was out of town, I was surprised to get a phone call from a friend informing me that Roger had a woman staying at his apartment—supposedly an airline stewardess from Kansas City—and that he was away with her that very moment.

As I say, I'm not a jealous person, but I sure as heck don't like somebody making a Hempstead County idiot of me. I must've been alone at home with Bill, who was probably three at the time, because I decided to take him with me while I went over to Roger's to investigate. So I packed up the future President of the United States and we drove across town to pursue my own domestic policy.

I let myself in and it was pretty obvious that Roger had been—well, let's just say "entertaining." There was expensive and extremely sexy lingerie all over the apartment—lacy bras draped over chairs, silk stockings on the floor, garter belts and filmy little slips cascading off the edge of the bed. The woman wasn't just a tart, she was *messy*. With all this underwear lying around, I wondered what she could've possibly been wearing right then.

On a table I found her return airline ticket. *Oh, no*, I thought, *you're here, you're going to stay*. And I tore the ticket into pieces the approximate size of English peas. Then I took them into the bathroom and flushed them down the toilet. *Let Roger pay for her to get home*, I thought.

Ah, but that was too easy, too private a penalty. I was after a public humiliation. With Bill in tow, I walked around the apartment thinking, *What's the worst thing I can do to him?* The wheels were really turning. It occurred to me that the only two tenants in this entire building were Roger and the old man who owned the place. No one would mistake all this lingerie as coming from the old man's apartment.

So I took it all and hung it outside on the clothesline. There was no way that anybody who drove by could miss it. I didn't see Roger's face when he pulled up the next day, but I heard that all week at work he was ribbed by people who had seen or been told about the display in his yard. Everybody in town saw that Roger Clinton was *seriously* in the doghouse.

❦

Mother knew it was coming, but she still wasn't ready. And when I told her I was marrying Roger, she reacted by trying to get legal custody of my son.

To her mind, Roger Clinton wasn't fit to be under the same roof with Bill, and she said she was going to stop the possibility of it if she could. I had seen my mother do some crazy things, but this went beyond anything she had ever even approached before. She was actually announcing that she was willing to rip this family apart. I remember thinking that the blackness inside her had finally taken over, and there was nothing left but the blackness itself.

I screamed that the only way she was going to get my child was over my dead body. But she didn't scream back: She was perfectly cool about it, and that scared me. She seemed so self-assured, and I was accustomed to her being able to do anything she said she would do. Daddy kept trying to reason with her, as he had all their married life, but her mind was made up. I clutched Bill, who was four years old. I probably thought he was too young to be seriously affected by even such scenes as this, but I was dead wrong, of course. Forty-one years later, during the presidential campaign, I would be flabbergasted to hear some of what he remembered about his early life in Hope. I don't know whether or not he remembers this part. In any case, Mother went downtown to consult an attorney. Fortunately, common sense—and the laws of the land—prevailed, and she was told there was no way in the world she could get my child.

In hindsight, I suppose you could make the case that Mother knew best—about Roger Clinton, I mean. But I don't think any of us can live our lives that way. I won't look back and say I was wrong to get into a marriage that exposed me to alcoholism and abuse, but also brought me my son Roger and helped shape Bill's life. And I know darn well that you can't live other people's lives for them, the way my mother was trying to do, and by the same token you can't relinquish responsibility for your life to anyone else. I don't blame Roger Clinton for making our nights miserable for two decades; *I* stayed in the marriage, and *I* made the best decisions I could at the time. I'm not a victim, and I never will be a victim.

Having said that, however, I'll also say this: Mother obviously saw a bit of herself in Roger Clinton, and it scared her. Later on, I would come to see a fair amount of Roger's manipulative, even evil, side, too. But I think both Mother and Roger were essentially good people who just weren't strong enough to fight off their demons.

We were married in the early evening of June 19, 1950, at a little white house that served as the parsonage of a church a few blocks from the racetrack in Hot Springs. To be honest with you, I can't remember what church it was, or why we chose that place or that preacher. Most likely we selected it for convenience. Roger certainly wasn't much of a churchgoer when I met him, nor was I at the time. I had grown up Baptist, but one thing and another—nursing jobs, most often—had kept me away from regular attendance.

What I do remember is that Gabe and Virginia stood up for us, and that I wore a white dress with a matching cloche hat, with my thick, dark hair pulled back. My parents weren't there, nor was Bill, nor were any of Roger's family besides his niece. We didn't invite anyone else. I knew my parents wouldn't come, so I didn't bother. What I didn't know is that Roger's family might've had a few problems with the wedding themselves.

We bought a little white wooden bungalow on a corner lot on Thirteenth Street in Hope, the kind of house that had been built all over the country to fill the demand of the soldiers coming home from World War II. It had a small concrete porch, and then you stepped into a tiny living room. To the left was a dining room just large enough for a table, and to the right of that was the kitchen—which had a door opening out to the carport. From the living room, you walked down a hall, past the kitchen on the left, then the bathroom, then the master bedroom at the end on the left-hand side. Across the hall were two other bedrooms. The back one opposite our bedroom was Bill's room, and the one next to that became a playroom. As soon as we got there, Roger went out and bought Bill a Lionel train and set it up in that playroom. The two of them would stay in there playing with that train for hours, and I began to wonder exactly which one of them Roger had bought it for.

❧

Even though this was my second marriage and I had been a mother for four years, I was as green as a blackjack table when it came to the business of being a homemaker. My mother had never let me do anything—cooking, cleaning, decorating, whatever—because, to her, anything I would do would just be wrong and it was easier to do it herself. After a little of that treatment, I stopped trying: It *was* easier for her to do it herself.

Fortunately, an elderly couple, the Williamses, lived next door to us on Thirteenth Street, and I tell people to this day that Alice Williams taught me everything I know about homemaking. The Williamses didn't have any children of their own, and I guess Alice sort of adopted me. Actually, I plunged in and tried my best to learn to cook on my own, but she would come over and rescue me whenever I got into a bind—which was nearly every meal. Of course the meals I served were balanced, with meat, potatoes, green vegetable, salad, and dessert. But I grew up on fried foods, as most of my generation did, so I confess that my taste ran to greasy, and as plentiful as I could serve up. Later on, as the world got more and more health conscious, I tried to adjust my cooking; later still, after I contracted cancer and had to curb my diet, I cut out the fried and greasy foods altogether. But I'll be honest with you: I sure do miss it. Give me a good old french fry over a stalk of celery any day.

Bill spent much of his time on Thirteenth Street out in the yard playing cowboys. Before John F. Kennedy rode into the picture, Hopalong Cassidy was Bill's hero, and I treasure a photograph I took of him standing on the sidewalk in front of the house wearing a black cowboy hat, boots, and a black, short-jacketed cowboy suit with Hoppy's picture on it. As a Cassidy myself, I heartily approved of Bill's taste. Our backyard was filled with pine trees, and Bill would roam that seeming forest chasing bad guys for hours on end.

From the beginning, Bill was a special child—smart, sensitive, mature beyond his years. He remembers my sitting him down in that house on Thirteenth Street and telling him about his real father. He must've been four or five at the time, but talking with him at that age was like talking with a grown friend. I told him how Bill Blythe and I had met, and how we had decided to get married before he went off to the service. I told him about Bill's family, as much as I knew. By this time, he was familiar with Earnest Blythe and his family, because they would sometimes drive over from Texas just to "see little Billy." I explained why I'd gone home from Chicago, and how his daddy had died in a wreck coming to get me. I showed him his father's citation for excellence in his military service. Bill Clinton still remembers all of that, and to this day he believes, as I do, in the possibility of love at first sight.

When he wasn't playing in the backyard or on the front walk, sometimes Bill would mosey over to the Williamses' house next door and visit with Mr. Williams—Ned—who was retired from the railroad and spent most of his days making scale-model trains out in his shop. But that wasn't all Ned did out there: He drank. And Alice would sometimes talk with me about it a little. Some nights, she said, Ned was worse than other nights, and on those occasions Alice was afraid for her own safety. Listening, I felt for her, of course—but I also began to feel a vague foreboding for myself. I never said anything to her or to anybody else, but her stories about Ned gave me my first inkling of the direction my own future might be heading.

Even then, Roger would sometimes come home with a little too much whiskey in him. He wasn't always abusive, though. Sometimes he would simply withdraw. Bill and I would be having a perfectly fine time and Roger would just go into the living room, or whatever room we weren't in, and sit by himself. He would do that occasionally even when he wasn't drunk. I know now that Roger had pressures on him during that time that I was oblivious to then.

It turns out that Roger was still married—to his second wife—when he and I met, which is why his family may not have looked too favorably on me at first. This wife was named Ina Mae, and they were married on December 23, 1933. Roger and Ina Mae had no children, though she had two sons, Roy and George Murphy, from a previous marriage. By all accounts, Roger was a good stepfather to the boys—both of whom I know as grown-ups today, and you won't find any finer men than Roy and George Murphy. But as early as August of 1948, the month Ina Mae filed for divorce from Roger, she had been garnishing his bank accounts in order to get support money that she said he owed her.

I never knew much about Roger's financial dealings—a fact that, as you'll see, would eventually get me into trouble. But Roger was one of those people who preferred to deal in cash, so the trails probably wouldn't have been very clear even if I'd had a mind to follow them. I do remember his secretary at the Buick dealership saying that Roger "kept stealing from himself"—in other words, he would just stick his hand in the cash drawer and take whatever he needed, whenever he needed. It was the secretary's job to keep him balanced, so whenever she would come up short, she would say to him: "Roger, have you been stealing from yourself again?" It was a joke between them.

Now I wonder if maybe Roger dealt in cash in order to hide his finances from Ina Mae. It's truly amazing to me what you can go down to the courthouse and find out about people—court records show that in July and September of 1951, and then again in September of 1952, Ina Mae filed against him for overdue child support. As of September 22, 1952, he was apparently $2,210 behind in his payments—a huge amount, considering that his salary at the dealership was $10,000 a year. And I didn't know a thing about it.

❧

We had fun, too, of course. Many weekends I would leave Bill with Mother and Daddy and we would drive to Gabe and Virginia's in Roger's little yellow 1952 Henry J. convertible. Actually, though we called it a Henry J., that car had burned in a fire, and Roger's dealership had rebuilt it from spare parts. The *majority* of it was Henry

J. It had fiberglass where the backseat had been, and no roof. If we got caught in the rain, we were in trouble.

By this time I was beginning to know my way around Hot Springs and was finding the place to my liking. I'm not one for rules, and the only rule in Hot Springs was to enjoy yourself—a rule I could handle quite nicely, thank you. Virginia and I would often leave the boys at home for a few hours and drive over to a place called Spencer's, where we'd get a couple of Scotch and waters and play the slot machines. There was still plenty of gambling action even after Mayor McLaughlin was thrown out of office. I guess some of the major gambling places had been closed down, and others operated deeper underground than before. But you could carry your drink around with you downtown, even on Sundays. After Spencer's we might get one to go and drive around seeing the sights for a while, and then we might stop off at the Southern Club and have another drink and play the slots some more. By the time we got back to Gabe's, he and Roger would be roaring drunk.

You know how it is with drinking: You do it to excess, you feel terrible—both physically and emotionally—and you vow to quit forever. Then, when you start to feel a little better, you squint your eyes and look at it a different way. *Oh, what the heck,* you rationalize to yourself. *I can have just one or two.* It's the same way living with an alcoholic. Drinking had been so much a part of Roger's and my relationship that I really hadn't worried about his excesses in any sustained way. There were times, of course, when it bothered me—and then it wouldn't be all that bad for a while. I would just busy myself with my work and forget about it.

Then one day Roger took a shot at me, and I couldn't ignore it anymore.

You've heard this story, no doubt. During the presidential campaign Bill told the press about this episode, and I almost fell out of my chair. Bill and I had never even talked about it, and I assumed he didn't remember it. He was probably five at the time.

My grandmother, my mother's mother, was in the hospital and wasn't expected to live; I wanted Bill to see her again before she died. Roger and I were in our little master bedroom, which also had a door out to the driveway, and Bill was in the hall about to walk into the room. I was sitting at my dresser brushing my hair. Roger was leaning against the far wall staring at me.

"Where do you think you're going?" Roger said.

"I'm taking Bill to the hospital," I said matter-of-factly, obviously not grasping the depth of his mood. "We're going to see Mammaw. She may not live through the night." I hadn't invited Roger to go because I always felt that he, or any other husband, was welcome on a visit to my family, but they weren't obligated to go.

"You're not going," he said.

"Well, of course I'm going," I said flippantly. "What in the world's wrong with you?"

Before I knew it, I heard a gunshot and a bullet smacked into the wall next to me, about two feet up from the floor. I was stunned: I didn't even know there was a pistol in the house.

Almost immediately Roger was sorry, but it was too late. In fact, I don't believe he was shooting *at* me, he was shooting just to scare me. It worked, too, but I didn't react the way Roger thought I might. I grabbed Bill by the hand and we got out of there. We went across the street to the neighbors' house, and they called the police. In a few minutes a squad car pulled up in front of my house and two policemen knocked on the door and arrested Roger.

That night Gabe Crawford and Roger's brother Raymond drove down to Hope and went to the jail, thinking they would just throw their weight around and get Roger out of this trouble the way they had so many times before. But the policeman had news for them. This was Hope, Arkansas, he said—Virginia Cassidy's hometown. Around here, they had known me since the day I was born. No hotshot from Hot Springs was going take a shot at me and get away with it. Raymond Clinton wasn't used to being talked to like that, but pretty soon it became obvious even to him that an act of Congress wouldn't get Roger out of the Hope jail that night.

Six

ROGER CLINTON WOULDN'T have known a soybean if he'd found one floating in his bourbon, but suddenly he decided he wanted to become a farmer.

The year was 1953. Bill was about to turn seven and was going into the second grade that fall. Suddenly Roger told us we were moving to Hot Springs—or, more precisely, we were moving a few miles outside Hot Springs to a four-hundred-acre farm on which there would be cattle and sheep. Roger, the man known far and wide as Dude, was going to manage this menagerie.

I was speechless. Not that I cared that we moved to Hot Springs, mind you. Back then, I'll admit, it never occurred to me that I had a choice or even a vote in the matter: You went where your husband went. But, in fact, I thought moving to Hot Springs was probably a pretty good idea. For one thing, it was time for me to live away from my parents; for another, I was beginning to really worry about the effects of Roger's drinking, and I didn't want anybody—especially my parents—to find out.

So far, the pistol shot had been the only violent episode, but other problems were developing. I want to make something clear about Roger Clinton, however: I know now that in Ina Mae's divorce petition she accused him of beating her with his fists and with the heel of her shoe, and it's clear that he did have a terrible violent streak running just below the surface; but in all the years Roger and I were together, he mostly kept it below the surface. I stress the word *mostly*. His real abuse was verbal, the way my mother's had been to my father.

Roger would keep me awake all night with his tantrums and his accusations of infidelity and his jealousy about everything under the sun. What I know now, but didn't then, is that this is the nature of an alcoholic. This helps him deal with his own conscience. If he can point out that you're guilty of some bad thing, it keeps the focus on you and not on him.

It's interesting, considering what I've learned about alcoholics, to think about the similarities between Roger, who drank to excess, and my mother, who preached against alcohol. During research for this book somebody told me that Mother sold bootleg whiskey out of our house on Hervey Street, but I don't believe it. Later in life she would in fact become addicted to a dangerous drug, so I'll grant you she had the capability of addiction in her. But if she ever had one thing to do with alcohol, she kept it so hidden that I find it impossible to conceive of such a thing.

In any case, I was happy to be leaving Hope—leaving, I prayed, with our family's secrets intact. On the other hand, I couldn't for the life of me imagine Roger Clinton on a farm. I tactfully tried to explain to him that, judging from what my grandfather and father—both farmers—had told me, it seemed that you really needed to *know* something about farming even to hope to turn a profit at it.

But Roger's mind was made up. This was just the kind of off-the-wall scheme that got his juices flowing. Of course Gabe Crawford was involved—it was his farm that Roger wanted us to buy. Van Hampton Lyell played a role, too. He would come over before we left Hope, and he and Roger would talk for hours about how it was going to be. After they'd had a few drinks, it was going to be dandy indeed. In Roger's mind, I think, he was moving back to Hot Springs to become a gentleman farmer.

My son Bill now reminds me the farm had an outhouse, a fact I had successfully repressed for forty years. When a friend of mine heard that, she asked, "And where, Virginia, did you keep your makeup in *that* bathroom?" No wonder my mother despised Roger Clinton so—she had insisted on leaving the farm so I would have a better life, and now Roger was taking me back.

But I decided to button my lip on the matter. It was late summer when we moved, and I figured that by wintertime, when Roger had to roll out of bed in the dark and the cold and go tend to some bleating lamb, he would probably rethink this whole silly plan.

&

When Roger was young, the Clinton clan was ruled by Roger's mother, Eula. In fact, now that I think about it, Roger's parents paralleled mine in some ways. His father, called Poppy Al, ran a grocery store, although at one time he had been a parole officer. He was a quiet man, as kind as the day is long, but he didn't have an iota of power in that family. Eula, whom I called Mama Clinton, was a bona fide matriarch. She had the kind of cunning that you see in women who were born just knowing all the tricks of manipulation: She bullied, she promised, she withheld, she threatened. She was an awful hypochondriac who used her imaginary illnesses to test your devotion. If you showed interest, you were in favor; if you didn't display enough concern, you found yourself an outcast. The funny thing is, everybody in that family will be mad at me for saying all this, and yet if you talked to each one of them individually, they would tell you the very same thing.

Mama Clinton and Poppy Al had five children—Robert, Roy, Ilaree, Raymond, and Roger. Ilaree was Virginia Crawford's mother. I have no idea why they started all the boys' names with the same letter and skipped the girl, but that's just the kind of thing Mama Clinton might've done to single out Ilaree's position in the family—either way. As the children became adults, the power shifted from Mama Clinton, bypassing the older brothers and their sister and settling in the waiting hands of Raymond. Robert and Roy were successful, all right—Robert worked in Texas for Kraft Foods, and Roy had a feedstore. Roy also served in the state legislature. But none of the siblings enjoyed the kind of overall success that Raymond did. Raymond Clinton had success Hot Springs style.

Among all the siblings, Raymond and Roger were the most alike. The older brothers were calm and easygoing, content to do their work and enjoy family life. But Raymond and Roger enjoyed the fast Hot Springs lifestyle. Both relished the rough-and-tumble of Hot Springs politics. Both measured success the Hot Springs way—by money and power.

Over the years, I've thought a lot about Raymond Clinton. He affected my life in profound ways, and it's only with the passing of the years—and of the people involved—that I've come to anything resembling conclusions about Raymond. Although I was an only child, I know that in most families there's always one sibling who assumes a leadership role; Raymond managed to put himself into a position where even his mother and father looked to him for every decision.

And Raymond loved his power. I remember soon after we moved to Hot Springs, Raymond called me one day and wanted to talk about the upcoming election for sheriff. My friend—and Raymond's, for that matter—Leonard Ellis had been sheriff for a term, and now he was about to run again. In fact, Raymond and Leonard had been part of the group that had finally thrown Mayor Leo P. McLaughlin out of office, after twenty years of corruption. I thought Raymond and Leonard were compatriots.

"You're going to vote for Duffy Searcy," Raymond told me. That's the way he put it to me.

"Well, no, I'm not," I said. "I'm going to vote for Leonard Ellis. Number one, I think he's been a good sheriff. Number two, I have a young son and Leonard has all these youth programs he's promoting. I have no reason in the world to vote against the man."

This was Raymond's first tip-off—or second, if you count that night Roger spent in the Hope jail—that he couldn't push me around, and I have no doubt that he came to respect me more than he did anybody in his family. But I couldn't believe what he was trying to get me to do; it turned out that Raymond's daughter was getting ready to marry Duffy Searcy's son.

The relationship between Raymond and Roger would fill a book all by itself. For whatever reasons, Roger was never as successful as Raymond was. It certainly wasn't for lack of working, because Roger worked hard all day long—even if he'd been stone drunk the night before. But the payoff for his efforts didn't amount to much compared to Raymond's, which must've eaten at Roger all the time. Not that Roger seemed to have any animosity toward his brother; it was just the opposite. He felt it was a privilege to work for him, to be around him, to be associated with him. In fact, he mimicked him, and once I got to Hot Springs and saw Raymond on a regular basis, I couldn't help noticing the similarity between him and the man I had met in Hope. Raymond even had an annual eggnog party.

But I've come to realize that Raymond Clinton enjoyed his mastery over his younger brother. I can't even tell you how I know that—there was just something in his attitude each time he would rescue Roger from yet another calamity—getting him out of jail, helping him buy a house, giving him a job. I wasn't in the family early enough to say why this was—and besides, I don't have a dozen doctorates in psychology, which is probably what it would take to figure it all out. But Roger was Mama Clinton's baby, and she called him that even when he was grown. To the disgust of his siblings, she forgave him each excess in turn, from childhood into adulthood—which of course kept him in that childish position. I think Raymond picked up where Mama Clinton left off, though without the blind motherly devotion. I've loved Hot Springs, but sometimes I wonder what Roger Clinton could've been if he'd had the courage to make his life somewhere else.

That first fall Bill started to school and Roger began "farming." Farmer Roger reminded me of an old story about when the city-slicker gangster Pretty Boy Floyd holed up in Hot Springs for a while in the 1930s, taking a cabin out by Lake Hamilton. He wanted to blend in, so he went to town and bought himself some overalls—which he wore with his pressed white shirts and patent leather shoes.

That was Roger: He would get up in the morning and put on dress pants, sport shirts, and good shoes to go check the animals. I never knew what, exactly, he did during the day, but whatever it was, it was accomplished with frequent supervisory visits from the eminent farming consultant Van Hampton Lyell.

As soon as we settled in, I made the rounds to see what kind of work I could find. The first place I went was St. Joseph's Hospital, an imposing blond-brick landmark just off Central Avenue in downtown Hot Springs. I had no appointment and didn't know a soul, but I just wanted to introduce myself to as many people as possible and gauge the need for someone with my credentials. I said hello to the doctors and the administrators and the nurses and other staff, and I dropped the name of my brother-in-law, Raymond Clinton. Everybody knew who he was.

I learned right away that there were only two certified nurse anesthetists in town, two women by the names of Margaret Lawton and Alice Cherdavoine. These two had the anesthesia for the entire county to themselves, but when I met them, they gave me the distinct impression that there really wasn't enough work for a third nurse anesthetist.

After my meetings at the hospital, I stopped by Raymond's Buick dealership to pick up something. While I was there, I got a phone call. It was from Dr. Frank Burton, a surgeon I had met at the hospital; he was a friend of Raymond's, and he had a message for me: "Mrs. Clinton, please don't let anybody tell you we don't need another anesthetist here. We need one very badly." On his word I decided to keep going, so I started letting the surgeons around town know that I was available.

Almost immediately I got a call from Lawton at the farm. Of the two nurse anesthetists, Lawton was the more forceful, and she was forceful indeed. "You don't work on Thursday afternoon," she told me. "We don't work on Thursday afternoon. Nobody works on Thursday afternoon."

Being ordered around like that doesn't set well with me. I feel a flash inside, and it's all I can do to control it. But I was admirably calm, I thought. "Well," I told Lawton, "I'm just as sorry as I can be, but I was trained that sometimes people get sick on Thursday afternoon just like they do the rest of the week. And when I work, I work. And I *will* be working Thursday afternoon."

Oh, they were furious. They wouldn't speak to me when I ran into either one of them in the hall. They must have hated the competition—hated dishing up a little sliver of their pie. But Dr. Burton was right, there was plenty of work. Pretty soon I was busy day and night.

I guess Lawton and Cherdavoine had heard the old saying that "Revenge is a dish best served cold," because once I got involved and was taking on what I thought was a reasonably heavy workload, they decided to teach me a lesson: They quit. They lived together, and they decided to take an extended vacation.

They were gone only a couple of months, as it turned out, but during that time I was the only nurse anesthetist for all of Garland County. I could hardly find time to paint on my eyebrows. Starting every morning at six-thirty, I would spend all day at one, and usually both, of the hospitals, St. Joseph's and Ouachita. Then I would drag myself home after dark and fix dinner for Roger and Bill, and after that I would fall into bed and start all over again when the alarm went off at four-thirty A.M. This, I decided, was the embarrassment of riches God was bestowing on me to make up for the lack of work in Hope.

One of the lasting benefits to come out of my early work years in Hot Springs is my friendship with Marge Mitchell. After a decade away, she and her husband, Bill, had just come back to Hot Springs. Bill had retired from the Judge Advocate section of the U.S. Army and was now in law practice with his father. Marge was obstetrics nurse supervisor at Ouachita Hospital. During racing season, she also manned the nurse's station at Oaklawn.

The moment I laid eyes on Marge Mitchell, I knew I had found a kindred spirit. She's outspoken and outgoing like I am—touching, hugging, always laughing. Marge is an only child, too, and we adopted each other. To this day, we call each other Sister, a single word that speaks volumes. Marge got me through those hard early years. We

•

would sit there late at night drinking coffee and filling ashtrays with Pall Malls, each feeling as though we were looking at a mirror image of ourself. Marge even taught me to knit, to help me pass the hours between surgery.

Though I didn't talk with her about Roger, I'm sure we discussed my work problems—one of the most maddening of which was that I found out I wasn't worth a flip at collecting. For the first six months I collected maybe 30 percent of my bills—which, as anybody will tell you, is no way to run a business. Looking back, it's easy to see why it was happening: My office was at home, and I was doing everything myself—scheduling, administering anesthetic, and getting the bills out. The first two tasks weren't a problem. They simply called and I went. But I was at the hospital so much, I didn't have time to pay enough attention to the third item.

Now money is not, has never been, all that important to me in and of itself. But when I work hard, I believe in being paid for it. I battled this problem for months, falling farther and farther behind. Then one day I was over at the Buick dealership and I happened to mention the billing snag to the bookkeeper there. "Why, Virginia," she said, "I've got some time. I can take that off your hands." I felt like falling to the ground and kissing her feet.

So the billing began to improve—slowly but surely. But as though we didn't have enough craziness in our lives, while all this was going on, my father got sick. He had what's called a ruptured esophageal varix, or a varicose vein in his esophagus. He was in a coma much of the time and had to be transfused something like thirty pints of blood. I was worried sick about him, afraid he was going to die, so after my days at the hospital I started driving to Hope every day to see him. I would visit with him in the hospital, get back in the car and drive back to Hot Springs in the middle of the night, and then close my eyes and try to get them open when that alarm went off again. This went on for three solid weeks. I remember one day, as I was getting ready to leave for Hope, I called the doctor whose surgery was my first case the next morning. I was exhausted, and I just didn't think I could get there on time to save my soul.

"Could we please start at eight o'clock instead of seven-thirty?" I asked him.

"Absolutely not," he said, the very voice of haughty self-importance. "Absolutely not." I never forgave that man for that. And I'll carry that grudge with me to my grave.

Life was just that much harder because of the distance from the farm to town, and with my workload I had also become worried about Bill being in Roger's care so much with no backup. Not that anything had happened: Roger got up every morning and fixed Bill's breakfast and took him to school and picked him up religiously in the afternoons. But I worried the way mothers worry—about how they were eating and so on—as I drove back and forth to Hope. And there was a bigger worry nagging at me—what if Roger's drinking buddies came around?

One day I was driving to work along this dirt road and I saw an older lady walking toward town. I stopped to pick her up, and she introduced herself as Mrs. Walters, one of our neighbors. I liked her immediately, and I said, "Mrs. Walters, I have a son who's seven years old, and I'm going to need somebody to care for him while I work. Do you know anybody?"

She looked at me. "Well, what about me?" She went on to tell me she had raised nine or ten children, I forget how many. "It's all I've ever done," she said, "and now my oldest is in high school and can take care of herself. What about me?"

You talk about heaven-sent. And you talk about somebody who's had a tremendous influence in Bill Clinton's life: Not only did Mrs. Walters take care of him for years, but the things she taught him were priceless. He's a mighty good man today, and it's not only due to my being perfect. Mrs. Walters was a Christian woman, maybe the most Christian person I've ever known. But she was the kind who *lived* her Christianity, not the more common kind who spends so much time bending your ear about how godly he or she is. Mrs. Walters taught Bill the Golden Rule and other lessons about how to live and get along and how to treat people in this world. She would eventually work for us for eleven years, and after that her daughter Maye would take over and work for me for thirty years. Both have had a tremendous influence on my children's lives.

Just the knowledge that Mrs. Walters was there when Bill got home from school relieved me tremendously. Besides taking care of him, she also cleaned. Once she saw how much I was working, she even tried to get me to let her make supper for us. But I was proud. I was determined to be what a later generation would call a superwoman. "Oh, no, thank you, Mrs. Walters," I said. "*I* should do it."

Now let me tell you something I've learned from long, hard experience: If anybody *ever* volunteers to cook your family's supper for you, by all means let her.

ﾋ

Sure enough, by the time we had our first frost, Roger had cooled on farm life. But not before we experienced what could've been a tragedy—not just for us, but, if you'll permit a mother her pride, for the future of the entire country.

I know it was a Sunday because Roger's parents and some of his brothers and their families were out at the farm. We had had a big noonday dinner, and afterwards the children had gone out to play and we adults were probably loosening our belts and looking for a place to take a nap.

Suddenly I heard the children screaming, and I ran outside, Roger and the others right behind me. When I saw what was happening, I almost died of fright. A big ram had Bill down, and every time he would try to get up, the ram would butt him again. The ram had the most gigantic head I had ever seen. Bill was screaming for help, but we all just stood there with our mouths open; it was as though we were paralyzed and couldn't make our bodies do what needed to be done.

And then I saw Poppy Al in the middle of it all. He reached over and picked up a huge rock—it looked like a small boulder almost— and he raised it over his head and smashed it into the ram's head right between his eyes. You could hear the thunk from where we stood. The ram reeled and backed away, and Bill got up and ran into my arms. We were both sobbing, and I held him tight for a long time. Then I felt so weak I thought I was going to faint, but I didn't. I sat down right in a huge fresh cowpatty. It didn't matter to me—I had a washing machine. My son was safe, that was the main thing.

I was not what you would call sorry to leave farm life behind me. Nor was Roger, though he put a spin on this move that matched anything the spin doctors in Washington could've come up with. He had an "opportunity," he said, one he couldn't pass up: He was going to work as parts manager for Clinton Buick Company. Not only that, but Gabe Crawford happened to have a great house for sale up on Park Avenue in town, a big old five-bedroom, four-bath house with a four-car garage. Just what the three of us needed.

We didn't intend to be three for long, however. Roger and I wanted a baby, and Bill was almost beside himself contemplating the possibility of a little brother or sister. It meant so much to him that he still remembers a miscarriage I had before little Roger was born. Even I had forgotten that. When I look back on those years, it's amazing I didn't have a dozen children: I don't recall ever using any kind of birth control. As a friend of mine points out, however, a husband's nightly alcoholic tantrums can work wonders in that regard.

The house at 1011 Park Avenue sat high on a hill. It was built in a kind of Tudor style, with lots of trim that at the time was painted a dark green. The front yard swooped down to the street far, far below, but most of our guests never walked through the iron front gate and up that long front sidewalk. We were a back-door family, opting always for comfort over formality. We came and went through the back door, entering the kitchen. The house had two stories, but we lived mostly on the first floor, which had spacious rooms divided by a wide hall that ran down the center.

Next to the kitchen was the dining room, and Bill's bedroom was next to that. I remember he had a double bed for a while, and then, as he got older and wanted to have friends over to spend the night, we got him twin beds. Just thinking about that room reminds me of the hours Bill and Rose Crane, whose house was on the street directly behind us, used to sit in there on the floor playing Chinese checkers; later, when Bill began to study music, he would plop himself up on the bed squeaking and squawking on his clarinet, and Rose would lie on the floor reading a book. She still remembers how once, after enduring hours and hours of his toot-toot-tooting, she looked up at him in surprise and said, "My God!"

"What?" said Bill.

"You're playing a real song. That's 'Old Rugged Cross.'"

Beyond Bill's room was a funny kind of room whose only use was to contain the stairs to the second floor. All I can figure is that this house was originally built as a single story, and when they added on, they couldn't come up with any better place to put the staircase. Across the hall was our living room, a room I loved. It was decorated with highlights of pink, and I remember I had a ceramic swan I used to keep on a table there. That was the room where we played dominoes on Sunday nights with Roger's brother Roy and his wife, Janet. That's where we gathered around the big console TV. That's where, during the Christmas season, I decorated our silver aluminum tree with blue lights and blue ornaments, and under it I wrapped all our presents in aluminum foil and tied them with blue ribbon. I loved that look, that crisp, elegant, frosted style that was like nobody else's I knew. I was so adamant about keeping it pristine that I wouldn't put the gifts anybody else gave us under the tree. Only silver and blue for our family Christmas.

Roger's and my bedroom was next to the living room, directly across the hall from Bill's. It was a comfortable room, or at least it should've been. There was a bay window, into which our headboard jutted. At the foot of the bed we had a game table, where Roger and I would sometimes sit and play cards. A ceiling fan circled lazily overhead. On the wall that backed up to the living room was where I had my dressing table with all my lipsticks and eyeliners and other makeup just so, and my radio where I would hear Patti Page singing "Cross Over the Bridge" while I got ready for work. We had a TV set in the corner, and a huge closet where I kept my clothes pressed and hung with exactly the right amount of space between them. On the floor, I stacked all my shoes in boxes labeled neatly on the ends telling me what was inside.

Our bedroom connected through a large bath to another bedroom, which eventually became little Roger's room. Beyond that, across from the kitchen, was the breakfast room. This was where we ate most of our meals, and it really doubled as what we would today call a family room.

Upstairs on one side were two big bedrooms and a bath. On the other side, the previous owner—Gabe—had built and furnished a party room to end all party rooms. It ran the entire length of the house, directly above the living room side, and included rattan sofas, Mexican leather barrel chairs, and several Mexican tables that could be used for cardplaying. But the real focal point was the built-in professional bar, complete with mirrored back wall and red-and-white-striped canvas awning. We used this room for big occasions, of course—Christmas parties mainly—and Bill and his friends loved to play in there. On the wall we had a print of dogs playing cards, which I always thought was a pretty good representation of Roger and his cronies. We also had two pictures I loved. From a distance they looked like skeletons, but if you got up close, you could see that they were really Victorian ladies.

&.

But I lived outside as much as possible. The back was where I put on my tube top and short shorts and went out and tended my rose garden, digging happily in the dirt on the side of the hill and sunning myself on those wonderful rare days when I had some blessed time off. Because I was so often on call, I had the phone company rig up a loud bell outside on the wall so that no matter where I was when the hospital called, I could hear the phone. Rose Crane says that because of that bell, everybody in the neighborhood knew to get out of the way because I would soon be tearing out of the driveway to go to work.

Bill and his pals Rose, David Leopoulos, and Ronnie Cecil played for hours in the backyard, too, along with Susie the German shepherd. They were always putting on productions. Circus was a big theme, and I remember they would decorate Susie's collar with whatever flowers happened to be growing, and they would also festoon the trapeze on the swing set. Rose would be the barker and Bill and Susie would be the trained-dog act. When they got thirsty, they simply walked into the garage, where we had a big red Coca-Cola box thanks to Van Hampton Lyell; he even sent the Coke truck by to refill it. And whenever I got called to the hospital, I had a brand-new black Buick convertible sitting right there next to the Coke box, thanks to my husband. It looked like a perfect life, and when I was at home with Bill and Roger was away at work, for a time I could believe it was.

The neighborhood was so much more convenient than the farm had been. Roger and I could be at work in five minutes, and Ramble Elementary School, which Bill attended starting in the third grade, was just a short hike up a couple of nearby hills. Bill had his haunts in the neighborhood, roaming alone or with friends to the grocery store for candy or to the barbecue place for an afternoon snack. Also, Park Place Baptist Church was just down the street, and Bill had decided he wanted to go to church even when Roger and I didn't. When he got to be about eight years old, he would get himself up and bathed and dressed in coat and tie on Sunday mornings. I would give him his breakfast, and then he would pick up his Bible and set out for Sunday school and church. For years, I had dropped Bill off at Baptist Sunday school—feeling guilty, of course, about only dropping him off. But I had found that I was so on edge dreading the inevitable beep of my beeper during the sermon that I didn't get as much out of it as I should have. I couldn't go anywhere—church, dinner, PTA meetings, out with friends—without that infernal beeper erupting. I've always said, though, that if I had attended church half as much as I've prayed, I'd be the saint Mrs. Walters was.

Bill frequently went to visit his grandparents in Hope, leaving by bus on Friday and coming back to Hot Springs on Sunday afternoon. He always loved Hope—he once said he felt like he was surrounded by a great big loving family when he was down there—and as he grew

older, he was probably repelled by much of what he saw in Hot
Springs. I, on the other hand, generally liked life in Hot Springs better than I did in Hope. There was more to entertain you in Hot
Springs, but of course that had its bad side as well as the good. For
someone working the hours I was working, nightlife was a strain. On
the other hand, how could you resist?

Even though gambling had ostensibly been closed down with
McLaughlin's ouster in 1947, the ban had lasted only a few years.
Hot Springs was addicted to gambling, since that's what the town's
economy had been based on for so long. When the tourist dollars
began dropping, the city fathers got together and decided that maybe
they had been a little hasty, and they instructed Sheriff Ellis and
others to "ease up," in Leonard's words. In fact, the years 1954 to
1965 were probably the "hottest" in all Hot Springs's long history.

During those years we went to such places as the Tower Club, the
Belvedere, the Wagon Wheel, the Southern Club—the names themselves conjure up memories of evening dresses and cigarette cases
and tangos and tuxes. By this time Lawton and Cherdavoine had
come back, so I could take every third night off. My favorite nightclub by far was the Vapors, which was as plush and glittery and showy
as anything Las Vegas ever dreamed of. The place was draped in red
velvet, and they had these imported chandeliers like nothing I had
ever seen in my life.

In the back room there was a sea of roulette wheels, craps tables,
blackjack dealers, slot machines. Roger would head for the back
room just as soon as he could. I liked that part, too, but I mainly
liked the entertainment. I never missed a show at the Vapors, because every big star in the country came there to perform. The Vapors was where I first saw Liberace, and I thought he was wonderful.
I loved his diamonds, I loved his furs, I loved his *makeup.* To be honest with you, I guess if Roger Clinton had been from Stamford, Con-
necticut, I might've turned out a little less flashy. But—nothing
against Stamford—I'm glad he was from Hot Springs, Arkansas. I
obviously was born with a flashy streak inside me just waiting to
burst free, and Hot Springs let me be me with a vengeance.

I stood up on the Vapors stage and sang "Ghost Riders in the Sky" with Frankie Laine. I wanted to join Patti Page when she sang "Tennessee Waltz," but I just couldn't—I was too carried away with her. She had—has—such a voice, such a presence. Nobody measured up to Patti Page in those days. So, sentimental me, I sat there at my table in the dark, crying while she sang about the night she lost her darlin' to an old friend she happened to see.

The event that cured me of getting onstage with the entertainers happened at the Tower Club sometime during the late 1950s. Back then you used to see a lot of variety acts, and the Tower had booked a performance of roller skaters. I tell you, it was the most beautiful sight you've ever seen, those skaters going round and round and round up there on the stage.

They made the mistake of asking for a volunteer from the audience, and in no time flat I had pranced up there to hog the spotlight. I should add, in case you hadn't figured it out, that I might've already had a cocktail or two. The star of the show wanted me to be his guinea pig, and what he did was to pick me up above his head and start to skate. He went faster and faster, and his circles were tighter and tighter, until he was spinning like a top. Suddenly he stopped—and all the tables, dishes, the people's faces started hitting me in the face. I thought I was going to lose my dinner in front of the entire audience. The crowd applauded, but that was one time when applause just wasn't worth it. I never again crashed another stage show.

Hot Springs wasn't just a nighttime town. In the afternoons, during season, there was horse racing. Roger and I had gone to Oaklawn with Gabe and Virginia a few times, but until I moved to Hot Springs, the track had been a peripheral part of my life. I'm not sure which I liked more, the gambling or the *scene*. In those days, everybody dressed for the races, and the characters who hung around were wild and colorful and larger-than-life.

On the other hand, I loved the challenge of trying to top that very first betting experience I had on my senior trip. To me, a day at the races is like life itself—every race is a new chance to win, and what went before doesn't count at all.

Except, of course, in the daily double.

Some of my best friends in the world are people I met or really got to know at the track. Dixie Seba is a woman I have lunch with almost every day of my life; she's the one who takes me to get my chemotherapy treatments; she laughs with me, worries with me, cries with me. We can't even remember exactly how we met, but it must've been at Oaklawn. In the early fifties, her husband, Mike, was a trainer there, so Dixie was always in her box. After I found out that I loved horse racing so much, I began to schedule my cases for the mornings during the racing season, just so I could be at Oaklawn every afternoon—in fact, the doctors and nurses used to joke, "God help the patients after the bugle blows." But Dixie and I just gravitated toward each other, and I consider her friendship the best payoff I've ever had at the track.

Racing creates as many strange bedfellows as politics does. For years, my Oaklawn buddies were Dixie Seba and Joe Crain, the one-time Hot Springs chief of police—and a man I owe a lot, as you'll soon see. We were a sight. Here's Dixie—tall, reserved, as refined as the day is long; me—well, you know what that's like; and Joe—a scrappy little ex-boxer from the New York Bronx, with forearms the size of hams. We would meet every day and sit in Dixie's box, and whenever anybody else would try to come sit with us, I'm afraid we were less than gracious. When we three got to the track, we were there for serious business—studying the racing form and figuring out our bets for the afternoon. At least Dixie and I were; Joe never seemed to get the hang of handicapping, so he served as our bouncer. When people would drop by wanting to talk, drink, eat, bet too much, give or get tips, or any number of other activities that disturbed our concentration, Joe would move them along as politely as possible. It was a great triumvirate. After years of experience, I've decided it may be about as hard to find compatible racing pals as it is to find a compatible husband. When you've got something that works, stick with it.

So on the surface, Hot Springs seemed to afford me a wonderful life. Occasionally, however, there would be a crack in the facade—such as the night I danced with a man at the Tower Club and Roger Clinton beat him to a pulp. Or the night at the Wagon Wheel when Roger got into a fight defending Gabe Crawford from some situation Gabe had created. Gabe, who drank as much as Roger did, was always starting things he couldn't finish, and I remember Roger shaking his head and saying, "God dang it, I don't know why Gabe gets into these things. He can't break an eggshell."

But Roger could—especially when he was mad at me, which was most of the time. It was in Hot Springs, as Roger's life got more and more out of control, that he began to terrorize me in earnest, making the same kinds of wild accusations my mother had tortured my father with. I'm sad to say that the self-destruction of Roger Clinton is a strong theme in this saga.

Working for Raymond at the Buick dealership, Roger happened to be right across the street from Van Lyell's Coca-Cola plant. After work most afternoons, Roger would amble over to Van's and they would proceed to do serious damage to a bottle of Yellowstone bourbon. Van had an apartment upstairs at the Coke plant, and that's where they would gather. Incidentally, I want to make it clear that I'm not blaming any of Roger's behavior on Van Hampton Lyell; Van was a running buddy, and Van drank, though I never saw it affect him the way it affected Roger. The bottom line, however, is that Roger was responsible for his actions, no matter who else was involved.

You never knew when Roger was going to lose control. For all those years Roy and Janet Clinton came over to our house on Sundays to play dominoes, Janet remembers to this day that Roger seldom seemed drunk on those evenings—even though he often would've had several drinks. It was the most amazing thing—whenever his family was around, Roger could walk straight lines and speak plain sentences and act like nothing was wrong. I've seen him stone drunk and his parents or one of his brothers would call, and Roger would get on the phone and sound as sober as a teetotaler.

I'm sure I drove him to anger on many nights when we were out. I won't try to pretend that I'm oblivious to the power of female sex appeal, and I certainly recognize a handsome man when I see one. I won't even deny that I was often put out with Roger and didn't mind seeing him suffer a little. But even though Roger liked to dance and was a good dancer, he usually left me sitting at the table while he went to the back room to throw dice with the boys. Then he would emerge, drunk, to find me dancing with someone else. That's what happened that night at the Tower Club. Roger came back and saw a gentleman helping me into my chair at the table, and after the man walked off, Roger just went up to him and hit him. He was in a rage, and it took several people to hold him back.

On nights like that, our house was just bedlam from the time we got home until dawn's early light, by which time Roger would usually have yelled himself to sleep. As I've said before, he seldom hit me; he mostly just hurled accusations of infidelity, pitiful rants about where-was-I-at-a-certain-time-when-I-was-supposed-to-be-some-where-else.

But it got so that it didn't take an actual incident to set him off. At around suppertime I would always be in the kitchen with Bill, and we would hear Roger's car drive up. As soon as those sound waves reached my ears, I would begin to tense up, and I could tell Bill would, too. The car door would slam, and we would hear footsteps crunching across the gravel. As Roger got almost to the door, we could hear him cursing to himself. At times like that, I knew we were in for a night of it.

None of the neighbors knew what was going on, of course. I was too embarrassed to tell anybody. Rose Crane, who was a child and couldn't be expected to know—although children sometimes pick up more than you give them credit for—remembers only that "Roger was sometimes very friendly to us, and sometimes he wouldn't have anything to do with us at all." On those occasions when Roger would curse and rail for no apparent reason, Bill, probably age eight or nine, would say, "Mother, what's the matter with Daddy?" I never knew an adequate answer to give him.

Finally, one night it got so bad that I was afraid for Bill's and my safety. With Roger staggering around behind me, shouting awful things and knocking pictures off the walls, I packed bags for Bill and me and drove off with him. I wasn't even sure where we were going. Worse yet, I had no money and no way to get any. Roger and I had been pooling our salaries, but he controlled the checking account.

We drove around for the longest time, but then I thought of some people I knew who owned an apartment house—the Cleveland Manor was the name of it. I knocked on their door and simply told them that Bill and I needed a room for a few nights, and that I didn't have any money but would get it for them when I could. Those good people didn't ask me any questions whatsoever. I guess they could guess the problem, since they knew I was married to Roger Clinton.

I did pay them shortly afterward. But that night was a turning point in my life. Earlier I said that money wasn't important to me for its own sake, and that's still true. For years I never paid the slightest attention to it, never wanted to worry about it: I was glad to have a husband to do that for me. But that night I realized that a woman needs her own money—money enough, to put a fine line on it, so that she can take care of herself and her children if need be—and she needs to pay enough attention to it so that she alone controls it.

Years ago, parents used to give teenage girls money to slip into their billfolds when they went out on dates. This was called "mad money," and it was to be used in case you got mad at your date and needed to pay for your own ride home. Well, mad money shouldn't stop once a girl is grown and married. What if it turns out your husband sometimes goes stark raving mad, like mine did? Too many women are economic slaves to their husbands, and too many husbands enjoy exercising that upper hand. I might've been a slave, too, without good friends and a backbone.

As Bill slept soundly next to me that night, I made a vow to him and to myself: *Never again will I be without money to protect us.*

Seven

THE YEARS RUN together. Sometime in here my mother became addicted to morphine.

I know it was after I moved to Hot Springs and before little Roger was born, which means it must've been 1954 or '55. She had had a stroke. She was still a young woman, of course—no more than fifty-four years old—but she was way too heavy. This was a massive stroke, and she was unconscious for several weeks. She would scream and thrash around and generally make problems for the doctors and the nurses and certainly for the other patients in the hospital. One of her doctors was a man none of the family had much use for, and how in heaven's name he had been put on her case, I'll never know. To keep her quiet, he gave her morphine.

And it worked—oh, boy, it worked. At first, I didn't say anything about it. But then, when I heard he was keeping it up, I called him and I strongly suggested that he stop prescribing that stuff for her. I mentioned his medical license and what might happen to it if he didn't. Obviously, he got my point, because he cut her off. But by that time, she was hooked.

So I brought her to Hot Springs. She and Daddy, who wasn't well himself—his bronchiectasis had steadily worsened, and we all knew he wasn't going to live long—left Hope and moved into a little apartment near us on Park Avenue. Daddy would've gone crazy sitting around the apartment, so he got a job running a liquor store.

Mother was even more of a problem now than she had been before the drugs. She wanted them, and she couldn't have them. I knew better than to put her into a private hospital. You think I'm strong? I'm nothing compared to my mother. I knew if I put her in a private hospital, it wouldn't be any time before she was calling the shots. I'd seen it happen too many times. And in a private hospital, where you're paying your own way, they're darn well going to listen to you because they don't want to lose any paying customers.

So I made what has to have been one of the most difficult decisions of my life. I made it alone, without consulting Daddy or Roger or anyone: I decided to commit Mother to the state mental hospital. Back then, there was no such thing as drug treatment available. Today, both drug treatment and mental health facilities are a thousand times better, but in the midfifties, the options were slim. As hard as that decision was for me to make, it was, I thought, her only chance.

Oh, God, it was an awful place. It nearly killed me to see her there. The state hospital was in Benton, about thirty miles from Hot Springs. She stayed there several months—until she could prove to me that she had control of herself.

I would drive up to see her on Sundays, and sometimes Bill would go with me. Mother would always act like everything was fine, like she was the very model of moderation. But I had these secret gauges that I would test her by. For example, if she would start in on me to let her come home and not even speak to Bill or pay him any attention at all, then I knew she wasn't ready. She worshiped Bill—when she wasn't obsessing about getting hold of that dope. And I'll tell you, I would cry every mile of the drive back to Hot Springs.

I'll never forget the happy day we went to pick her up. And do you know, I never had another minute's problem with her. God bless her, one time after she got out of the hospital, she cut her hand badly and I had to take her to the emergency room. As soon as she saw the doctor, she said, "Whatever you do, don't give me anything for pain. That's okay, you just go right ahead and sew that up. Don't give me *any*thing for pain."

Roger Clinton probably could've used something for his pain, however, because with Mother in Hot Springs he was reminded every time he saw her how much she loathed him. Roger had wanted to adopt Bill, but I wouldn't let him because of his drinking. And I never did. I don't know whether Bill knows that, since so many news reports have stated otherwise. Bill went by the name Billy Clinton at school just because it was less confusing. Back then, not many children had names different from their parents'.

Mother didn't like Bill's going by the name Clinton. Even Rose Crane remembers that when she and Bill would be playing and my mother was over at our house, Mother would always make the point about what a fine, handsome man Bill Blythe had been. "And he was Bill's *real* father," she added.

&.

So what do you guess happened next? I got pregnant, that's what.

Isn't that just the way we women do things? Here I was, married to an alcoholic who was abusing me and my son, and I go and let the man make me pregnant.

Close friends have asked if I was hoping a baby could help heal the problems between Roger and me, and nothing could be further from the truth. (Anybody who believes a new baby will fix a bad marriage is kidding herself, anyway.) The fact is, I wanted another baby for *me*, and Roger wanted a child of his own, too. I've already told you how excited Bill was at the idea of having a brother or sister.

And I suppose I did still love Roger at that point. It was the fall of 1955. We had been in Hot Springs two years. In spite of the fact that I had grown and changed and learned some hard lessons about life—many of them thanks to Mr. Roger Clinton himself—I still retained my innate optimism about people. On occasions when Roger would get so out of control that I would threaten to leave him, he would plead with me not to. He would promise that he wasn't going to drink anymore, that he wouldn't even think of doing the things that were driving me away. Looking back, I really don't know if I believed him or if I just wanted to believe him in order to keep our family together. But I would give in, hoping that Roger would come around and miraculously turn into a responsible human being.

Instead, he was getting worse. He was insanely jealous, not just of any man I might look at, but even of my women friends. He would've preferred that I stay safely at home. When he was angry at me, he would try to make me believe that my friends didn't like me. He knew that was my soft spot. It would've destroyed me if I had believed it.

The sad thing is, everybody knew how to press Roger's buttons, too, and sometimes even his closest friends and relatives would do it. One day Virginia Crawford called Gabe's drugstore and he wasn't there. Then she called my house and *I* wasn't there—never mind that I was always at the hospital in the middle of the day. Virginia put two and two together and called Roger, and he was livid with suspicion. Of course, the fallout took place inside the walls of 1011 Park Avenue.

Another time, after little Roger was born, I was taking him for an afternoon drive and passed Lawton and Cherdavoine. There were periods, even considering our ongoing professional battles, when we could all be civil to one another, and this happened to be one of those times. They flagged me down and wanted little Roger and me to get into their car so they could drive me out and show me their new house. So I left my car parked on the side of the road out near the Belvedere Country Club. It was just my luck that Van Hampton Lyell happened to drive by and see my car. Well, why would Virginia's car be parked on a country road unless she had met a man and gone off with him? So Van called Roger, who was in Jackson, Mississippi, on business. Roger practically burned up the highway getting home, and when he arrived, he had worked himself up into such a state that I was surprised he didn't tear the door off the hinges.

After that he took to following me occasionally. I would be driving home from work and I would see him in my rearview mirror, back in the traffic but definitely watching every move I made. Sometimes, out of sheer meanness, I would lead him on a wild-goose chase around a few blocks and then I'd disappear on Quapaw Avenue, because that's where Janet and Roy Clinton lived. They had a little narrow drive that I could whip into and hide my car around back. Janet and I would drink coffee and look out the window laughing ourselves silly as Roger drove up and down the street wondering where on earth I had disappeared to.

I guess by the mid-1950s Roger was beyond being happy; all he could hope for was being numb. He'd get drunk nearly every single day until I would threaten him with leaving, and then he would try to straighten himself up. But he was the type of alcoholic who's as bad when he's not drinking. He was miserable just being himself.

Roger didn't buy big bottles of whiskey; instead, he traded in pints and half-pints, the better to hide them, my dear. One day, soon after Roger had done something so awful to me that he'd been moved to swear off alcohol, Gabe dropped by. Roger greeted him at the kitchen door and immediately affected a hangdog persona that made me want to throw up. "I'm sorry, Gabe, but the way things are around here, I don't have anything at all to offer you to drink." *Oh, spare me,* I thought. So while those two sad sacks were moping around feeling sorry for themselves, I got a shopping bag and made the rounds of the house—behind this book, under that cushion, way back in this drawer, high up there on that shelf—picking up Roger's hidden stash of whiskey bottles. If they thought I was falling for their act, they were sadly mistaken.

I walked back into the kitchen, where they were sitting morosely at the table, and I dumped the contents of the bag all over the tabletop. "Yes, Gabe, Roger *does* have something to offer you," I said. The embarrassment seemed to ruin the mood for drinking.

For a time, I was rescued from this intolerable situation by an unlikely savior—Joe Crain, my racetrack buddy. I had first met Joe in the early mornings when I would stop in for breakfast at the Southern Grill. He had been on the graveyard shift then, before he became a bigwig at the police station, and he would stop in and say hello and sit for a cup of coffee. Later, of course, we had gotten to know each other at the track. I had never told Joe anything about Roger's nightly tirades, but Joe knew Roger. Being a policeman, he also knew something about the darker sides of human nature. And he may've gotten an inkling from his wife, Louise, an emergency-room nurse with whom I had spent many an intense evening. I didn't really confide in Louise, either, but, given her profession, she also was no stranger to the ugly results of anger and drinking and domestic discord. Louise knew how hard I worked, and she knew I needed my sleep. Maybe she told Joe.

In any case, Joe Crain took to driving Roger around town several nights a week. The way Joe tells it today, Roger would walk into the police station around nine P.M. and ask for Joe. Roger would be drunk, of course, having logged a few hours at Van Hampton's and God knows where else, and Joe would suggest they go for a drive. Louise bows less to Joe's modesty: She says Joe knew how much I needed my rest, so he arranged to drive Roger around to keep him from going home drunk. They would get into the squad car and cruise downtown. Then they would head out to the lake to check the clubs there. They didn't talk much. The police radio was often the only sound in the car for long stretches at a time. It wasn't that Roger wanted to talk, he just wanted to be with somebody. Sometimes they would stop at a club or two, and Roger would have a drink, but they would always end up at Moore's Steak House, where Roger would wolf down a huge T-bone. By about midnight when Joe dropped Roger off at his car, he would pretty much be sober.

I can't tell you how much I appreciated Joe Crain's quiet, steady support. Most of the time when Roger was gone late at night, I would sleep fitfully, with one eye open. I always felt like he was going to burst in the door at any minute. But after I got used to Joe driving Roger around, I began to sleep a little more soundly. It was a precious gift.

I said earlier that I threatened Roger with leaving him. The truth is, divorce wasn't a real option with me. Not yet. I've since come to believe that sometimes a divorce is necessary, but back then I had almost Catholic views on the subject. This may seem odd, considering that so many of the people I knew and ran around with in racy Hot Springs had been divorced. In fact, by this time Virginia Craw-

ford had divorced Gabe, having had enough of his antics. Gabe Crawford was probably the best male friend I ever had. I admired his gen-
erosity, I loved his sense of humor, I respected his business sense,
I marveled at his ability—like Roger's—to stay out drinking until
all hours and still be on the job and functioning by starting time the
next morning. Roger Clinton never missed a day of work until he got
terminally ill, and Gabe was just as diligent. I used to go have coffee with Gabe, and I could get there before many cars were even out
on the street—five-thirty A.M., maybe—and Gabe would be out
sweeping the sidewalk in front of his drugstore. He didn't seem to
be using the broom to prop himself up.

But for all my admiration for Gabe otherwise, he was probably as
difficult to be married to as Roger was—or so Gabe's wives have told
me. One day Virginia came over to our house and said, "That's it.
We're through." She wasn't tentative, like me. And she was as good
as her word—she divorced him and never looked back.

What others did, however, didn't matter to me—I didn't pass judgment. For me, though, it just felt wrong to bail out of an agreement
made for life. Work harder at it, that was the answer.

But leave yourself an escape hatch.

Since the Cleveland Manor episode, I had begun rat-holing some
of my paycheck every week. Because my income varied according
to how many cases I'd had, Roger never missed a single dime. I remember going downtown and opening a checking account just for
myself. There wasn't much in it at first, but the simple act of opening it made me feel like I suddenly had power over my life.

&.

Life, however, has a way of disabusing you of such a notion. I was
working at the hospital one day in 1956 when one of the ob-gyn surgeons, Dr. Walter Klugh, Sr., pulled me aside and told me that his
son—Walter Klugh, Jr., known as Buddy—was about to finish his
residency in anesthesiology and would soon be coming back to Hot
Springs. My interpretation of that news was that Buddy Klugh intended to take over the anesthetics business in this town.

I was stunned. There really were very few MDs who specialized in anesthesiology at that time. We nurse anesthetists used to joke that the only doctors who did that were doctors who couldn't make it in some other field. That wasn't true, of course, and the very fact that we would say such a thing belies our fears about our future. Eight years earlier, when I had gotten my nurse-anesthetist training, I had been ahead of the curve. Now the curve was catching up with me.

Dr. Klugh—junior—and I remember some of the events of the ensuing three decades a little differently from each other, and I'm going to do my best to tell how each of us was viewing the other during that time. Dr. Klugh remembers that I drove up to see him in Little Rock, where he was doing his residency. He says we went for lunch or dinner and I asked how *he* would like to come into business with *me*.

I don't remember this, but it sure sounds like me, doesn't it?

Actually, it wouldn't have been such an outlandish suggestion. In the three years I had been in town, I had built up quite a business. I was still working alone, but business was so good that I had to preface every invitation we got with, "If I'm not working." That even went for Bill when he'd ask me to attend some play or something at school. Now here I was pregnant again; maybe it wouldn't be such a bad idea to go into partnership with somebody.

Dr. Klugh recalls that he gently passed on that offer. He had other plans.

He returned to Hot Springs and went into practice for himself. After a couple of years—during which he had been "urged by various doctors in town"—he decided the time was right for him to make his move. One day he invited me to a meeting at his office. When I arrived, Lawton and Cherdavoine were there: This wasn't a meeting, it was a summit. The subject on the agenda was the direction of anesthesia in Hot Springs. Dr. Klugh laid out his vision, which involved the creation of what he called a "department of anesthesia" at St. Joseph's Hospital—a department in which nurse anesthetists would administer the anesthesia, supervised by an MD.

That was the spiel. To my mind, however, it basically boiled down to this: If any lawsuits were ever to be filed against a surgeon, he would be in a stronger position if the surgery reports had been signed by an MD, even if that MD hadn't actually been in the room. Therefore, since Klugh was an MD and we weren't, we would work for him.

I was incredulous. Here I had been slaving for more than a decade, and now this. He would put us on a salary, he said. And I said to him—knowing full well that I wasn't about to go for any of this—I said, "Look, Dr. Klugh, I don't mind working, and if I work very hard, what's the chance for advancement under your plan?"

"Oh, well," he said, "I'll be the one who decides that." It would all depend on how much money we made, blah, blah, blah. After listening to a few minutes of that malarkey, I said, "You know something, Dr. Klugh? I wouldn't any more help you do this than I would help Hitler take our country."

There are some—many—people today, some of them my supporters, who say that I brought my thirty-year battle with Dr. Klugh upon myself. Certainly I could've handled things differently—could've maybe been more "politic" in my way of dealing with him and others. But my response was just me. When you threaten me or mine, I'm going to come at you with everything I've got, and in my mind Dr. Klugh was threatening my very livelihood. I won't deny that before this drama was to play itself out, pride, gender, and personality also entered into the mix—on both sides. As Dr. Klugh says today: "You had two people with strong wills and their own ways of doing things."

The irony is, Buddy Klugh is a charming man—tall, handsome, smart. He's somebody I could've been friends with. But it was hard for me to think kindly of him when I felt that he had come to town to cut my throat.

Lawton and Cherdavoine accepted Dr. Klugh's offer. Maybe they were simply intimidated. Here they had been working in Hot Springs much longer than I had, and yet they didn't stand up to a new competitor. It's rare for me to run across anybody that I can't warm up to eventually, but I never could with Lawton and Cherdavoine. I al-

ways felt a coolness from them and toward them, and this event sealed
my feelings about them forever. To give them their due, however, it's
true that Roger Clinton made a good income, so I didn't *have* to work.
That gave me independence, although no one but me knew how much
my work meant to me. But I had that card to play, and I played it.

On the other hand, I think Lawton and Cherdavoine didn't have
the personality I had, didn't have the fight. My patients loved me,
probably because I treated them the way I would've wanted to be
treated. Shirleen Adcock, a woman who runs the dry cleaners I
take my clothes to, still talks about how, thirty-two years ago when
her son was in for surgery, he wanted a Coca-Cola and the nurse
wouldn't let him have one. She said she'd have to check with the
doctor. I didn't see one bit of harm in that child's having a Coke if
it would make him feel better, so I got him one. Just so you know,
the boy is still alive—he's now a strapping thirty-five-year-old man
with children of his own.

Another time we were about to do some kind of surgery on a woman
who happened to have terrible acne. When you go into surgery,
you're generally scrubbed of all makeup. That terrified this poor
woman because in all their years of marriage, her husband had never
once seen her without makeup. When I went to see her before the
operation, she pleaded with me to try to do something about it. She
couldn't stand for her husband to look at those awful scars.

Well, now, she'd lucked out, hadn't she? How was *I* going to stand
there and deny somebody the use of a little makeup? Besides, I understood her feelings—her vanity, her fear, her love. I even understood such things on a more practical level. We were supposed to
remove all fingernail polish when we anesthetized a patient, because you look at their fingernails to detect a lack of oxygen. Well,
dear Lord, there are a thousand ways to tell if you're not getting
enough oxygen—for one, you show it in your face before your fingernails. It's expensive to get manicures, and there's no telling how
many manicures I've saved by not paying attention to such nonsense.

I know I was going to be the only one working around this particular patient's face, and besides, you don't upset a patient like that

before they go to the operating room. Even from a medical stand-point, there wasn't a reason in the world that this lady couldn't wear her makeup. It was just a silly rule. So I told her she could keep it on, and I raised such a fit about it that the doctors just threw up their hands and said okay. I never saw a patient go under the anesthesia so happy in all my life.

I mentioned stopping by to see that woman before surgery: that wasn't an isolated incident. I used to go to the hospital and make the rounds of *all* the patients I was going to anesthetize the next day; then I'd make rounds the day after surgery to see how they were feel-ing, and I would keep that up every day until they left the hospital. To me, this was professionalism, this was commitment. In fact, later this very practice of my making rounds became another battle be-tween Dr. Klugh and me. He complained to the hospital that I was "practicing medicine," and they made me stop it. "It was just a mat-ter of protocol," Dr. Klugh says today. "Making rounds is something MDs do."

In any event, the skirmishing that had begun two years earlier with Lawton and Cherdavoine now escalated to full warfare. I loved my work, and I wasn't going to go down without a fight.

&.

Roger Cassidy Clinton was born on July 25, 1956, at Ouachita Hos-pital in Hot Springs. Buddy Klugh administered my anesthesia.

Some men, when they become fathers, settle down and begin to take the world a little more seriously. Alcoholics, however, can't bear even to think about that kind of responsibility. Suffice it to say that Roger Clinton didn't miraculously change overnight.

In fact, my first night in the hospital was awful, thanks to him. My baby had been born by cesarean section, and of course I had been visited by all the family. Roger brought Bill over, and the Clinton clan showed up en masse to celebrate the momentous arrival of the Baby's baby. Mama Clinton had even taken a bit of a shine toward me by this point: Janet Clinton says it's because I indulged her about all her imaginary ailments.

But after visiting hours were over, I lay there for a while and suddenly I began to feel like something was wrong. My motherly instincts were operating on overdrive. The problem wasn't at the hospital, it was at home.

The switchboard had turned off the phone in my room, so I got myself up and put on my robe and went down the hall to a pay phone. It was probably ten P.M. I called home, and Bill answered. I asked how everything was, and he said fine. Now, Bill had been brought up not to story about anything—total honesty, that was the policy I had instilled in him. "Bill," I said, "are you alone?"

He hated to tattle on his stepfather, but he didn't lie: "Yes, ma'am," he said. Imagine that: ten years old, and all alone in that big house. Obviously, Roger was out strutting his manhood over the birth of his son.

So I did what everybody who wanted responsibility from Roger Clinton eventually had to do: I called his brother. "Raymond," I said, "I have to get back to bed. I'll trust you to go and see about my son and make sure he's safe the rest of the night." And of course he did.

Now where was Roger? I have no idea. For much of the time I was married to him I had no idea of Roger's whereabouts. He would go off for what were supposed to be one-day business trips, and it might be several days before he would come home. When he did, he'd be packing the lamest excuses you've ever heard in your life. Actually, in hindsight, some of them were pretty funny. Once, for example, he had gone to Memphis. When he reappeared three days later, he said the Mississippi River bridge linking Tennessee and Arkansas had burned, and it had taken all this time to make it passable. This was a *concrete* bridge, mind you. I beg your pardon? I may've been born at night, but it wasn't *last* night.

Another time—this was back when we lived in Hope—he said he was driving home and ran upon a bunch of county workers moving a cemetery from one side of the highway to another. Well, it would've been a *sacrilege* to cross, Roger said—he related this with impressive piety—so he stopped and waited for them to finish, which took two or three days. Roger told these stories so often I think he began to believe they were actually true.

More often, he would be missing in action on certain occasions—such as the death of his father in the midsixties. Poppy Al was on his deathbed, and it was just a matter of hours before he would be gone. The entire Clinton clan had gathered—except Roger. Nobody had any idea where he was, and they had called all over town looking for him. Raymond was really exasperated. Finally, he turned to me and said, "Well, *you* must know where to look."

"I do not," I told him. "I've never rolled the first wheel looking for Roger Clinton." Number one, I was always relieved that I was going to get some quiet time. Let carousing dogs carouse, you know. And number two, it's just not my nature to chase off looking for some man. Women who run around trying to find their husbands doing this, that, and the other thing just kill me. I was always too busy for that.

There *was* one time, though. I was at home on Park Avenue and a friend called and told me Roger was downtown at a fancy bar—like I cared where he was or what he was doing. But this friend said he was drunk, of course, and that he had gathered a crowd around him and was holding forth and playing the big man. I hung up the phone and tried to forget about it, but all I could think was, *What's the meanest thing I can possibly do to him?* When I channel my mind in such a direction, I usually come up with something—a legacy from my mother, I guess.

So I blacked out one of my teeth with mascara, and I put on the worst clothes you could possibly imagine. I drove downtown and walked into that fancy nightclub, and it wasn't hard to find Roger. He was at the bar bragging and boasting to everybody within the sound of his voice how rich he was, how cute he was, how smart and charming and successful he was. A crowd of men and women were standing around drinking—on Roger's tab, no doubt.

I walked up to them looking like the meekest little thing you've ever seen, and I stood there on the periphery a second. "Roger?" I said in a timid squeak. "Roger?"

Pretty soon people started to notice me. The crowd parted slightly and I stepped in from the shadows. That's when Roger saw me. At first, he had no idea what was happening. Then I said, "Roger, I need some money to get the baby some milk." Some of these people didn't know Roger, and I guess they were appalled. Roger himself went pale—then red. I turned around and walked out, and I didn't look back. But I bet Roger's boasting came to a screeching halt *that* night.

On the night of his father's death they finally found Roger, many hours too late, sound asleep out at the house of a lady friend who lived on Lake Hamilton.

The word I was hearing was that surgeons around town were becoming alarmed by the specter of malpractice lawsuits. There was a time, you may remember, before fear of malpractice had completely taken over and started running the entire medical profession. Back then, doctors were friends with their patients. Patients were friends with their doctors. There wasn't the slightest thought of lawsuits. Back then, people still respected common sense, too. When I was in nursing, we would have patients come in with a terrible pain in their abdomen. The doctor would feel around and say, "This patient has appendicitis." It wasn't any time before we would be in the operating room cutting the patient open and finding that, yes, indeed, he did have appendicitis.

Now, however, doctors have to replace common sense with reams of paper documenting jillions of tests. I was always critical of the number of tests they run on patients: No matter what's wrong with you, you've got to have all these tests. It's stupid, it's expensive, it's a waste of time. But doctors will tell you that it's absolutely necessary now—because if a patient sues, one of the first things his attorney will ask is, "Did you run such and such a test?"

I hate it, but I can see the doctors' point. You know something, though? It seems to me that the patients who actually have a case— the people who've been neglected or let down or harmed in some way by the doctor or hospital or anesthetist—those patients usually don't file. The people who file are those with frivolous cases that don't have a leg to stand on. That's why so few lawsuits are won. But they still have to be protected against, and that's terribly costly.

When Dr. Klugh came home to Hot Springs, the world was a more trusting place than it is today—even in Hot Springs. But surgeons have a lot to lose. They've put in all that time and money getting through medical school, and then they've set up offices and clinics and bought homes and cars and boats and started sending their children to expensive schools. It's a nice life, and they don't want to lose it. So when someone plants—even inadvertently—the seed of a possibility that their carefully cultivated world might someday be taken from them, those doctors listen. And they talk among themselves.

That's what I think was happening in clinics all over town. Dr. Klugh says today that he was simply arguing the merits of his plan, which were that nurse anesthetists would be backed up by someone with a superior education—someone who could come to their rescue if need be. That someone, of course, would be Walter Klugh, MD. In any case, I think it's safe to say that Dr. Klugh's medical degree was beginning to be seen by some surgeons as a buffer between the good life and the threat of losing it.

Along with Dr. Klugh, Lawton and Cherdavoine profited from such a perception. As for me, my phone began to be silent for long stretches at a time.

Roger, bless him, decided I needed a vacation. I hadn't really had one for years, other than maybe a weekend trip to Memphis. Lying on my back in the hospital having a baby and worrying about my other son didn't really count. A real vacation sounded exactly right. I had never been to Las Vegas, and Roger had been telling me I needed to go. If you loved Hot Springs the way it was from the 1930s through the 1960s, then the only place better was Las Vegas. We decided to head there.

Little Roger was no more than two months old, and Mrs. Walters had agreed to stay at our house to take care of him and Bill. Roger couldn't take a lot of time off, and neither could I—if I wanted to have any work at all when I got back—so we wouldn't be gone long.

I knew Mrs. Walters and my boys would be fine.

But I hadn't thought about how I might be. By the time we got a mile out of town I was missing that baby so much I thought I would die. I had said I would go, though, and I did need a break. And besides, Roger was in such a good frame of mind that I felt like I shouldn't ruin the trip for him. Instead of saying anything, I looked out the window at the passing pine trees and kept my mouth shut.

We drove straight through, trading the driving on and off. When we started getting closer to the real West, I remember seeing these odd things hanging down from the hoods of the few cars coming toward us. Finally I said, "What in the dickens are those things, Roger?"

"They're canteens," he said. People bought canteens and hung them on their cars in order to drive through this hot, desolate country. Later, I remember sitting behind the wheel deep in the middle of the New Mexico night—how strange it felt to be there rolling through that alien place I had never laid eyes on and couldn't see very well now, aside from the flatness that lay right in front of the high beams. Every now and then some critter would dart across the road or just off to the edge of the headlights, and I would grip the wheel tighter. If you had a wreck in a place like that, you'd be buzzard food before anybody had a chance to rescue you.

On the evening of the second day we pulled into Las Vegas. We had spotted the glow earlier from a distance and followed it to the very center of the light. I was truly unprepared for all that neon, that brightness, and for a time it energized me. I remember we checked into the Sands Hotel, which was one of the first hotels on the Strip, for $10 a night. Roger couldn't wait to go hit the craps tables, so we got cleaned up and headed out. Back then I had more energy than I do now, but even today I can stay up later in Las Vegas than I can anywhere else in the world. There's just an electricity about the place, and no matter what time of the day or night, you can step through the door of any casino and be greeted by the click of the dice and the snap of the cards and the clatter of the roulette ball bouncing against the spinning wheel.

My father,
Eldridge Cassidy,
working at the
Bruner-Ivory
Handle Company
in Hope,
Arkansas, 1925.

My mother, Edith Grisham Cassidy.
I would've killed for eyes like
hers—eyes so intense they
could kill *you* with just a glance.

Daddy (*at right*) in his grocery store in Hope in the midforties. The county had just
gone dry, but Daddy kept a little something for sale beneath the apples.

Me, age twelve. I got caught in the rain going home from school, so I ducked in and had my picture taken.

I gave this portrait to Richard Fenwick, my first serious boyfriend. Note that I had colored the gray streak that was already showing in my hair. (Richard Fenwick)

Richard Fenwick in Hope, late thirties. He worked at the movie theater and gave me extra popcorn.
(Richard Fenwick)

Bill Blythe as a soldier; I wrote to him every single day.

Senior-class bathing beauties about to dive into real life.
That's me at the very top. *(Hope Star)*

Bill Blythe and me *(above)* with Bill's friends Max and Rosalie
Williams at Chicago's Palmer House, spring 1946.

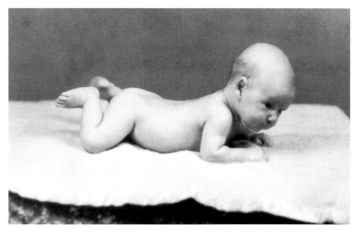

William Jefferson Blythe III, born August 19, 1946, in Hope.

Roger Clinton with one of Hope's world-famous watermelons. Maybe this is what inspired Roger's brief stint as a gentleman farmer.

My new family, circa 1951.

Roger and me with his parents on their wedding anniversary. To Mama Clinton, her baby—Roger—could do no wrong.

The Wild Bunch rides
again: Gabe and Roger,
Virginia and me, and
Roger and me—in a prophetic pose.

Roger Clinton could be hilarious at times. He
used to say, "Let's all get drunk and talk about
the chances we had to marry."

Virginia Crawford,
Roger, me, Gabe Crawford,
and another friend.

Nobody ever loved Bill Clinton more than Roger
did—and Bill never stopped loving Roger, in spite
of all that happened.

Roger and Bill
with their respec-
tive reading
selections. Bill
broke his leg in
the spring of 1952.

Roger Cassidy Clinton, born
July 25, 1956, in Hot Springs.

A joint birthday party. Somebody forgot
to tell them to smile.

The two Rogers at home at 1011
Park Avenue in Hot Springs.

A rare Hot Springs snowstorm.
Incidentally, I *love* furs—politically
correct or not.

On the way to Las Vegas, fall 1956. I missed my baby so much that we spent one night and came home.

If the puppy was inside, big Roger must've been in the doghouse.

After my sons, my career as a nurse anesthetist was the most important thing in my life.

Mother in the midfifties. As stern as she was with us, she spoiled her patients rotten.

Bill never once
complained
about his
little brother's
company.

My family, circa 1958.

The party room at 1011 Park Avenue was a favorite hangout for Bill and his friends.

Bill, 1958. Can you spot the Elvis influence?

Roger in second grade at Oaklawn School, 1963.

Little Roger visiting his big brother at Georgetown, 1968.

King and me at Scully Street, 1960s. This is the outfit the Reverend Yeldell said was the true "harbinger of spring."

Roger, Gabe, and me, summer 1962. Though Roger and I were divorced at the time, we ended up at the same party. (Nancy Adkins)

My wedding to Jeff Dwire, January 3, 1969. Marge Mitchell was my maid of honor, Bill was Jeff's best man, and Reverend John Miles did the honors.

Jeff treated me like a queen. Here we are on the way to an Elks Club luau—Jeff designed our outfits.

With Bill and Marge
Mitchell, midseventies.

Bill and Hillary's wedding day,
October 1975.

Bill, Roger, and me with Dick
Kelley, my future husband.

The Birthday Club, my
pals through thick and
thin. *Left to right:* Nancy
Adkins (the former Nancy
Crawford), Edith Irons,
Clover Gibson, Estelle
Blair, me, Dixie Seba,
Johnette Taylor, Marge
Mitchell, Virginia
Livingston, Edie West.
Not pictured: Berenice
Lyon, Elizabeth Ross.

(Harry Benson)

Bill being sworn in as the youngest governor in the nation, January 1979. (Donald R. Broyles)

I spent years in smoky clubs watching Roger get his singing career off the ground. Isn't he handsome here?

The new First Family of Arkansas. Chelsea was born February 27, 1980.
(Donald R. Broyles)

The day Roger got out of prison was one of the happiest of my life.

Barbra Streisand and I hit it off immediately. She calls me her "Southern mother." Here we are with Dick in Vegas at New Year's, 1994.

(Firooz Zahedi)

Carmen Miranda, eat your heart out.

(Nancy Adkins)

Elvis gave this Stutz automobile to his good friend Elias Ghanem— who gave me a ride. What a thrill!

(Elias Ghanem)

At Santa Anita racetrack for the Don McBeth Memorial Jockey Fund, summer 1993. (Benoit & Associates)

For someone who could never stay on a horse, I've sure stayed a long time at the track. (Harry Benson)

A visit with Col. Tom Parker, Elvis's longtime manager and friend, at the Parkers' Nevada home. (Kenn Wynn)

If you really want to push my buttons, say something against my sons. Bob Dole, I'm watching you.
(© David D. Vann, Hot Springs *Sentinel-Record*)

Dick, Champ, and me at home in Hot Springs. (© David D. Vann, Hot Springs *Sentinel-Record*)

Christmas 1993, with my beloved Chelsea.

Hillary and I—so different, and yet so much alike. (© 1993 Jorden Davie)

I've been a lucky woman. I've had love, work, friends, and the two most wonderful sons a mother could hope for.

(Harry Benson)

The next morning I woke up before Roger. I slipped on my bathing suit and went down to sit by the pool. I missed my baby so much I couldn't stand it. And Roger walked down and found me there, crying.

"What's the matter with you?" he said.

"This is the biggest mistake I ever made," I blubbered through my tears. "To leave that baby as young as he is." I looked at Roger looming over me. "I don't think I can stand it."

I'd thought he would surely argue, but he didn't. Who knows—maybe he was hurting, too. "Well, you sure can't enjoy it under these circumstances," he said. "Let's go home."

We went right upstairs and packed and left, pointing the Buick toward Arkansas. Ever since then, I've always told people that my first trip to Las Vegas was a U-turn.

&.

It was in these mid to late 1950s that two other men came into my life. One was Elvis Presley. The other was Jeff Dwire.

I need to clarify some things about my feelings for Elvis. Since Bill ran for President, the Elvis story has been blown out of all proportion. People still send me Elvis pictures, Elvis books, Elvis albums. But I was never a fan-club member. I'm not one of those people who believes Elvis is alive and living in the attic of the White House. I don't dream about him. I don't even listen to his music much anymore.

That being said, however, I'll admit to several things: I own a puka-shell necklace that Elvis once wore, and sometimes I can still smell Elvis's Brut cologne coming from the porous shells. I've ridden in a black Stutz automobile that Elvis gave to his best friend, who's now a friend of mine. I've been to the home of Col. Tom Parker, Elvis's longtime manager. I've even got a bust of Elvis in the corner of my dining room. But I ask you: Does any of that make me an Elvis nut?

I do remember being dumbstruck the first time I saw the man. I had heard people at the hospital talking about him, but I somehow hadn't heard him. And I sure hadn't laid eyes on him until Sunday night, September 9, 1956, on "The Ed Sullivan Show." Elvis had been on other shows—the Dorsey Brothers, Milton Berle, Steve Allen—several times during that spring and summer, and at first, Ed Sullivan had vowed not to have such a "lewd" act on his show. Then when Elvis appeared on Steve Allen and got terrific ratings, Sullivan reconsidered.

As we sat there in the living room watching Elvis sing "Don't Be Cruel" and "Hound Dog," I'm sure Roger had no idea that anything special had happened to me. But I'm telling you, I had never heard such a spiritual sound coming from anyone; it was the sweetest, most beautiful singing in the world. And of course you can't discount the man's sex appeal. I've told my girlfriends, if I hadn't had children and a job, I'd have spent the rest of my days traveling around from Elvis concert to Elvis concert.

I know a lot of people don't like Elvis, but he's my taste, the way horse racing and Vegas and bright makeup and leather boots are my taste. In my opinion, Frank Sinatra just couldn't produce the notes Elvis could. I used to like Dean Martin, but he couldn't measure up, either, once I heard Elvis. Later, in the 1970s, I would like Tom Jones. But nobody I've ever heard comes even close to Elvis in my mind.

Bill used to laugh and say that I loved Elvis so much because he was so good to his mother. He's right, I did like that. I also liked that he worked hard and pulled himself up to the top from a small town in the South. But none of those things had anything to do with his voice.

I never once discussed Elvis with Roger Clinton; he wouldn't have understood, and he would've been jealous. But from then on, whenever Roger gave me problems, I would go listen to my Elvis 45s. That fall he sang "Love Me Tender" and followed up with "Too Much." By the next summer he was on every radio station in the land with "Teddy Bear." And in the fall of 1957 he cut the record that's my all-time favorite Elvis song—"Jailhouse Rock." I remember I'd be tooling along in my Buick convertible down Park or Central Avenue, my perennial Pall Mall held between painted nails, and every time that

song would come on I'd start slapping time on the dashboard so hard
I thought I was going to have to drop the car off with Roger to get me
a new dash.

The second man who entered my life about that time was Jeff
Dwire. Little did I know that he would eventually become my third
husband.

When I met Jeff, however, he had just come to Hot Springs to open
a beauty shop. He was the first male hairdresser in town, a distinction that naturally brought out the boor in most of the local males.
Jeff was a tall, handsome man with movie-star looks and the flashy
clothes to match. He was meticulous about his appearance, and he
had impeccable manners. Since those weren't things you could read-
ily say about most of the men I knew, it's no wonder that there were
rumors, awful rumors, about Jeff—that, for example, he'd grown up
in a whorehouse in Louisiana, or that his shop was a front for prostitution. Actually, I never even heard those rumors until later, when
Jeff got into some trouble with the law. And I never believed them
for a minute.

To me, Jeff Dwire was simply and always a gentleman. The ladies
who came to his shop were treated like queens, and more than once
I heard him rebuke an employee if he or she didn't light a client's
cigarette or failed to be totally attentive in some other seemingly in-
consequential, but to Jeff absolutely unforgivable, way. One of his
operators once told me she had heard of white-glove inspections,
but she thought that was just a manner of speech—until she met
Jeff, who actually did go over the place with white gloves. He was a
perfectionist.

All the women in town were thrilled at having a male hairdresser—
it was such a sophisticated idea, you know, and we wondered why it
had taken so long in such a sophisticated town as Hot Springs. Right
away, Jeff had all the business he could handle.

I went to him looking for a new me. I was thirty-five, thirty-six,
and still wearing my thick, dark hair long down my back. I couldn't
exactly put it in words, but it felt unseemly. The hair didn't match
the grown-up woman inside.

Jeff was nothing if not decisive. He told me I ought to cut it. And there was one other matter of business, too: that gray streak in the front that I had been coloring for years. He thought it was wonderful, a hint of the mature me peeking out. Well, yes, that was why I'd been covering it up—it looked a little *too* mature. No, he said. He absolutely refused to color it. "Go somewhere else if you insist on doing that," he told me. "I won't do it."

That night after supper I brought up Jeff's ideas with Roger and Bill, both of whom liked my hair exactly the way it was. Men are always the last to know who you are *today,* aren't they? They get an image in their heads and that's it. But surprisingly, they didn't fight too hard on behalf of the status quo.

Back in Jeff's chair I remember being at once thrilled and petrified as I felt the clumps of dark hair falling on my arms, then floating down to the floor. It was the end of the 1950s and the beginning of the '60s. I, for one, was ready for a change. As Jeff clipped, I felt that an old self was surely being shed—even though a new one had yet to be formed.

Eight

NINETEEN SIXTY WAS the beginning of the end for Roger and me.

By this time, he was drinking tumblers of whiskey at the table during Sunday dinner—and when we in the South say Sunday dinner, we mean the midday meal. He even got drunk at Gabe's daughter's birthday party. While the children were cutting the cake and playing with their favors on the deck, Roger was screaming obscenities at me in the not-exactly-soundproof kitchen. It had gotten almost impossible to go out to eat with him. I have a good friend who remembers seeing Roger and me at a restaurant in about this period; she says I was sitting there looking into space while Roger dragged his fork through his food, his head bobbing precariously just inches above his plate.

And all over the radio that fall, Elvis was singing "Are You Lonesome Tonight?"

Nineteen fifty-nine had been bad—Roger had become violent at a dance, and later the same month he had actually beaten me on a couple of different nights and Bill had had to call my lawyer, Bill Mitchell, who summoned the police. One time I even filed for divorce, only to relent and take him back.

But it was two events in 1960 that were really pivotal. The first was the night Bill and little Roger both had to come to my rescue. Roger

had arrived home after work terribly, terribly drunk. It wasn't late—
maybe seven-thirty or so. How he had become so drunk so fast I'll
never know, but he was spitting fire when he walked in the door. He
started right in on me, yelling awful things, accusing me of seeing
other people. With years of practice, I had gotten so I could just tune
him out most of the time—as long as he didn't touch me, I could ignore him. But this time was different. He was making a scene like
this in front of the boys, who were horrified. Little Roger was screaming his head off, and so, for that matter, was big Roger. We were in
the kitchen, and I kept moving to stay away from him. Eventually he
got me into the bedroom and locked the door. I was really afraid he
was going to touch me this time, and I kept moving, kept dodging
him, kept pushing chairs in his way.

After what seemed like hours of this, poor Bill, whose room was
directly across the hall from ours, couldn't stand it any longer. His
little brother was terrified and crying, and behind his parents' door
what sounded like bloody murder was taking place. Roger had just
finished a tirade and he was slumped in a chair at the game table at
the foot of the bed when suddenly the door burst open and there was
Bill. Bill was fourteen and a good-sized boy by then—an inch or so
taller than Roger. I'll never forget the scene that followed as long as
I live.

Bill said, "Daddy, stand up."

And of course Roger couldn't. He mumbled and snarled and
slurred and stumbled, but his legs wouldn't lift him.

"You must stand up to hear what I have to say to you," Bill told
him. "Daddy, I want you on your feet."

Roger, reeling, looked at Bill, and Bill caught him by the arms.
"If you can't stand up, I'll help you." Bill lifted Roger from his seat
and held him up as Roger wobbled, scowling. And I'll never forget
how straight Bill looked him in the eye. "Hear me," he said to Roger.
"Never . . . ever . . . touch my mother again."

That night I had to call the police and have them come take Roger
to jail. He refused to get dressed, so they hauled him downtown in

his boxer shorts. Joe Crain was at the station that night, and he put Roger in the cell.

Of all the images of that awful episode that still haunt my memory, the saddest and most forceful is this one. When I was standing in the hall with Roger going berserk, before he cornered me in the bedroom, I remember seeing little Roger—age four, mind you—go out the back door and pick up a stick. It was as big as he was, and he had to drag it back into the house, but he was desperately determined to protect his mother. That moment was the turning point. *I may be married,* I thought, *but I'm a single mother nevertheless. And this is no way to bring up my children.*

The other pivotal event in 1960 was that I found out we didn't own the house on Park Avenue—Raymond did. I can't remember how this fact came to light, but it was devastating to me. If anything ever made me feel like a foolish woman, that was it—and all because I had relinquished to Roger all my financial rights and responsibilities. All those years, from 1954 to 1960, I had been turning over my paycheck to Roger, thinking it was getting us somewhere. And, in the end, it was really Raymond who was the owner. We were just renters. I asked Roger, "How could you deceive me this way?" He didn't have an answer.

But I did. Those two episodes sealed it for me. I was going to leave Roger, just as soon as I could manage it.

&.

If I had been the kind of person to beat myself up about things, by 1960 I would've had quite a bit of reason to be disappointed in myself. On the personal side, I was ashamed of what I had put up with, what I had allowed my sons to endure for so long. Little Roger was the same age Bill had been when Roger had fired that pistol in Hope. I was letting another child be drawn into my husband's sickness.

In 1957 my father's illness had finally won out. I missed him more than words can say, but I was glad he had died without having to know the extent to which Roger Clinton was terrorizing us. Daddy was now lying one grave away from Bill Blythe in Hope. Mother was in Hot Springs, still in her little apartment. She visited us often at Park Avenue, but mostly during the day when Roger wasn't at home. She could hardly stand to look at him. Mother and I didn't talk about Roger. There wasn't, there never had been, much point in it.

My work life had deteriorated, too. Instead of losing myself in the joy of the job—as I had for so long—I had begun to retaliate in the war with Dr. Klugh. By the late 1950s, the skirmishing had spread and gone underground, and the weapon of choice was innuendo. Hot Springs was a political town, and this was backroom politics at its best. Dr. Klugh and I were still both working at both St. Joseph's and Ouachita hospitals. In typical Hot Springs tradition, we would smile and say hello when we ran into each other in the corridor; then, as soon as we were out of each other's sight, we would be digging for all the dirt we could find on the other. At least, I know that's what I was doing, and I assume it was going on on his side, as well.

You could hardly have avoided it even if you'd been a saint. Nurses and doctors who supported me couldn't wait to tell me about the slightest mistake or misstep they'd perceived among Dr. Klugh's anesthetists during surgery, and I feel certain other nurses and doctors were critiquing my operating-room procedures to him. This wasn't really about competence, however. In fact, Dr. Martin Eisele, a surgeon and longtime friend of mine, says he never heard one question about my competence during these early days of the war. This was about personality, about power, about turf.

But whatever it was, it wasn't a happy atmosphere to work in. This isn't the way medicine ought to be practiced. Even though I thought I was right, deep down this all disgusted me. It reminded me of the way my mother had been. It made me feel like taking a shower when I got home.

But, fortunately, I'm not one to beat myself up. Life wasn't all bad, by a long shot. I had my support group. Everybody needs people to talk with, to laugh with, to cry with. People who believe in you. People who'll keep you believing in you. There are many messages I want to get across in this book, but none of them is any more important than this: Life is hard; don't try to go it alone.

My support group began with my sons. Simply by looking at them I could remember that I hadn't done *everything* wrong. Of course, because they're so different they lifted my spirits in different ways. Little Roger was a charmer from the day he was born. I remember at Park Avenue he would come sit by me on the stool when I was putting on my makeup, and I would ask him to sing me a song. Inevitably, he would croon, "Bring me some red roses / For a blue ladyyyy." He knew I loved that song.

Roger called me Dado, as distinguished from Daddy. He would say, "Dado, can we go get some ice cream?" He had trouble pronouncing his *r*s, so he referred to himself as Odgie. From the beginning, he had the kind of bad-boy streak that steals women's—even mothers'—hearts. One time I thought maybe he was telling me a fib, and I said to him, "Roger, are you storying to Dado? If you are, you're going to be in big trouble." He cut his eyes up at me and said, "Odgie likes trouble."

I can't say he never warned me.

It's funny how differently my two boys responded to parental discipline. When he was little, Bill would do everything in the world to avoid a spanking—and he never needed but one—because that was *such* an insult to his dignity. Whereas Roger would seem to say, okay, let's get it over with so I can go right back to whatever I was doing that got me the spanking in the first place. I guess Roger and I respond to authority in similar ways.

But though he didn't like trouble, Bill sure didn't run from it when it found him. Even when he was growing up, Bill was father, brother, and son in this family. He took care of Roger and me. By the early sixties he had grown into quite an impressive young man—imaginative, inquisitive, involved, always concerned with the world beyond our doors. He was also a pretty straight arrow. Later on, I would tell off-color jokes to Roger, but not to Bill. Who knows why people are the way they are? Maybe some of it had to do with Roger's formative years being spent in Hot Springs, while Bill's were in Hope—largely with his grandparents. His Mammaw Cassidy was a stickler for making you keep your nose clean, both figuratively and literally. Rose Crane remembers that no matter where she and Bill might be going, when they got ready to leave the house, Mammaw Cassidy would ask, "Have you got a handkerchief?" I recently ran across a postcard Bill wrote to his grandmother from band camp in 1960: "Dear Mammaw, I'm having a wonderful time with my two roommates. Am keeping my nose blowed," he kidded her.

Bill's reactions to Hot Springs's excesses have also probably helped shape him. He is simply not a gambler, nor is he a drinker. He's always been a religious person, but he's like Mrs. Walters—he lives his Christianity, he doesn't talk about it. He never gave any overt indication that he didn't approve of my gambling, or of our social drinking; he just simply moved quietly in the other direction.

In the afternoons when I would come home, he and I would sometimes have discussions that I was amazed at—talk about racial injustice, about history. He educated me, not the other way around. At Park Avenue and later at Scully Street, he always had a crew of friends over to listen to music or shoot baskets or raid the refrigerator or, sometimes, just to do nothing together. They played a lot of card games, and I'm proud to say that Bill inherited my competitiveness at game playing. I've heard my husband, Dick, say that he plays golf for fun. Well, I play any game to win—and I hope I have fun doing it. Bill is the same way. And on those afternoons when they would play marathon card games at the kitchen table, little Roger would always be right there with them. Bill never once complained about having his little brother around. That, to me, was the most amazing thing. I realize how suspicious this sounds coming from his mother, but Bill Clinton was always a remarkable boy.

My support group extended to my close friends, even though I didn't confide all my troubles to them. At work, there was still my "sister," Marge Mitchell, to smoke with and laugh with through the worst calamities. Dixie and I had our afternoons at the track, but our relationship went deeper than watching a bunch of horses running in circles. As different as we are personally, we just touched some chord in each other.

Back before he began withdrawing so, big Roger and I would sometimes go nightclubbing or out to eat with Marge and Bill Mitchell,
and also with Dixie and Mike Seba. But I met another of my great,
good, lifetime friends after Virginia Crawford divorced Gabe and he
began dating a young woman named Nancy Belinge. Gabe brought
her to the Hot Springs Yacht Club one night in 1957, and Roger and
I hooked up with them there. I thought Nancy was the cutest thing
I'd ever seen. Gabe seemed smitten by her, though you couldn't always tell with Gabe. He wasn't the sort of man who was short of girlfriends.

Naturally, that fact was always torturous to those women, such as
Nancy, who aspired to be Gabe's one-and-only. Nancy and I hit it off
from the start, and before long she was getting together with me or
even with other girlfriends and me. Still, Gabe was always present
in spirit. Nancy was absolutely crazy about him, and she would make
us drive all around Hot Springs trying to catch a glimpse of Gabe,
or at least of Gabe's car. The rest of us thought Nancy was a little
nuts to pursue Gabe so, but we loved her anyway and still do.

One night in 1958 I got a frantic call from Gabe. Nancy had tried
to commit suicide, and he had gone to her place and found her. This
hadn't been some pathetic ruse to get attention: She had been so de-
spondent over Gabe's treatment of her that she really wanted to end
it all. She had swallowed pills on a timed basis. When Gabe had
happened upon her, she was unconscious. He had called an ambulance and then me. I jumped in my car and tore over to the hospital
to meet them.

For seventy-two hours Nancy lay in a coma. The doctors said that
even if she did come out of it, they had no idea what kind of condition she would be in. For three days I hardly left her side. I talked
to her constantly, trying to breathe life into her spirit. I told her that
life was worth living—that no matter what troubles come your way,
life is a positive thing. I didn't know if she could hear me, but she
could. She did. In the end, Nancy says, "God didn't want me and
the Devil didn't want me, so they gave me back to Gabe."

And to me. What a bond Nancy and I have. That happened thirty-five years ago, and—as you'll see—through all those years she's breathed life into my spirit time and time again, just the way I did for her in that hospital room. Nancy eventually caught Gabe and became Mrs. Crawford and stayed married to him for seventeen years, though they separated after fourteen.

Beyond my close, tight circle of friends, I've relied on so many people through the years that I can't begin to name them all. I'll tell you this, though: Whenever my son Roger brings a new friend to visit Hot Springs, he never fails to take them to see Charlie and Ann Tyler. Bill, Roger, and I lived with them for a few weeks in 1962. But I'm getting ahead of my story.

ౌ

Dr. Klugh had a well-known expression: "The fainthearted never whipped a wildcat's ass." Not pretty, but true enough.

And maybe that statement is a clue to how he and I arrived at the situation we were in. Both of us were strong-willed, both of us were inclined to believe we were right. And both of us were determined not to back down.

The more the phone didn't ring, the more fight I felt welling up inside me. By the early 1960s, the war had returned to the surface a little, in that at least the battle lines were becoming clear. Medicine in Hot Springs was basically split right down the middle. We had two feuding factions of anesthetists, Dr. Klugh and me; that had produced two feuding clinics, Burton-Eisele and Sammons; which in turn had ignited a feud between two hospitals, St. Joseph's and Ouachita. Sammons and St. Joseph's supported Dr. Klugh. Burton-Eisele and Ouachita supported me—although, in certain touchy cases, they called in Dr. Klugh.

Over the years I had tried everything I could to hold on to what I had. To counter Dr. Klugh's plan for an anesthesia department at St. Joseph's—which he was pressing hard for now—I had persuaded the Burton-Eisele surgeons to write a letter to the hospital saying they thought anesthesia in Hot Springs should remain as it always had. In other words, that independent contractors such as myself should be able to operate without interference from anyone. I'm sure the letter drew guffaws from the administrators at St. Joseph's.

I had also tried to get the American Association of Nurse Anesthetists (AANA) involved on my behalf. You think when you belong to a group that they'll stand behind you whenever you get into trouble. Well, they stood behind me all right—so far behind me nobody could even see them.

I was, and still am, disappointed in the AANA. The onetime leader, a Mrs. McQuillen, had died by this time, and that made all the difference. Mrs. McQuillen had been a fighter. This situation would've been a long time coming if she had still been around. Instead, a new breed of administrators simply caved in and basically refused to help. At the time, I wasn't sure why they let me down: Were they intimidated, or did they actually see Dr. Klugh's point?

I've pondered that one for years, and I've finally come to this conclusion: They knuckled under because their opponents in this fight were doctors, and they were male.

&

The grapevine burns fast in Hot Springs. You've heard of a New York minute? Slow, slow. They haven't invented the stopwatch that can time Hot Springs spreading gossip. Never does it move faster than when conveying word on such torrid topics as love affairs, unwanted pregnancies, fistfights between grown-ups, and the threat of prison bars.

One day in 1961, the grapevine seared me with the news that Jeff Dwire had been indicted. Admittedly, few things in life are more disturbing to a woman than hearing that her hairdresser might have to leave town, but my reaction was sparked by something deeper than selfishness. Jeff was my friend, I felt, and I don't care what you say, you can't make me believe a friend of mine has done something wrong if I didn't see it with my own two eyes. I decided that this had to be some kind of trumped-up charge.

His other clients agreed with me. What we could actually learn about the complaint itself sounded crazy enough. I remember we

found out it had something to do with Oklahoma, the movie industry, money, and the sale of stock across state lines. The one thing
we knew for sure was that the movie was about the gangster Pretty
Boy Floyd.

Other than that, we were in the dark—and so was just about everybody else in town. But do you think that kept the rumor mill from
trying and convicting poor Jeff Dwire before he had even gone to
court? Hot Springs can be a mean little town, and this was a case
right down Hot Springs's alley. It wasn't murder or rape or robbery
or assault; no, it was apparently a con game gone bad, something
plenty of the rumormongers in town knew a thing or two about firsthand. For those who had disliked or distrusted Jeff from the beginning, this was proof positive that he was the con man they had
suspected he was.

But we were determined to help him, so some of us organized a
letter-writing campaign. My friend Sam Anderson was Jeff's attorney, and he gave us names—judges, prosecutors, people like that.
We sent letters to them and to everybody else we could think of, at-
testing to Jeff's sterling character. Meantime, Jeff remained his usual
quiet, polite, slightly distant self. He appreciated our efforts, but I
could tell he was embarrassed by the need for them.

Sometimes I think people in Hot Springs believe that I don't know
what they're saying about Jeff, but of course I do. He would go to
prison a year later, and over time I would finally have to accept that
he—duped by others—had indeed done something against the law.
But to my mind, that one mistake wasn't a reflection of the inner
man. Seven years later I would get to know him well enough to con-
firm my feelings: Jeff Dwire was good and kind and decent. In no
way was he the venal, opportunistic manipulator others make him
out to be.

The Hot Springs grapevine was burning again in the spring of
1962: That was when I announced to Roger Clinton that I was divorcing him.

Ever since I learned the truth about the Park Avenue house, I had
been searching for a place for the boys and me. With my workload,

though, I house-hunted in hit-or-miss fashion, sometimes doing it intensely for several days and then maybe not at all for weeks at a stretch. I wasn't ready to register with a realtor—that would've gotten back to Roger. Instead, I would go alone or with a friend, Ann Tyler. Ann and her husband, Charlie, owned the Motel Capri on Central Avenue, and Ann and I had been friends since I had put her to sleep a couple of years before.

I say that my hit-or-miss house-hunting was due to the demands of my job, but that's not entirely true. Breaking up a family is a frightening decision, and even though I had made it in my head, I still vacillated in my heart. Roger would be sweet and funny one day and I'd think, *Maybe he's changed.* When he was sober and feeling well, Roger could be amazingly funny. I remember he used to say one thing that Bill would laugh at every time: "You can't tell which way a frog'll jump until you punch him." Bill and I still laugh about that, and I've heard Bill use it when he's trying to guess how some senator might vote or something. Roger also used to tease Janet Clinton when they came over to play dominoes. She wasn't exactly a natural domino player, so one night she showed up with a book she had checked out of the library—*How to Play Dominoes,* I think it was called. Roger had fun with that. "Okay, Janet," he'd say when it was her turn, "what's that book say about what you should play here?" And he would crack up laughing.

Ninety-nine percent of the time he was sweet to the boys. He loved them and loved being with them, though as the years progressed he withdrew more and more, even from them. He would just sit by himself, looking off into space, not even wanting to go out. All these years later it still hurts Bill tremendously to remember him like that. "I loved having a father," Bill told me one day at the White House when I was working on this book. "I loved having a man around the house that I could just be with. And it pained me to see him as withdrawn as he became, just unable to get outside of himself anymore."

Sometimes Roger would take little Roger to the Buick dealership, where he would be entrusted to a man named Early, a mechanic. While Roger was working, Early would put little Roger up on the rack for a ride or would let him lie on his back on one of those rolling carts, upon which he could glide under a car and study the secrets of how it worked. Later, Roger would take him across the street to see Van Hampton Lyell, a man little Roger adored. Van was like a second father to him. And one of my son's fondest memories is of standing there with his daddy and Van Lyell watching that constant parade of six-ounce Coke bottles coming around and around on the conveyor belt, being filled and then marching off toward the bottle-top station. It was a man's world of grease and machinery, and Roger loved sharing that with his son.

There were other good times, too. Recently I came across little Roger's first billfold, which we must've given him when he was four or five. I flipped it open and there, still in their cracking plastic sleeves, were several faded pictures that forever freeze a few of the good moments: Roger lifting his son out of an inflatable pool; Roger, little Roger, and our German shepherd puppy King; big Roger, me, and Bill in a cowboy suit, standing in front of a new Buick; big Roger alone, but apparently happy, posing by a palm tree on one of our few family vacations, this one to the Mississippi Gulf Coast.

Whenever I would think I was dead set on a divorce, such sweet memories of *family*—no matter how rare—would give me pause. And then Roger would do something to return me to my senses— such as disappearing from work on the day he had taken little Roger with him, and somebody else would have to bring the child home.

D day was April 9, 1962. That was the day I finally told Roger I was divorcing him. I was nervous, of course, but when I've got something to do, I can steel myself and get it done. I made sure the children were in another room, and I stood at the kitchen sink waiting for Roger to come home. I knew that how this went would depend partly on whether or not he was drunk when he got there, and I was relieved to find that he wasn't. As soon as he walked in the door, I told him we needed to talk. And at that second he *knew*. He sat down warily, and I told him I wanted a divorce. Not only that, I said I wanted him to move out until our house was ready. At first he pleaded, and then he got snarling, dig-in-your-heels mad. When it was obvious that I wasn't going to change my mind, he salvaged what he could: He refused to leave.

The next day I packed suitcases for the boys and me, and we left the Park Avenue house, essentially for the last time. We drove directly to the Motel Capri, where Charlie and Ann Tyler took us in without question. We took two adjoining rooms, and for the next three weeks this was our home.

During that time, I found a house, a wonderful new brick ranch-style house. In 1962, builders were putting up what they called Gold Medallion homes, which were constructed using all the latest amenities. They were show houses, essentially. I bought the very first Gold Medallion house in Hot Springs—bought it all by myself, with the money I had been rat-holing out of my paycheck.

᠀

I filed against Roger on April 14. Less than a month later, Bill and I would be called to give a deposition. Mine, in part, read as follows:

Q: What was the cause of the separation?
A: Since we have been married, my husband has had a continuous drinking problem. It has become steadily worse for the last three or four years. On the first of March, 1959, while we were out at a dance, my husband became quite drunk and kicked me and struck me. Then on the twenty-sixth of March, 1959, my husband slapped me around without any just cause or reason and, on the twenty-seventh of March, 1959, threw me to the floor and began to stomp me, pulled my shoe off, and hit me on the head several times. At that time I separated from him and filed for a divorce, however, because of our child's age and the promises made on behalf of the defendant to quit drinking and to treat me with love and respect, I reconciled with him. After the reconciliation, the defendant did not quit drinking and the periods became greater and longer and it has become impossible for me to live with him any longer. We had gone to a party given by Mrs. Perry, Christmas, 1961, attended

by other people, and my husband became so intoxicated that I was unable to get him home. I finally was able to get my oldest son, Billy, to help me with the car and we were finally able to get him home. He has continually by his drinking and his attitude and actions toward other people continually and systematically embarrassed me in the presence of my friends and other people. I have worked practically the whole time that we have been married as an anesthetist, causing me to have to leave the house at different hours of the day and night. He is very jealous, continually calling to check on my whereabouts, which is causing me considerable embarrassment with the people with whom I have to work. When I am free and able to go out to be with my friends, he doesn't want to go, doesn't want me to go by myself, and has refused to let me associate or to have many close friends. Because of his drinking, he has kept me up at all hours trying to reason and take care of him, and I have a difficult time the following days trying to continue my employment. He even resents the fact that I began knitting, and he continually nagged and argued about this and almost every pursuit that I attempted to have. He has continually tried to do bodily harm to myself and my son, Bill, whenever he attempts to attack me when he has been drinking. Since our reconciliation, he has continually argued, quarreled, and nagged me until I can stand it no longer. I am afraid of him when he is drinking because of the physical abuse that I have received at his hands in the past.

Then Bill told his story:

Q: Do you know what the cause of the separation was?
A: Yes, I have lived in the home and am familiar with the defendant's systematic habitual drinking, and I know that when he gets this way that he has struck my mother on a number of occasions. I was present on March 27, 1959, and it was I who called my mother's attorney, who in turn had to get the police

to come to the house to arrest the defendant. For the last four or five years the physical abuse, nagging, and drinking has become much worse. On one occasion in the last month I again had to call my mother's attorney because of the defendant's conduct causing physical abuse to my mother, and the police again had to be summoned to the house. He has threatened my mother on a number of occasions, and because of his nagging, arguing with my mother, I can tell that she is very unhappy and it is impossible in my opinion for them to continue to live together as husband and wife. The last occasion in which I went to my mother's aid, when he was abusing my mother, he threatened to mash my face in if I took her part.

All the Clintons were upset about the divorce. Mama Clinton was on the phone to me immediately, weeping and wailing like I had never heard her before. "Please don't do this to my baby," she pleaded. "Please don't do this."

I was nice to her, as usual, but I thought to myself, *Me doing this to him?*

Nine

ROGER AND I stayed divorced three months. He was pitiful that summer, the summer of 1962. He lost thirty-five pounds, and everybody said it was from grief. He started going to church. At night he would come sleep on our concrete front porch, curled up under the living room picture window like a derelict.

He would park his car across the street from our house and sit there in the long summer twilights, until finally I would break down and go get in the car with him. We would talk for hours, hashing and rehashing the same old story. Roger promised to really change this time. He loved us so, he said, and I know he did. I just wish I had known then what I know now about alcoholism. Not that Roger was of a temperament to be helped by any group like Alcoholics Anonymous. Though I might wish otherwise, I always come back to believing that Roger would never have found the courage to stand up and say, "I am an alcoholic. I am powerless over alcohol." He was too vain, too proud, too much a product of his Hot Springs.

In the end I felt sorry for him. I know Bill did, too—and maybe that helps to explain something Bill decided to do in June, after the divorce was final.

One afternoon the phone rang and it was a judge I knew. "Virginia," he said, "Bill's in my office."

"Whatever for?" I said.

"He wants to change his name. To Clinton."

I thought about it for maybe three seconds, and then I said, "If he wants to change his name, please allow him to do it. It's fine with me."

On the surface, this may not seem like such a big thing—he'd been using the name Clinton for years. But here I was, just divorced from Roger Clinton, and Bill picks that moment to go and change his name officially.

When he got home, I asked him why he did it. He told me it was because little Roger would be starting to school that fall and Bill thought it would be confusing for them not to have the same name. That's a nice, pat story, and I know it's *part* of the reason. Bill has always been one for the extraordinary gesture, and I believe this was his statement about family solidarity: He wanted to have the same name his mother and brother had. On a deeper and more personal level, though, I suspect it was a kind of tribute to big Roger, whom Bill loved and never stopped loving. I do remember one thing Bill said about the name change: "A man's name doesn't make any difference in the world, Mother. It's the man." I thought that was amazing coming from a fifteen-year-old.

Of all of us, Bill may've had the most conflicted feelings about the divorce—as evidenced by what came next. Bill Clinton had never once intruded in my personal business, even though he had been dragged into it since the day he was born. But when I told him I was going to take his stepfather back, he made his feelings clear: "Mother, in my opinion, that would be a mistake." That's all he said. In our family, we don't nag. That's the way I brought my boys up—say it one time, and one time only. After that, you're nagging, and nagging is counterproductive.

"Thank you," I said to Bill, "but it's something I feel I have to do."

&

Two thirteen Scully Street was my house, earned by my own tears, and maybe that's why I love it more than anyplace I've ever lived. It was a home *I* made for *my* family.

My friend Toni Karber, who still lives at the other end of the block, describes Scully as "a *Saturday Evening Post*" street back then. Whereas Park Avenue was old Hot Springs, the area surrounding Scully Street had been a farm just a decade before. The Karber house was the first one built on Scully Street, and that was in 1952. Gradually the block filled in, mostly with young families looking for more room for less money—as well as for a safe street where their children could roam free. In those days, in neighborhoods like that, kids had the run of the entire street. Boundaries were a concept imposed by adults.

You enter Scully by turning right off Wheatley Street. The Yeldells lived on the corner facing Wheatley, and we were the first house to the right on Scully. Our back and side yards butted up to the Yeldells' backyard. On the other side of us were the Clarks, and beyond them were the Frasers, the Hassins, the Karbers. Ethel Street dead-ended at Scully in front of the Karbers' house, and the two corners formed by the joining of Scully and Ethel were important points of interest in my boys' young lives. On the right corner lived the Housleys— little Roger practically adopted Charley Housley as his surrogate father. On the left corner was a vacant lot known to all the neighborhood as "the playground." That's where baseball and football games were played, usually until darkness settled so deeply that you could only see the ball by throwing it high against the sky. Other attractions were the railroad tracks, which slashed through the area just beyond the Karbers', and Stokes Creek, which ran behind our houses a block or so away. Over the years, many a penny has probably been flattened on those tracks, many a rock chucked into that meandering stream.

By the time we arrived on Scully Street, most of the children were closer to Bill's age than to Roger's. As Toni Karber puts it, "Roger was kind of the caboose." Once again, I think she's described it exactly right. Roger was always allowed to tail along behind Bill and his crowd, which included Mike Karber and Guido Hassin among the boys, and Carolyn Yeldell—now Carolyn Staley—as, literally, the girl next door.

Bill's group was of driving age by then, so other friends from school, such as David Leopoulos and Joe Newman, would often be at the house when I would get home from work. In those days, even though some of them would have what they considered girlfriends or boyfriends, Bill's crowd was mostly just that—a crowd. They went places as a group, they enjoyed one another as members of the group. As a parent who was gone much of the time, I thought it was a very healthy atmosphere.

I don't mean that Bill didn't have dates. He did. Mary Jo Nelson was one he went out with; Mauria Jackson was another. (Small world, Hot Springs: Mauria happened to be Buddy Klugh's niece.) I liked both girls very much, and still do. Back in those days, Bill's taste ran toward the strikingly attractive, a bent I wholeheartedly agreed with. I liked what I called beauty queens—girls who wanted to look pretty. Bill was a handsome young man himself. I've got a photograph of him playing cards on a band bus, and he looks remarkably like the young Elvis Presley. Even *I* can see that.

Neither of my sons ever got the standard parental lecture about sex. At the times it seemed appropriate, I always happened to be between husbands—and I never could summon up the courage to do it myself. I wasn't one for lectures anyway—I believed my sons were of above-average intelligence, and if I told them something one time, that would be it. But with sex, I couldn't make myself tell them even once. If I'd had daughters, I think it would've been easier: I'd have told them sex could be a sweet and beautiful thing—but that precautions had to be taken.

By that age, though, I guess the lecture doesn't count as much as the values you've instilled during all the preceding years. Bill seemed to do all right. He kept himself incredibly busy during his high school career. He was active in DeMolay. He was president of Key Club and Beta Club and was a member of the National Honor Society. He was a major in the band. He was a National Merit Scholarship semifinalist. I trusted Bill implicitly and so imposed very few rules on him. Carolyn Staley remembers that "tell the truth" was about it. When the boys would tell me something, I would say, "Honest Injun?" If they could reply, "Honest Injun," that meant it was absolutely true, no more questions asked.

I never put a curfew on either of my boys because I didn't want them taking chances with their lives or anybody else's by rushing home to meet some arbitrary hour of the clock. So my rule was simple: no curfew—but you know a decent hour to be home. And if anything detains you, you call.

Bill was always very conscientious about checking in, letting me know where he was. Much of that was due, of course, to Bill's natural sense of responsibility. But part of it was because big Roger was still alive then, and Bill was always a little worried about me and his little brother. He would sometimes call home two or three times a night, as much to check on us as for me to check on him.

Once again, we were a back-door family—or, in the case of Scully Street, a garage-door family. The house was basically a one-story rectangle. On the left was a two-car garage with a laundry room at the end of it. A door from the garage/laundry led into the kitchen, a good-sized room divided roughly in two by a breakfast bar. On one side was the kitchen area, on the other a family room with a dining table, a TV set, and several lounge chairs. To the left of that were sliding glass patio doors, which opened out onto a small concrete slab, around which I had planted my roses.

Parallel to the kitchen/family room was the dining/living-room area. I've always had portraits of my children on the walls of my living room, and by this time I had framed Bill's colorful band medals, too. They took up a huge frame, there were so many of them, and I combined that with portraits of Bill and arranged them on the wall just inside the living room. Carolyn Yeldell and David Leopoulos used to refer to that area as "the shrine."

From the front entry you could jog left into the living room or go a bit farther and make a left to the family room or a right toward the bedrooms. Going down that short hall, the first door on the left was the main bathroom, a big, luxurious space with a sunken tub that I used to love to soak in. Across from the bath was little Roger's room At the end of the hall was the master bedroom, which we gave to Bill.

Big Roger and I used a smaller room between Bill's and little Roger's.

It wasn't a huge house, but it was plenty big enough for us and all our friends. Bill, Roger, and I all like to have people around us, and seldom was the day that I would roll in after work and find only Bill and little Roger at home. Carolyn Staley recalls that Bill would call and invite her and David Leopoulos over even if he didn't want to do anything in particular. One time when David was at Carolyn's and Bill called, David told Carolyn, "Oh, okay, let's go on over and watch Bill read."

More often, however, I would drive up and there might be a crowd of boys—girls, too, sometimes—shooting baskets in the driveway or practicing their music in the garage or playing cards at the dining room table or making a snack in the kitchen. In addition to his beloved peanut-butter-and-banana sandwiches, Bill craved tuna fish on rye bread, and I used to keep a big bowl of tuna salad in the refrigerator for after-school snacks. I would brew a pot of coffee and light a cigarette and just join the group. Carolyn remembers that Bill and I would have "philosophical" conversations, often spurred by heartbreaking stories I had heard at the hospital. Somebody couldn't get credit, somebody couldn't get health care. Carolyn says it was a seminar in Ethics 101. I would sort of lay out the problem, and then all the kids would talk about the way it ought to be. Bill and I talked most, Carolyn remembers. He and I had done that kind of thing all his life.

Carolyn also recalls, I'm flattered to say, that I was a "cheerleader for their dreams"—that I would probe to find out what they most wanted to do in the world and urge them to follow their hearts and keep on working. I knew I had done that with my sons, but to think that I might've had an influence on some of their friends makes me very proud indeed. I do recall that these were the times when I would caution them about jealousy or temper or whatever else was my soapbox topic for the day. I guess I thought of myself as a kind of unofficial den mother.

One afternoon my beeper went off when Carolyn was there alone with me. As I headed for the car, I asked if she wanted to ride to the hospital, and she said she'd love to. When we got there, I had her wait in the car for a few minutes while I went into the operating room and checked with the doctors and the patient. Then I had someone go out and ask Carolyn if she wanted to see a baby being born. She was about a junior in high school at that point. She was flabbergasted, but game. We put a gown on her and she stood in the operating room openmouthed, watching the entire miracle.

All these years later I find that Carolyn's mother, Kay, wasn't exactly pleased with me in that case. "It was personal," Carolyn says. "It was seeing the most private part of a woman's body. It was sex." Mr. Yeldell was a Baptist preacher, and their house was apparently run a lot differently than ours was. Carolyn says she could tell that just by looking at our driveway: We had three cars—two new Buicks and Roger's old Henry J., and all three of them were convertibles. There were other, more subtle differences. In her house, there was no such thing as spare time; duties always beckoned. When she got to know us, she marveled at how loosely our household was run. Bill and Roger didn't really have busywork-type duties; big Roger and I had always felt that their studying and making good grades and being involved with their school was enough.

Carolyn says her parents weren't a hundred percent sure how safe it was for Carolyn to be over at our house. We drank and went to the track. We gambled at the Vapors. They saw Bill, she says, as a fairly mature young man who had lots of girlfriends and a convertible to drive and all the freedom anybody could want. One night Bill and Carolyn stayed up late watching an old movie in our den, and they both fell asleep in the chairs. Carolyn remembers hearing a loud knock at the glass sliding door and waking up to see her father's disapproving face on the other side of the glass. You just didn't fall asleep with a boy, even in separate chairs. "Time to come home, Carolyn," the preacher intoned.

On the other hand, she says her parents "knew there was something remarkable going on" at our house, and that they noticed Carolyn gaining self-confidence from being exposed to it. I like to think that increased self-confidence came from being treated as an adult at our house—from being trusted. Bill and Roger were on their own so much of the time that I really had no choice with them. Early on, I had taught them to be self-sufficient because I was gone and big Roger was basically unreliable. When we moved to Scully Street, I even had to take little Roger to school before dawn so as not to entrust him to his father. Once again, I got a break when I needed it most. There was a janitor at the elementary school, and he told me, "You don't worry about your son. I'll keep him with me until the other students get here." And he did. The way my life has run, I've had to place my trust in people. What I've found is that most people respond to that, if you offer them the chance.

So I gave my sons the phone numbers to call if they needed to, and I tried my best to instill in them the kinds of values that would make them trustworthy. I conversed with them as adults, I treated them the way I wanted to be treated. I was never a disciplinarian, but I always expected self-discipline and respect. Seldom did anything happen that made me wonder about my judgment.

Both boys were told in no uncertain terms that they were never to call me at the hospital unless it was an emergency. But one day when Roger was about six, the nurse came to me in the operating room and said Roger was on the phone. I told her I was busy and to find out what he wanted. She came back and announced—so everyone in surgery could hear—that Roger wanted to tell me we were out of bologna. If there was ever a time I came close to killing him, that was it. "Roger," I said, when I got home, "what do you mean calling me like that? You know better than to call me unless it's an emergency."

"But Dado," he said, "it *was* an emergency."

I don't know where Bill was in that particular instance. Bill was always in charge of Roger after school, and I felt that I couldn't do any better than that. In fact, Carolyn recalls that her impression was that there were three adults who lived in our house—big Roger, Bill, and me—and only one child.

No wonder, then, that she enjoyed coming over so much. We enjoyed her, too, and she's probably Bill Clinton's best female friend, aside from his wife. But we loved all the Yeldells, no matter how different they were from us. I've always been able to find some way to connect with just about everybody, and on those rare days when I had some time off from the hospital, I would sometimes go have coffee with Kay. We found plenty to talk about—our children, our yards, the school, the town, anything but my life with Roger Clinton.

Not that I really think they would've been judgmental. I'll never forget Reverend Yeldell's remark to me one spring day when I was out working in my yard. As I've told you, I liked being as tan as I could possibly get, and my way of accomplishing that was to tend my roses and putter in the yard wearing a pair of shorts and a tube top. I still laugh when I consider the image I must've presented to a Baptist minister: dark bare limbs, stomach and cleavage showing, painted eyebrows, long wispy eyelashes, dark eyeliner, bright glossy lipstick, fingernails and toenails as vibrant as the flowers in my garden.

"Virginia," he said to me that warm April afternoon, "I've decided that the truest harbinger of spring isn't the robin or the daffodil. It's you out here working in the yard with short shorts and a tube top."

Most of us never get to know how we're really perceived by others, and sometimes that's a blessing.

For me, though, one of the joys of doing this book has been reminiscing with some of my longtime friends and hearing how my life looked to them at various points in the past. Toni Karber is one of the smartest, most articulate people I know, and she's a loyal friend who held her tongue during Bill's presidential campaign when scores of news agencies had identified her as someone who could give them details about Bill Clinton's boyhood.

I had actually met Toni long before we moved to Scully Street. For twenty-five years she handled public relations for Ouachita Hospital, and that's where I first got to know her. Her office was right by the rear elevator, and she used to get to work early so she could concentrate on any writing she had to do. Toni remembers that I would roll in with my game face on: "Good morning! Good morning, every-body!" The truth is, it wasn't all a game face; as I've told you before, just being at the hospital gave me an emotional lift.

If Toni didn't look too busy, I would stop and smoke a cigarette with her. Otherwise, I would make the rounds of my patients and get set for surgery.

I was, Toni says, "a lightning rod" for gossip. Even though I never uttered a syllable to her about Roger's behavior, she says it—and I—were the talk of the hospital. Gossip is an interesting phenome-non, isn't it? It's a waste of time, and much more demeaning to the person talking than to the one being talked about. Imagine, all those people devoting their dull little lives thinking so much about inter-esting old me.

The truth is, gossip—about me—doesn't bother me at all. Never has. I've always known that people speculate about strong people. People speculate about leaders. I think it's one of the trade-offs for being who you want to be. That's something I taught my sons: Be who you want to be, and don't worry about what people say about you. You wear your armor on the inside.

Even before Bill became a public official, I had what might be called a "public persona," and maybe that's why I've been able to deal with the spotlight that's fallen on me since Bill was elected President. Ever since I was a girl, when I've showed up someplace, I've wanted people to know I'm there. So when you go out of your way to look and act the way I do, gossip comes with the territory. I can walk into a room and see it happening in my peripheral vision: Someone leans closer to someone else; a cupped hand pretends to stifle a cough; an opinion is shared while the speaker looks the other way.

Toni recalls that the gossip came in layers. The top layer was ap-pearance: "Is that gray streak real?" "Can you believe those eye-lashes?" "Why does she do that with her eyebrows?" "Look at"—take your pick—"that tan, that lipstick, those diamonds, that big con-vertible, those white penny loafers instead of nurse shoes."

It apparently threatened a lot of people that I could sit down with a cup of coffee in the cafeteria, and before long a crowd would've pulled their chairs up to my table. It threatened them that I was loud and funny, that both men and women sought me out. Another layer of the gossip involved those other people, of course. I was supposed to be doing this with this person, and that with that one. It's been that way all my life. Poor Roger Clinton: no telling what all he must've heard.

At its deepest level, says Toni, the gossip was transformed into resentment of what appeared to be "a charmed life." Is that not funny? Is that not ironic? Over the years I've lost three husbands, had a son go to prison, developed cancer, and people in Hot Springs have been offended that nothing seems to touch me. What this says to me is that the gossipers want me to fall down and wail, to reveal a vulnerability that they can then feel sorry for—and therefore superior to. That's what gossipers are about, and that's why you can't worry about them. In fact, I *do* believe I've led a charmed life, but it's not because bad things didn't happen to me. It's because I made it my prime business every single day to rise above the bad things— to be positive, to look on the bright side, to spread cheer and not gloom. That'll strike some people as Pollyannaish, I know. But I'll guarantee that being positive in this world takes more grit than giving in to cynicism any day.

The one area in which the gossip bothered me was my work. I wanted my work to be above that. However, if you're a lightning rod, you can't screen out certain channels the way you can with cable TV. Seeing Dr. Klugh on a daily basis became wearisome to me, and not necessarily because of him personally. It was the electricity produced by our proximity to each other that got to me—the charged atmosphere, the constant buzz, the crackling sparks of innuendo. It was as though both hospitals were wired with an extra circuit.

❧

Toni Karber has a writer's way with words. It was her impression that Roger Clinton "moved around the periphery" of our lives.

I think that's true, especially after we settled in on Scully Street. So much was out in the open by then. It was clear that Roger wasn't the man I had met so many years before in Hope, and in fact never had been. Who was he? He was his mother's baby. He was Raymond's little brother.

I felt sorry for Roger, but I didn't love him anymore. Roger was my husband, but he was no longer central to my life. My sons, my work, my friends—that's what I concentrated on.

Roger didn't really change much. He went to work every day and toiled for his brother. Toni Karber remembers how it was at the Buick dealership when she or her husband, Jon, would take their car in for service. Raymond's dealership was a gathering place for powerful, politically savvy men in Hot Springs. The big wheels. They would drop by to have a cup of coffee with Raymond, and they would all puff on their cigars and dissect the current state of the world. Raymond—tall, handsome, magnetic—would be in his element, presiding over this smoke-filled room while taking phone calls, doing deals, making more money. Roger wouldn't be out there sitting down with the big boys; he would be in the back with the mechanics, standing behind a counter looking up automobile parts in a catalog.

Toni says she always trusted Roger more than Raymond when it came to getting her car repaired right and without unnecessary cost. Roger had a good heart. Carolyn Staley remembers one day when she had dropped by the dealership, probably with Bill—though if Bill was there, he was occupied doing something else.

"Carolyn, come here," Roger said to her. "I want to show you something." He walked her out to the lot where a wrecked car had just been towed in. She remembers how slow moving he was then, how there seemed to be no energy left in him, how he looked so much older than his years. The wreck he wanted to show her was the most god-awful wreck you can imagine, with the front end all jammed back through the front seat and the top twisted and the windshield nothing but a memory. They stood there staring at it for a long time.

"Look inside it," he told her. "I want you to look real good." She did, and there was flesh hanging from the steering column. Of course, she was shocked, but Roger smiled at her lovingly. "Be careful," he said.

People who remember Roger from this era tend to recall the quietness, the passivity about him, more than anything else. He had just withdrawn from life more and more.

Then, suddenly, he would erupt, spewing anger. He would go berserk if he went to retrieve one of his hidden bottles and I had thrown it away—which I did with regularity. Another thing that would set him off was when little Roger, who lived in fear of him, would ask why he drank so much. He was humiliated, I guess, that the children knew how weak he was. One night he came home stone drunk and bounced from one side of the hall to the other trying to get to the bedroom. Later he chewed me out for "telling the kids I've been drinking."

Little Roger used to play with Steve Housley down at the other end of the street, and sometimes Mr. Housley—Charley—would take them fishing. They called themselves "Charley's Navy."

Charley was one of little Roger's boyhood heroes, and to hear him talk about Charley is like hearing someone with a normal life talking about his father. Charley and his brother were roofers, and they could do anything. Charley had built cabin cruisers, put together Jeeps from the ground up. He taught little Roger how to hunt and fish and camp. At one time Charley had been an auctioneer, and he loved to sing country music. Charley used to ask little Roger to sing "Gentle on My Mind" all the time, because that was his favorite song. Roger says Charley Housley was the first person who ever told him to keep following his musical career.

If Bill or I weren't there, Charley was the person little Roger would run to when his fear of big Roger became too great. On a couple of occasions Roger says Charley even stood big Roger down, though I never saw any of that. "Don't touch him. Don't you lay a hand on him," Charley would say, and Roger would turn away.

One day Roger came home early, drunk and furious, and he got me down in the laundry room with a pair of scissors at my throat. He bent me backwards over the washing machine, and he was practically lying on top of me. Who knows what the fight was about—and yet it was about the same thing that *all* the fights were about.

Bill was next door at the Yeldells, but little Roger, who was six at the time, was in his bedroom. He heard the screaming and ran to the end of the hall—from where he could see all the way through the den and the kitchen to the utility room. He saw Roger, he saw me, he saw the scissors.

He dashed out the front door like a bullet, not caring that he was wearing nothing but his underwear. He burst into the Yeldells' well-ordered household screaming for his brother: "Bubba! Bubba! Daddy's killing Dado!"

Roger says Bill went absolutely crazy. He grabbed his little brother's hand and ran back across the yard to our house, crashing through the garage door, screaming all the way. Big Roger threw me down and wheeled to face Bill, who pulled little Roger behind him with one hand and me behind him with the other. Bill was seething. "You're not going to hurt them anymore," he said to his stepfather. "You're not going to hit Mother and you're not going to hit Rog anymore. We're not going to take it anymore. If you hit them, you're going to have to go through me."

Bill walked us into the living room and sat us down on the couch. Little Roger was crying and so was I, and all of us were shaking with fear and rage and the sheer indignity of what we had been forced to endure. Big Roger tried to follow, laying down the scissors and taking off his belt as though he was going to hit Bill, but Bill shut the door in his face. He knelt down and comforted us. "I want you to stay right here," he said. "Everything is going to be all right."

Then he stood up and went to the kitchen to deal with Roger. We could hear them shouting, but Roger was no match for Bill anymore. This time it *was* over. Before long we heard the door slam and Roger left the house.

&

Bill's graduation affected me in ways too complex to fully understand. On the one hand, I was thrilled for him to be going off to Georgetown to follow his dream. On the other hand, I hated to think of life without seeing him every single day. And somewhere in there a little fear was probably mixed in, too.

I'll never forget the day of commencement. I was ironing Bill's graduation gown and these huge tears kept plopping all over it. Bill walked by and saw the splotches on the fabric. "What're those stains?" he said.

"Oh, just a little water to get out the wrinkles," I said, keeping my head low and steaming out the tears.

After Bill left home, Mother came to live with us at Scully Street for a while, if you can believe that. What on earth was I thinking?

Well, I was thinking that since we now had an extra room, there wasn't any point in Mother spending money to rent that apartment. She was reasonably healthy, so that wasn't a major consideration— though I did also feel it wouldn't be a bad idea for her to be where people could watch her. Also, she loved little Roger and vice versa, and since he missed his big brother so much, I thought they might welcome each other's company. I also thought it might have a quieting effect on my husband.

He hadn't changed, other than to shrink into himself more. He still got drunk and he still ripped off his belt and threatened to hit us, though he never followed through with it. He just enjoyed inflicting the fear, especially on little Roger. He still raved, still accused me of cheating on him, though there was a kind of emptiness about it now. I no longer paid much attention to his shouting; I had reached the stage where, as long as he didn't touch me, I could lie there and think about something else. His shouting was just a vague noise coming from someplace very far away.

Even though we were still a couple in the eyes of the outside world, our marriage was basically over. We were just marking time—toward what, I wasn't sure. I hardly talked to Roger when we were alone. I hardly even looked at him.

One day, tired of his accusations, I had decided to put them to

rest once and for all. I brought him a month's worth of documenta-
tion of my whereabouts, signed by people at the hospital. Roger
wouldn't even acknowledge it, wouldn't even admit that it was in the
room with him. That was my final turning point. That's when I knew
that all his accusations weren't about me and never had been. They
were about him. He didn't want to hear that I hadn't done anything
wrong—because only by keeping a finger pointed at me could he
avoid turning it on himself.

It didn't take Mother long to decide that this wasn't exactly the
best possible arrangement for her. After a few months of living in
our madhouse, she was probably even homesick for the state hospital. One day she came to me and said she wanted to move back to
Hope, into a nursing home. I told her I thought that would be fine.
The truth is, I was delighted. She had been crabby and rude ever
since she got to our house. Little Roger and his friends would be
watching television and she would simply get up and change the
channel. Of course, the boys were too courteous to say anything to
Roger's grandmother, but I hated it. *She's going to make him not
want to have his friends over here,* I thought—*just the way she did
me when I was little.* I wasn't going to put up with that.

But she saved me the chore of having to confront her. At our first
opportunity we drove to Hope to see what was available. What we
found was ideal: The old Julia Chester Hospital, where Bill had been
born, was now a nursing home. Mother's room would be the very
room I had stayed in when I had had Bill.

So little Roger and I were alone again—except for Roger, of course.
We all three missed Bill. Roy and Janet still came over for dominoes, and if Bill would call while we were playing, big Roger would
shout from the table, "Tell Bubba hello!" Little Roger spent long,
happy hours composing letters to his brother, telling him what he
thought about the Arkansas Razorbacks' chances and which teacher
he hoped to get in school. Bill understood better than anyone the
void his leaving had created in little Roger's life. I had my work, and
I could sit drinking coffee and smoking with my girlfriends, and I
could brag with justification about Bill's latest brilliant accom-

plishment. Little Roger had his own friends, and of course he had
Charley Housley. But there was nobody left whom he knew could
protect him *all* the time.

Bill was good about writing to little Roger, too. Inevitably, his letters challenged and inspired. In one, he told about a wonderful experience he had just had, and then promised Roger that he could
have it, too: "Someday you'll have a great opportunity like that—
only remember to treat everyone fairly and honestly. Be good as you
can to everyone. Write me soon. Love, Bubba" In another, he responded to Roger's letter about not doing well in a football competition: "I'm sorry you didn't win the pass, punt and kick contest, but
you know things like that take time. Bubba finished last the first two
times I went to tryouts on my horn. But I finished first 10 out of the
last 11 times—lost only my sophomore year in high school at district clinic. So you see, determination will finally pay off—*if* you
want to win bad enough."

Those letters meant the world to little Roger, whose life at home
wasn't nearly so inspiring.

Even though Bill was fully engaged in his new world, conditions
back at 213 Scully Street were never far from his mind. He worried
about me and about his little brother, and that worry often came
through in his letters. The source of the concern was, of course, big
Roger. Early in Bill's junior year, after Roger had developed cancer and his moods had become even more unpredictable, Bill sat
down to confront *and* encourage his stepfather. The result is this remarkable letter:

Dear Daddy,
    . . . Mother told me you all went to church Sunday. If both of
you would just make up your mind to do that every Sunday, no
matter what, it would sure help. I believe, Daddy, that none of
us can have any peace unless they can face life with God, knowing that good always outweighs bad and even death doesn't end
a man's life.

You ought to look everywhere for help, Daddy. You ought to write me more—people—even some of my political enemies—confide in me, but the last real conversation we had alone was parked in a car behind an old house on Circle Drive. That was 6 years ago, and you and Mother were getting a divorce. I had hoped that things would be better after you got back together, but you just couldn't seem to quit drinking, and since then I have often wondered if you really wanted to.

Of course I know I have never been much help to you—never had the courage to come and talk about it. The reason I'm writing now is because I couldn't stand it if you and Mother were to break up after all these years. I just want to help you help yourself if I can.

I think I ought to close this letter now and wait for your answer but there are a couple of things I ought to say first—1) I don't think you have ever realized how much we all love you and need you. 2) I don't think you have ever realized either how we have all been hurt . . . but still really have *not* turned against you.

In spite of this you must do better. You have perhaps 20 years to live. They ought to be the happiest of your life. They could be misery if you keep drinking and drive Mother and Rog away from you.

Please write me soon Daddy—I want to hear from you. And remember, don't be afraid to look for help *before* you do something you're sorry for—Don't be ashamed to admit your problem. . . . We all have so much to live for; let's start doing it—together.

> Your son,
> Bill

᪣

Roger's cancer had first shown up one morning in 1965. He and I had been sitting at the breakfast table and I noticed something dis-

turbing about his neck. In truth, this was the first time in months
that I had bothered to really look at him. "Roger," I said, "your neck
is swollen."

"Yes, I know," he said.

"And I can't help noticing that you're getting hoarse."

He just stared at me. Finally, as I would have with a patient, I
said, "I really think you ought to see a doctor."

He didn't argue, and in fact we went right away to see Dr. Vic
Bennett, a close family friend and a brilliant orthopedist. Dr. Bennett discovered a big lesion underneath Roger's tongue that had
metastasized to his carotid gland, or vice versa. I say "discovered,"
but really there wasn't much discovering to it: the lesion was obvious. I think Roger had known about it but had been avoiding dealing with it.

"In my opinion," Dr. Bennett said to both of us, "this is squamous-
cell carcinoma, but we need to biopsy it to be sure. And to see what
methods we're going to use for treatment."

Roger began shaking his head. "I will never," he rasped, "have a
disfiguring operation." Of course, even if they had operated and
taken off half his face, they couldn't have promised that that would
save his life. With Roger, it was moot anyway, I knew. Live by vanity, die by vanity. He meant what he said about a disfiguring operation.

Dr. Bennett was astonished. "Roger, something *has* to be done
about this. You're going to die."

Roger wouldn't budge.

Finally, Dr. Bennett said, "Over at Duke they've just started working with laser." He had graduated at the top of his class from Duke,
and at a younger age than anybody I had ever heard of getting through
medical school. "Would you agree to let me take you there for an examination? Maybe they can do something with laser."

Roger and I were both touched by the kindness of this man. Here
he was, willing to shut down his medical office and go with Roger
all the way to North Carolina. "Yes," Roger said. "I'll do that."

They got into Vic Bennett's car and drove to Durham, almost a thousand miles. The diagnosis was very bad. The Duke doctors agreed to try laser, but they still strongly recommended the radical surgery and the chemotherapy and all that. Roger wouldn't sit still for it. After a week, they turned around and drove home.

A few weeks later they had to go back for more laser treatments, but Roger's condition had deteriorated so much that a car trip was out of the question. From then on they flew. He was there another seven days, living in the hospital and receiving his treatment daily. Dr. Bennett stayed with him the entire time.

In all, Roger made four or five trips to Duke over the next couple of years. Each time, we thought surely it would be his last, but somehow he managed to hang on. One time he was there over a weekend and little Roger and I drove to North Carolina to be with him. They had hospice quarters where we stayed, and Roger moved in with us during that visit. He was sweet that weekend—sweet but sad.

Though Duke was too far away for me to go regularly, Bill didn't miss an opportunity to come down from Washington, D.C., whenever Roger was in Durham. Roger made an extended trip to Duke in the spring of 1967, Bill's junior year. I think Roger was there six weeks. Even though Bill was working as well as going to school that semester, he would finish up as early as possible every one of those Friday afternoons and then start out in his 1963 Buick for the five- or six-hour drive through the Virginia hills into North Carolina. First thing Saturday morning, he would go to the hospital and pick up Roger. He would stay as late as possible on Sunday afternoon, then would set out on that long, lonely drive back to Washington.

Bill wrote to me often during that difficult year. He was running for class office, but took time to try to lift my spirits:

Dear Mother,
. . . How have you been, Miss Nightingale—and life on the homefront. I sure know just how Roger felt about the Math test. Story of my life.

Please write soon and tell me how very happy you are—but only if it's true—I hope you will be proud of me in the next few months: win or lose, I'll try to reflect the honor and courage with which I've been raised.

I love you,
Bill

During the spring when he was spending weekends with his step-father, he would jot me an update:

Dear Mother,
   . . . Daddy seems better but so very anxious to get home. He is mentally and physically more alert than I have seen him since he started having eye trouble. Of course, the treatments take away his appetite and make him sick but that goes with it. . . .
   Hope you will have some time to yourself other than the races now—probably you will never win that much. What a girl!—I know how hard this has been for you—my goodness, your life has been a succession of crises, all of which you've weathered.
   Surely I am prouder of you than you could ever be of me. . . . Keep your chin up—tell Rog to practice; I must write to him.

As sad as those weekends were, they were a healing time for both Bill and Roger. On those one and a half precious days a week, they'd drive together for hours, just the two of them, searching for a common ground amid the rich, green North Carolina countryside. Bill believes they found it on a sunny Easter Sunday, the last, and most peaceful, of the nearly twenty Easters they had spent together. "I never will forget it," he says. "We went to Easter service at the Duke chapel, and then I drove him slowly around the Triangle there. After that, we went over to Chapel Hill and saw all the dogwoods, the redbud trees. It was just stunningly beautiful. It was one of the most beautiful days I can ever remember in my entire life. And it was a wonderful experience we had, just the two of us."
   There was no "true confession" on Roger's part, nor any demands

by Bill. By that time, so much that had gone between them was too
obvious for mere words. Bill never once stopped loving Roger Clinton. He says he always knew that Roger loved me with all of his
heart—which made his story all the more tragic. In the end, Bill forgave him, and Roger may've even forgiven himself. "Somehow, that
prolonged battle with cancer was quite liberating for him," says Bill,
"and he was fine. I think he finally figured it out at the end."

Eventually, the doctors at Duke told Roger that unless he allowed
them to operate, there was nothing more they could do for him. So
he came home.

He lived for six months after that. For a time he was in the hospital in Hot Springs, but he told me he wanted to die at home, so I
brought him back to Scully Street. Once he got there, he hardly left
again. For probably the last month of his life he didn't set foot outside the house. He had started drooling and didn't want anyone to
see him like that. Van Hampton Lyell didn't come around much anymore.

We were living a virtual wake—always expecting death, but death
never seemed to arrive. In early November Bill came home from
school to be with us. Every night for the last three weeks of Roger's
life, Bill would take his eleven-year-old brother over to stay with
friends. We never expected Roger to live through the night, and Bill
didn't want little Roger there when Roger died. Then, the next morning, there Roger would be. In the afternoon, Bill would go get his
brother and take him for a drive, and they would have a long talk the
way they always had when Bill was home.

Today, Roger remembers wanting more than anything for his father to die. At the end, part of that was kindness—he wanted his father not to suffer so much. But a major part of it was something other
than kindness. For years, Roger says, he had prayed for his father
to die in order to end *our* suffering. To have his father hanging on
when it was obvious he was at death's doorstep seemed like one last
act of terrorism. "It was maybe two or three weeks of 'the last day
he can possibly live,'" Roger says, "and every day I'd wake up wondering if he was dead—and he would still be alive. I just said, 'God,

what are you doing to us?' I got so I didn't want anything to do with God. For years I had prayed that our family would stay together and stay strong and that Daddy would get well, and it seemed that none of my prayers would be answered. I'd pray he wouldn't get drunk—he'd go get drunk. I'd pray he wouldn't hit us—he'd come home and hit us. I'd pray we would have a happy household—we wouldn't. Now I prayed for him to die, and he wouldn't die. That's when I got tired of praying. And it took me many years to come back around. I did, finally, because I really believed in God the whole time. I hated Him, and you can't hate something you don't believe in."

The last week, Roger didn't even want me to see him. Once again, my good friends came to my rescue. So many of them are nurses, and they attended to him around the clock. Bill sat up with Roger all night every night. As for little Roger, he remembers being ushered into that back bedroom once during that week; it was a shock because he hadn't seen his father in so long.

One of the nurses placed little Roger's hand in Roger's palm, and Roger squeezed. Soon after that, his son's deepest, darkest prayer was answered.

Ten

FORGIVENESS ISN'T A talent I was born with; I had to learn it.

Where I come from, people tend to have long memories. By that, I mean they hold grudges. Usually, the problem develops over some matter of loyalty or the breaking of it. Loyalty still counts for a lot in Arkansas, where, for so long, family was all the insulation anybody had against the indifference of the frontier and the unyielding hardness of the land. Life was more clear-cut than in more complex places: This person is your friend, then he's mine; this person is your enemy, then he's mine. Arkansas has softened with progress, but some of the old habits die hard.

By far the most difficult job I had in raising my sons with Roger Clinton was in conveying to them that what their father was doing was wrong—but that he was still their father, and therefore worthy of respect. That was hard for me, because much of the time I felt he *wasn't* worthy of respect. There were days when I would've loved to turn his sons against him—as though I could've done a better job of that than he was doing. (Which reminds me of the old line, "No, I didn't tell them you were a son of a bitch; I don't know how they found out.")

My problem, though, was that I happen to believe in respect for your parents. Simple as that. So during the week that Bill and I spent away from Roger after he fired the pistol in Hope, I told Bill, "If you see your daddy, you speak to him. He did wrong, but he's still your daddy." And when little Roger would ask why his daddy was being mean, I told him, "Your daddy is sick. But he loves you." At the time, I didn't have a real understanding of alcoholism as an illness—that would come later. But I did know, beyond the shadow of a doubt, that Roger Clinton loved both his sons and would've done anything within his power to make them happy. The key words are *within his power*. Unfortunately, staying sober didn't fall into that category.

During Bill's presidential campaign, some members of the Clinton clan got angry at Bill for exposing Roger's abusive behavior. It would've come out anyway, and Bill knew that. But my hope is that when they read this book, those injured Clintons will finally understand that Bill would never do anything to hurt the memory of his stepfather. Roger Clinton was who he was, for whatever reasons. Bill had as much reason as anyone to hate him, to hold a grudge, but he didn't. He loved and forgave him—as clear a demonstration of unconditional love as any you'll ever encounter.

In fact, Bill was instrumental in making me put aside my own anger at Roger. "Mother," he's told me time and time again, whenever I fall back on my black-white view of the world, "Mother, there are two sides to every story." So later I learned about alcoholism, and I forgave Roger for putting us through what he did. As bad as it was, it was nothing compared to what he put himself through.

It pains me to say this, but the obvious casualty of Roger Clinton's abuse has been his son Roger. Bill—aside from being a different person altogether—had the memory of a mythical father out there somewhere, one who died young and who had been good and kind and hadn't abused his mother. Roger didn't have that kind of emotional space to operate in. This man had been *his* father, and that fact left as strong an emotional mark on him as it did a biological one.

I saw it coming early on. I remember one night when Roger was screaming at me in front of little Roger, who must've been four or five at the time. I looked Roger Clinton in the eye and I said, "It won't be Bill that deals with you, it'll be your own son."

And so he has: He's had to deal with the legacy of Roger Clinton every day of his life. There've been many rough spots, but life is much better now. Life is full of promise. Still, I don't think my son has ever forgiven his father. I won't nag, I'll just tell him this: He needs to forgive if he's ever going to be free.

⁊

Roger's death came in a year that also marked the end of Hot Springs as he knew and loved it. In 1967, then governor Winthrop Rockefeller finally put the kibosh on illegal gambling. It may not've been as simple as that, but the effect was the same: The games closed, the big spenders moved on, the town suddenly woke up and it was The Day After. By the 1970s, much of once-grand Central Avenue would be boarded up, and the upper part, between the elegant Arlington and Majestic hotels, would degenerate into a strip of topless bars attracting a clientele much different from the Hot Springs revelers of the glory days. There would be open prostitution, open drug sales. Hell's Angels from Dallas would bike in for drugged-up weekend sprees. There would be bad characters on nearly every corner.

Such was the backdrop against which my second son lived out his teenage years.

After Roger's death, I was more numb than anything else. We laid him to rest in Greenwood Cemetery, an old, tree-shaded burial ground not far from Scully Street. He's all alone in a large plot across a gravel driveway from the rest of the Clinton clan. Following the funeral, all our friends came by and we had the usual bittersweet session, part of the process, everyone taking turns telling stories about when Roger did this or when Roger said that. There was a lot of drinking, laughing, and crying—in this case, a particularly fitting end.

Then the people were gone, and I was left with my numbness. Roger and I had been together for twenty years, married for seventeen of them. My close friends rallied around me, of course—Nancy and Gabe came by and called. Marge and Bill Mitchell, Dixie and Mike Seba—I saw them all, sometimes in the evenings going out to dinner, and sometimes just the women for a drink or a cup of coffee.

But I had little Roger to look after, so I pretty much stayed close to home. In time, the numbness turned to relief. Earlier that year, in March of 1967, a tremendous tornado had roared through Hot Springs, destroying many homes, including Nancy and Gabe's. I remember the numbness we felt after that—and how eventually we were relieved not to hear the roar, or to have to anticipate more destruction. We were relieved to have the peace and quiet. The aftermath of Roger's death was like that.

Relief isn't the same thing as serenity, however, and I couldn't help feeling a disturbing current of change in the air. If you remember the late sixties, early seventies, you know what I'm talking about. All I had to do was turn on my car radio to tune in the changes: Where was poor Elvis? In his place was somebody named Strawberry Alarm Clock. Hair was getting longer, looking less well kept, less meticulous—less *controlled*. I never will forget a story Toni Karber told me about Bill sometime during this period. He had come home from college, and it must've been summer, because he was wearing shorts and a T-shirt and those big, ugly rope sandals people used to wear back then. His hair was thick and wild and sticking out to there. Late one afternoon Toni and a friend were sitting in Toni's living room, and Bill came walking down Ethel Street toward Scully. Ethel Street, you'll remember, runs perpendicular to Scully and stops directly in front of Toni's house. Suddenly Toni looked up and saw the most amazing sight. There came Bill sauntering down the street with the sun setting behind him, and the long hair and the sunset produced a halo effect. Then they saw the sandals, and that did it. "Look," Toni said to her friend, "Bill looks just like Jesus." That was always my problem with my boys and their long hair: Every time I tried to get them to cut it, some girl would tell Roger never to lose those beautiful locks, and somebody else would tell Bill he looked like Jesus.

The changes kept blowing my way, too. My mother died two months after Roger. She waited him out, I suppose, stubborn thing that she was. She died in that room I had stayed in when Bill was born. A circle was closed. Roger was fifty-seven, Mother sixty-six. It occurred

to me that heavenly nights had suddenly become a whole lot noisier—though I prayed that Heaven meant neither one of them would
ever feel the need to shriek through the night again.

Bill's calls and letters comforted me during those hard days, and
I tried to comfort him, too. I could tell that all our travails had shaken
him:

> Dear Mother,
>   . . . Never have I been so sorry to be away from you as I was
> when Mammaw died— Surely you will have some years of peace
> now . . . I suppose that, the older one gets, the more death be-
> comes a part of life, a reality that comes to friends and rela-
> tives and famous people and finally to the self. It is just coming
> to play a major role in my life and I am going to have to learn
> how to handle it—at least I'll have the advantage of you as a
> model—how you have been so strong I do not know, but the les-
> son was not lost on me, nor on Roger, I'll bet. . . .

Later that spring he tried to cheer me up: "Good luck with the
ponies," he said. "Try to keep the family alive."

As usual, I tried to lose myself in my work—but there, too, the
world felt even more unsettled than before. One night in the late
sixties I was working a case in the operating room at Ouachita, and
I got in trouble with the patient. We were right in the middle of
surgery, and something didn't seem right. I can't remember exactly
what the problem was—maybe an irregular pulse; I can't even remember whether we were using cardiogram machines at the time.
I always said I didn't need a darned cardiogram because I have such
educated fingers that I could *feel* a change in pulse. But something
wasn't right, and I said to the circulating nurse, "Please call Dr.
Klugh and ask him to come."

I tell you, he must've set a new speed record getting across town.
He was there as quickly as humanly possible, and he straightened
out the problem immediately. As I recall, he prescribed some medicine, which I wasn't allowed to do. Friends I've told that story to al-

ways ask how the other doctors reacted to me afterwards. I may be naïve, but I don't think they thought one thing about it. They weren't at all surprised that I called Dr. Klugh if I thought I needed the help. After all, he did have more extensive training than I did—I never argued about that. And those doctors never had a question about my judgment.

Dr. Klugh was gracious, too—gracious in the sense that he acted like there was nothing to the episode. He felt the same way toward patients that I did, and calling him in was just the right thing to do. He never even sent a bill.

Looking back on it now, maybe the changes in the air—and especially Hot Springs' continuing decline—were making us all a little skittish in those days. How could they not? Some people have characterized that period in Hot Springs' life as a time of desperation. Desperation isn't a feeling I like to admit to, but I've occasionally felt it nipping around the edges of my life. Whenever that happened, I instinctively turned to that airtight box inside my head. I blocked out the bad and focused on all the good things that had happened to me. I reminded myself that whenever I've been down the most, something or somebody always comes along to help me up.

ها

The phone rang on Scully Street. It was early in the evening, probably in the spring of 1968. Roger had been dead six months or so.

I had had a horrendous day in the operating room and had come home early. I was drained in that good way—beyond tension, just tired and looking forward to crawling under the covers. Tomorrow was going to be another hard day.

I picked up the phone and a voice said, "Hello, Virginia. This is Jeff Dwire." *Jeff Dwire.* I hadn't seen him in years. He had spent much of 1961 and 1962 trying to avoid having to go to prison; that's when we wrote the letters on his behalf. But eventually he ended up serving nine months. He had turned his beauty shop over to one of his associates, and I had found another hairdresser.

Then one day in the midsixties he had come into the beauty shop while I was having a manicure. His wife was with him, and he introduced her around to all his old clients. I remember thinking how good Jeff looked—happy, healthy. The old trouble seemed to be behind him.

And that was the last I had heard of Jeff Dwire before this phone call. "I've just heard about your loss," he was saying, "and I'd like to come by and say hello to you."

Tired as I was, I heard myself answering, "Well, sure, Jeff. Come on."

Mentioning Jeff in this context makes me think about love, and the ways I've experienced it in my lifetime. I'm convinced that—assuming you're open to it—there are different kinds of love that come to you at different stages of your life, bringing you exactly what you need at each stage. I know that's been the case with me. With Bill Blythe, I needed the wild, impetuous, idealistic love of youth; with Roger Clinton, I needed someone older to embrace both me and my fatherless son. And, as you'll see, both Jeff Dwire and Dick Kelley stepped into my life at precisely the right time.

Does this mean that I think one marriage can't work for life? I think nothing of the kind. I can't imagine anything finer and more rewarding than a rich, loving, lifetime relationship between two people who've grown together over the years. Unfortunately, I've not been privileged to have such a relationship.

After twenty years of Roger Clinton, I needed tenderness. I needed respect. I needed to be treated like a queen. Jeff Dwire was exactly the man I needed.

He came over and I fixed him a drink. The stereo was on—I remember a song called "Love Is Blue" was big that spring, and "Honey," about a man whose young wife has just died and gone to heaven. Oh, what a tearjerker that one was. Jeff and I sat at the dining room table, and before I knew it I was feeling like I had been sitting across from this man all my life. It was just so natural, so comfortable—so *comforting*. He was obviously very touched by the fact that I had lost my second husband, and that I had a young son. He wondered how he might help, how he might ease my pain.

That night we sat at the table until very, very late, just catching up on what had happened to each of us over the past six years. He told me he was divorced and that his ex-wife had moved to Nevada. We didn't discuss his prison sentence in detail; he had made a mistake, he said, and had taken the rap for some other people. It was a subject that was obviously painful for him to talk about. Also, because of his prison sentence, he had lost his license to do hairdressing in Arkansas, and he was trying to get that back. For the past few years he had worked at several home-building companies around the South, but his real love was hairdressing. He saw it as, essentially, the fashion business, since hair style and fashion were so intertwined.

I was surprised at how attracted I was to Jeff that night. *All these years I've known him,* I thought. *Why am I feeling this way now?* But after such a grueling time with Roger, it was wonderful to have a Southern gentleman sitting there giving me all his attention. Jeff was a master at that. He liked women, and he enjoyed lavishing the little niceties on them—flowers, perfume, dinner, dancing. But all of those are mere symbols of the thing a woman wants most: attention. Even if Jeff hadn't had a dime to spend on all those other things, he would still have been charming, because he gave whomever he was talking to his undivided attention. He sat there across that table looking me straight in the eye, watching every nuance of my reaction.

He was a handsome man—close to six feet tall, with dark, dark hair, a product of his Cajun genes. During this period he wore his sideburns down to the bottom of his ears. I thought of Rhett Butler.

We had many evenings like that. After that first night, Jeff began coming over regularly and I would fix dinner and we would listen to music and talk. Sometimes we went out, but since I needed to be near the phone anyway, staying home was easier. Cozier, too.

Whenever we did go out on the town, the experience was such a contrast to evenings with Roger that I could hardly believe this was now my life. Jeff loved music and dancing, and obviously everybody at the various clubs in town knew it. One of the top dance places was the lobby of the Arlington Hotel, an elegant room that evoked the grand style of the thirties and forties. When Jeff and I would walk through the door, the orchestra would stop the number they were playing and launch into a haunting rendition of "The Shadow of Your Smile." Somehow, that had become Jeff's theme song. Looking back on it, I guess it was perfect. When I asked Jeff about it, he just smiled enigmatically and said people knew he liked that tune. It soon became *our* song, and to this day I think of Jeff whenever I hear it.

Jeff was a marvelous dancer. Most artists are, I think. It's been my observation that if you have talent in one thing in the art world, you have it in others as well. In addition to his artistry with hair, Jeff had a tremendous sense of music and rhythm. Of all my husbands, he was easily the best dancer. Bill Blythe was next. Roger liked to dance, but, as with Dick, it didn't come naturally to him. Fortunately, I can follow anybody doing anything. With Jeff, I got to indulge my long-dormant passion for exotic dances like the tango. You should've seen us out there, cheek to cheek, arms outstretched, the very picture of Latin drama.

There was one disturbing note amid all this revelry: Jeff had diabetes. He didn't take insulin, he took another drug. He preferred swallowing a pill to sticking himself with a needle. I could understand that. He told me he was absolutely religious about taking his medicine, and he seemed to be as healthy as could be. He had a wonderful physique and kept himself in perfect shape. At first I worried about the diabetes, but after a while I decided it wasn't anything to get alarmed about.

When it became obvious that our relationship was serious, I began to break the news to my friends. I knew that was going to be touchy, for a variety of reasons. One, Roger hadn't been gone a year. Two, Jeff had been in prison. Underlying both those reasons is the one that never varies: My friends care about me and don't want me to be harmed in any way.

But I wasn't prepared for the intensity of the responses. One night Dixie and Mike Seba happened to be at the airport when Jeff and I were there, and I told them I wanted them to meet someone who had become very important in my life. To this day, Dixie remembers their first impression of Jeff: friendly, charming, well mannered—and they didn't trust him for a second. They thought he was too good to be true—a con man—and they asked around about him. In the end, they loved Jeff just like everybody who ever knew him did.

Marge was indulgent, and so was Nancy—if being with Jeff made me happy, then it made them happy, too. But Gabe Crawford was livid on the subject. I won't even try to analyze the reasons for his response. Obviously it had to do with more than just Jeff—after all, Gabe had been Roger's friend for decades. Maybe this looked to him like a betrayal. Of course, Jeff and Gabe were almost total opposites: Gabe mistreated women, while Jeff adored them. Gabe mingled easily in the rough-and-tumble world of men, while Jeff preferred the company of women. I'm not even sure I knew how strongly Gabe felt at the time, but Nancy now tells me he absolutely refused to go to Jeff's and my wedding.

My sons had their axes—however slight—to grind, too. In the summer of 1968, when Bill was getting ready to leave for Oxford, he met Jeff. Jeff told Bill right off the bat that he had spent time in prison. Maybe because he wasn't going to be around, Bill was apprehensive about our relationship. But as the summer wore on, he began to like Jeff more and more. Later, when I called Bill in England and told him Jeff and I were getting married, he was supportive. It was just, "Whatever, Mother." And I don't think he ever felt that I made the wrong decision—for me.

But one thing Bill said to me later, after he got to know Jeff even better, has stuck in my head for decades: "You know, it must be very frustrating to him to be working in a beauty shop, as capable as he is." That *could* be read as Bill looking down his nose at Jeff, but knowing Bill Clinton, I know that's not the case. He came to love and respect Jeff Dwire, as you'll see. But the reason that statement has stuck in my head is because it was so on target. Bill observed Jeff and understood things I didn't even see at the time.

Little Roger's reaction was in some ways the easiest to understand and the most difficult to deal with. Roger was now twelve. All his life he had been under some other man's thumb—Bill's, however benign, and big Roger's, a true instrument of fear and oppression. Now both of those men were gone, and as much as Roger loved his big brother, he was happy to be, finally, the man of the house. As Roger says today, "A man had mistreated my mother for many years, and I intended to take care of her. All of a sudden there's another man wanting to be in my mother's life."

I explained to Roger that this man was different. How did I know? I guess you never know for sure, but Roger Clinton had taught me a thing or two about judging men. I've been accused of being attracted to smooth talkers, and I don't deny that. But smooth doesn't equal corrupt. If a man is nothing but smooth talk, that's one thing; but I haven't had that experience. The smooth-talking men I've fallen for have meant what they said.

So I wasn't necessarily leery of smooth talkers. On the other hand, if I caught one single whiff of possessiveness, I would turn and run like Secretariat. I was even warier of drinking—I wasn't about to get into a relationship with another alcoholic. After Roger, that was the first thing I checked for. I kept a constant vigil with Jeff, as I did later with Dick.

Not that I would've been happy with a teetotaler, either. Teetotalers sometimes develop a personality—judgmental, moralistic, holier-than-thou. I've got no tolerance for that. To my mind, there's nothing in this world wrong with a man or a woman having a few drinks, as long as you control it instead of vice versa. That's not what I was watching for. I was looking to see if drinking changed the man's personality. And I could keep an eye on that and still be cute enough to keep his interest.

The second thing I looked for was how much the man loved me. It's not what he says, it's how he acts. Of course, there are no more dedicated actors than two people who're courting, but I figure that if you go with someone for six months or so, sooner or later he'll tip his hand—if there's a hand to tip. With Jeff, I always felt adored.

The third criterion was how much I loved and respected him. That was no problem with Jeff—I was head over heels in love again, for the first time in years. You who're reading this, I hope you know the feeling of being in love. It's the most wonderful feeling in the world: There's no hurdle you can't leap, no pinnacle you can't reach, as long as you're together. Once again, Jeff's past didn't matter to me. My heart *and* my head told me he was a good, decent man, one worthy of my respect.

Jeff was a Methodist, which was fine with me. One of my favorite people was the Reverend John Miles, who preached at Oaklawn Methodist and whose son John was Roger's best friend. John Miles also coached Roger's team in football. But the thing I liked best about John Miles was that he was *human:* He had a tolerance for human frailty that I found refreshing among the clergy. John wasn't judgmental. As a man of the cloth, however, he did have a certain obligation to try to nudge God's flock in a pious direction. After Jeff and I were married and I started going—occasionally—to his church, John used to say to me, "Virginia, why don't you go to church as much as you go to the racetrack?" He had a smile on his face and a twinkle in his eye when he said it.

Then one day I was at the track and who should I spot but John Miles. That was funny for a couple of reasons: I happened to know he was supposed to be in Little Rock at some church meeting. "Brother John!" I said, a tad louder than necessary. "What's the world coming to when I run into my favorite preacher at the racetrack!" He laughed and said he just hadn't felt like going to that church meeting. "Well, if you won't confess, I won't tell," I told him, and I laughed all the way to the betting window.

Jeff and I wanted John Miles to marry us. If you've ever been divorced, getting permission to remarry in a church can be like passing through the proverbial needle's eye. Church brass tend to frown on divorce, and I was surprised to find that the Methodists were almost as adamant as the Catholics on that score. At least, that's my recollection. John claims not to recall any such problems. In any case, God obviously wanted this wedding to happen. Bill flew home to be best man, Roger was an usher. The date was January 3, 1969. Marking a new year and a new life, I marched down the aisle at Oaklawn Methodist Church, and before long Brother John pronounced me the new Mrs. George Jefferson Dwire.

&

I thought I was picky. I thought I was a fanatic about neatness. I hang my clothes up at night. If I use a pair of scissors, I put them back where they belong when I'm finished with them. If I drink out of a coffee cup, I put it in the dishwasher instead of leaving it on the counter. In general, my husbands haven't shared this trait. Take tools, for example: Dick is likely to leave a good saw outside to be rained on. Roger never picked up a tool in the first place, so he didn't have to worry about putting it back. I wasn't with Bill Blythe long enough to know his habits on that score.

But none of them compare to Jeff Dwire. He color-coordinated his closet—black suits, then blue, then brown, then tan, and so on. He liked just *that much* space between his clothes, no more, no less. Every single night he took his shoes off and replaced the shoe trees.

And Lord, bless my lucky soul, the man was *handy*. Who'd have thought a tango-dancing hairdresser would be any good with a hammer and nails? But Jeff was a whiz. One of the first things he did was enclose the patio on our Scully Street house and put a pool table in it. He named the room Roger's Roost, and he and Roger would spend hours out there playing eight-ball.

Jeff was as generous as he was talented. He built shelves for Marge Mitchell's boathouse. He helped Joe and Louise Crain panel their kitchen. He cut a hundred-year-old board from a barn on some property he owned and made it into a mantel for Charlie and Ann Tyler's new house. There didn't seem to be anything Jeff Dwire couldn't do.

He even taught me to fish. I had never cared about fishing at all, but Jeff loved it. There was something peaceful about it to him— about being on the lake all alone, which is the way he usually went. The fact that he wanted to share that private time with me was just another declaration of his love. Jeff and I usually fished from the end of Marge Mitchell's dock. Of course, as Ann Tyler says, once Jeff taught me to fish, I acted as though I had invented the sport.

I've never let being a novice at something get in the way of my professional act, and I talked about crappie and bass and baiting hooks till I probably bored my friends silly. They were glad to see me so happy, though, after all those years.

During racing season, Jeff and I both began scheduling our afternoons free so we could go to the track together. He also liked dog racing, and we would occasionally spend weekends in West Memphis watching the greyhounds run. Frankly, I've always felt that once you've seen a horse race, dogs are a very poor second. But Jeff was a good dog handicapper, and if doing that made him happy, then I was happy to be there with him.

Jeff was as good with Roger as he was with everyone else. He told me soon after we were married, "Roger is the son I never had." He seemed close to only one of his own children. Kip was her name, and she and her husband came from Oklahoma to visit us two or three times. But the other girls Jeff seemed strangely reluctant about. One of them lived in Louisiana—in Shreveport, which wasn't very far—but he showed little interest in going to see her. As close as my sons and I were, I never could understand that, and I used to try to get him to go for a visit. I even said I would go with him, but he *really* didn't want that. He seemed to want to keep us all separated.

Jeff doted on Roger, and yet he was a strict disciplinarian with him, especially at mealtimes. Oh, Jeff's manners were wonderful, and his manners reflect in Roger Clinton today. Every time we'd sit down at the table, it was, "Roger, your left hand belongs in your lap. Don't bring your left hand out. Roger, do not lean on the table. Roger, Roger, Roger."

One time Bill was home, and I'm sure he was tired of hearing all Jeff's admonitions. "How long," Bill said, exasperated, "is it going to take this child to learn?"

And I said, "Well, if he learns as fast as you did, we've got about six more years."

That's the truth. If I had to say which of my sons has the better table manners, I'd say Roger. And that's all Jeff's doing. To give Bill his due, however, I think he has an excuse. From the time he was a little boy, his mind has always been in perpetual motion: He was thinking of this, figuring out that, analyzing the other. Now I'm not saying he's going to embarrass the nation at any state dinners, but his mind's just as busy at mealtimes as it is any other time, and sometimes the little niceties—such as keeping his hand in his lap or not talking with his mouth full—take a backseat to whatever brilliant idea his mind has seized on.

Away from the table, Jeff didn't have to discipline Roger much. The one time I can remember, however, was quite a scene. Roger was about thirteen, and I had just started letting him go out at night. It happened to be during racing season, which is an awfully busy time in Hot Springs. Lots of out-of-town people, lots of traffic, lots of partying. With Bill, because of my no-curfew/check-in rule, I felt comfortable enough to go on to bed, knowing he would be home at a responsible hour. But because this was one of Roger's first times out with a group of boys, I couldn't sleep. So Jeff and I sat up watching TV and reading, and I sat and I sat, and the longer I sat, the less I could concentrate on the TV or the book.

Then I started pacing. It was getting later and later, and I was working myself into a frenzy. I began crying. All I could think about was how many thugs were in town during racing season. Finally, I just knelt down by the front window with my nose to the pane, tears dripping off my chin.

At about three A.M., a car pulled up out in the front and Roger got out. The boys waved and laughed and Roger walked up the sidewalk whistling, just as happy as you please, not a care in the world. The second he opened the door, Jeff grabbed him by the shirt collar and practically threw him across the room. Jeff's face was mere inches from Roger's as he said in no uncertain terms, "Roger, you have scared your mother to death. If you ever—*ever*—do this to her again, you'll have to deal with me. Do you understand what I'm saying?"

Roger got the message. Of course, he sulked for a day or two and told himself that he hated Jeff Dwire's guts. But many years later, as he faced a prison sentence, Roger thought back on this very incident and said, "Had Jeff lived, I never would've had this problem."

&

Despite Jeff's courtliness and his gestures of kindness toward our many friends, I came to see that he was essentially a loner. While I was working, he would go out to Marge Mitchell's dock and fish alone for hours. Sometimes he even drove over to West Memphis to the dog track by himself. He seemed to need this solitude. There was a part of him that he didn't share with anybody, even his wife.

He may've come closest with Roger. They talked a lot, and Jeff opened up in small ways, hinting at a full and varied past. At different times he told Roger he had flown bombers in the war, been a judo instructor, built houses, fought oil-well fires. But whatever dreams Jeff may've had for his life, the private humiliation of going to prison seemed to rob him of some spark, some sense of himself necessary to the pursuit of such dreams. I can see that now, having watched my son endure the same indignities.

I didn't know the details of the events that led to Jeff's incarceration until I was writing this book, and maybe I still don't know the whole story. But what I do know is this: In February of 1956, Jeff was named president of something called Southwestern Productions Investment Company, of Muskogee, Oklahoma. The company was ostensibly established to raise money for the making of movies about Oklahoma characters, beginning with the onetime FBI-most-wanted gangster Pretty Boy Floyd.

In the Southwestern Productions prospectus, this is what it says about Jeff:

G. J. Dwire—Has had extensive administrative experience throughout his career. He was reared in Louisiana and educated in Louisiana and Oklahoma. Mr. Dwire served with the U.S. Air Force during World War II, completing combat missions in the Pacific theatre of operations before being honorably discharged in 1946. From 1946 to 1948, Dwire was completing the necessary college credits for an engineering degree. From 1948 to 1950, he served as division manager with Welex Jet Services, Oklahoma division, with home offices in Fort Worth, Texas. From 1950 to 1951, Dwire accepted a twelve-month contract with Spartan Tool and Service Company of Houston, Texas, as Superintendent in charge of sales and service of the Electrical Well Service Department. Upon completion of this contract, Dwire was self-employed as Consulting Engineer and independent Sales Analyses work. He also retained personal business in Duncan, Oklahoma. Mr. Dwire moved his residence to Fort Worth, Texas, and entered the securities business in 1953 as an independent securities salesman. January 1955, he accepted the position of Vice-President of Legal Reserve Investment Company in charge of securities sales in Fort Worth, Texas, and served in this position until he was contracted to investigate the potential prospects and feasibilities of the success of an operation of this type, along with direction of the management and general business of Southwestern Productions Investment Company.

Mr. Dwire is married and has three daughters and is a member of the Baptist Church, American Legion, VFW, and many other civic organizations.

Jeff had two partners in this venture—a veteran showman named Kroger Babb, and a securities salesman named Albert Johnston. Babb, executive vice president of Southwestern Productions, was also president of Hallmark Productions, Inc., of Hollywood, California, the company contracting to actually make the Pretty Boy Floyd picture. In the Southwestern Productions prospectus, Babb's philosophy of moviemaking was outlined:

"The story's the thing," is Showman Babb's formula of picture-making. The finest of proven, experienced writers will be assigned to this screen story. Babb favors stories which "teach but do not preach," which end on "the up-beat," and point up a moral. Although "Pretty Boy" Floyd's life was one of defiance of the law, yet through the proper telling of it, a motion picture can provide a fine moral, while supplying delightful entertainment for all ages.

The prospectus went on to say that Babb had big plans for this particular movie—the "new" Eastman color, prints by Technicolor, wide screen, and no fewer than two name stars. The potential benefits to eastern Oklahoma's tourist business were mentioned, since many of the state's landmarks would "come in for close-up treatment." Finally, Babb's credits as a moviemaker were listed: *Prince of Peace* (The Lawton Story), *Karamoja, Mom and Dad, Mixed Up Women, Monika, Redheads vs. Blondes,* and *Halfway to Hell.*

Southwestern Productions Investment Company sold $32,807.92 worth of stock in the movie, at $10 a share. Johnston had sold about $8,000 before Jeff was hired, and then Jeff got busy and sold $24,000 worth of stock. As Sam Anderson, Jeff's lawyer, says, "Thirty-five years ago in Muskogee you couldn't raise corn, much less money. If you raised thirty-two thousand dollars, you had hit the bottom of the well."

Jeff left the company in July, but it was too late. The federal grand jury eventually charged him and Albert Johnston with twenty-five counts of stock fraud, saying essentially that Southwestern Productions never really intended to make the movie and, in fact, spent all the money practically as soon as it was raised. Kroger Babb was never charged with any wrongdoing.

Unfortunately for Jeff and Albert Johnston, one of the people who bought the stock was a relative of Pretty Boy Floyd. When it was obvious that no movie or refunds were forthcoming, he latched onto the case like a terrier with a bone. Five years later, the grand jury returned its indictments.

"Jeff Dwire," says Sam, "was the most embarrassed at being convicted of any client I ever had."

Eleven

ONE OF THE nicest things Bill Clinton says about me is that I've never lost the capacity to grow.

I should add that he also says I've occasionally become stuck in a rut for years—gotten so emotionally invested in a course of action that I can't, or won't, examine my position or consider others'. He even uses the word *hardheaded*.

I can't imagine what he's talking about. Unless maybe it's Hillary.

Oh, Lord, yes: I confess that for me, Hillary has been a growth experience. I love her dearly now, and I believe she loves me. Unbelievable as it may seem, we've never talked about this. But when we first laid eyes on each other, it was like the old immovable object running up against the irresistible force.

I knew Bill's taste in girlfriends had been changing. Not long after he got to Oxford, he sent me a letter saying he had met someone he found very attractive—though not in the traditional sense of the word. "You wouldn't understand, Mother," he had the audacity to write to me.

Bill finished at Oxford in 1970 and went to Yale Law School the following year. His meeting with Hillary has been well documented. Early in the term they found themselves staring at each other nightly across the book-lined expanse of the library. This went on for some time—electricity crackling between them, but no connection. And then one night Hillary pushed back her chair, stood up, and walked across the room. "If we're going to keep staring at each other like this," she told my son, "we ought to at least know each other's names."

My first meeting with Hillary was just as electrifying. Well, actually, I guess I met her first in New Haven, but that's not the time I'm thinking of. The meeting I'll never forget is when she came to Hot Springs for her very first visit. I don't remember the exact date, but it was the early 1970s. Now, just think back to how people looked then: beards, scraggly hair, dirty jeans, tie-dyed T-shirts, clunky sandals. Suffice it to say that Bill and Hillary were very much of their time.

They had been on a trip to California. Maybe it had something to do with George McGovern's campaign for President, which they were both involved in. In any case, Bill wanted Hillary to see Hot Springs. That alone didn't indicate anything special: Bill had brought girls from all over back to visit, and he would drive them around and show them his favorite haunts—one of which was Marge and Bill Mitchell's house on Lake Hamilton. Marge would give him the keys to their speedboat, and Bill and the girl would zip off across the lake, the sun beating down on their shoulders, Bill laughing and the girl's long hair flying, a curl of water in their wake. So this new relationship wasn't necessarily serious. Bill had so much ambition, so many goals, that he wasn't about to sidetrack his education. Still, he'd completed a degree at Georgetown and had studied for two years at Oxford. The old college-education obstacle had been cleared. Sooner or later the right girl was going to come along.

When Bill and Hillary walked through the door at Scully Street, Roger and I didn't know what to think. Roger, you should know, was almost fifteen by this time, and he was turning into a good-looking young man with chiseled features. He worked out all the time, keeping himself in movie-star shape, and the girls had begun responding—in droves. As he got older, we would watch a never-ending procession of young ladies parade through his life, and they were all beauties in the classic Hot Springs beauty-pageant mold. This was the image of womanhood my boys grew up with—starting at home with their coiffed and painted mother, and extending to the girls they squired to the proms.

Hillary, however, was different. No makeup. Coke-bottle glasses. Brown hair with no apparent style. Even though Roger and I were polite, I guess our expressions gave us away, because the minute Hillary went to her bedroom to unpack her bag, Bill shot us a withering look. "Come here, you two," he said, and you could tell he meant *right now*. It was like he was the father and we were two bad children.

He got us into the kitchen, and he told us in no uncertain terms, "Look, I want you to know that I've had it up to *here* with beauty queens. I have to have somebody I can talk with. Do you understand that?" His eyes bored through us like my mother's used to do.

In my defense—and I'll hasten to add that there isn't much in this particular episode that I can bring to my defense—I think this was all much bigger than Hillary and me. All of us are partly a product of our upbringing, of the time and place we came of age, and in Hillary's and my case those two times and places could hardly have been further apart. I was reared in the Depression-era South. I had never really been anyplace else, had never, for any extended period of time, had any dealings with—well, let me just come out and say it—with Yankees. Bill may be appalled to read this, though I think he understood what was happening better than Hillary and I did. I know he's told a friend, "There was almost a kind of cultural tension between Mother and Hillary." I guess that's as good a way to put it as any.

I was from Hope, she was from Chicago. I grew up in the war years, she in the antiwar years. Rural vs. city, South vs. North, makeup vs. the natural look. And one other thing: I might have resented her being a lot smarter than I am. I've told you that I've never been jealous in my life, and I'm not going to admit to it here. But I might've been intimidated a little bit. There's no question that this was—and is—the smartest woman I've ever encountered.

So as Bill buttonholed Roger and me in the kitchen, we agreed that, yes, we absolutely understood what he was saying about having had it with beauty queens, about needing someone to talk with. We understood it intellectually, at least; emotionally we had a long, long road ahead of us.

For Hillary's part, she didn't seem particularly taken with me *or* Roger. She was quiet, cool, unresponsive. Maybe she was simply reflecting back the vibrations she felt from us. Or maybe she was as confused by us Arkansans as we were by this Chicagoan. Just think about what *she* was seeing: a mahogany brown woman with hot pink lipstick and a skunk stripe in her hair. And that woman's son, a budding rock musician. Today I can understand how offended Hillary must've been—here she was in darkest Arkansas, and the first people she met were acting like they wished she would hop the next plane out.

Alone among us self-righteous Southerners, Jeff Dwire saw beyond the differences between Hillary and me. What he saw, in fact, were two women so much alike it was funny.

⸰

Marge and Bill Mitchell's parties were legendary. Twice a year—on July 4 and New Year's Day—people from all over Hot Springs would gather at their rambling lakefront house for an all-day bash. Sometimes they would have three hundred people out there, so it was really a lot of little parties going on at one time. Jeff and I never missed one of the Mitchells' parties. They were potluck, and Marge knew a lot of good cooks. On New Year's, they would have TV sets everywhere. You could plop down on the carpet and watch the game, or you could wander through the house, sampling the bowl-day buffet. I was a wanderer, of course. I've never liked sitting in one place for very long—especially when there are so many people to talk and laugh with.

It was at one of these bashes, sometime in the early 1970s, that Jeff and I met Dick Kelley. Dick was a good friend and golfing buddy of Bill Mitchell's, and Dick and his wife, Jane, would sometimes go to football games with Bill and Marge. But Jane didn't like these huge crowd scenes, or at least that's what I've been told. Dick did—

he's a laugher, a joker, a people person. Much of the time, Dick would show up at the Mitchells' parties by himself.

Jeff and I also spent a good bit of time with the Mitchells after we were married, and much less time with Nancy and Gabe. Gabe just didn't want to have anything to do with Jeff. Nobody actually told us that, but we could feel it.

If such ostracism bothered Jeff, you'd never see it on the surface. He was unfailingly pleasant, fun, charming. Life seemed to be going well for him. He had, in fact, gotten his hairdressing license back, and in the summer of 1969 he opened Jeff's Hair Fashions. I always thought it was funny that it was on Beard Street. He also opened a wig shop—this was the era of wigs and falls, remember, and he was wonderful at designing wigs and matching colors. But the gossip mill never left him alone. Some society ladies sniped about the fact that showgirls, who played Hot Springs in those days, came to Jeff to get their hair done. In the narrow minds of some people—mostly the look-down-the-nose, wife-of-the-civic-leader types—it's not a big leap from "showgirl" to "prostitute." That's not right, but it's still so. Well, I have news for them. At the hospital, I've administered anesthesia to prostitutes. There was a famous madame in Hot Springs known as Maxine, and whenever one of these girls would come in with appendicitis or whatever, somebody on staff would whisper, "She's one of Maxine's girls." When I heard that, I was ecstatic—because I've found that the people who paid their bills best were the prostitutes. They paid *before* they left the hospital. Mr. President of the Bank might not pay me on time, but I knew one of Maxine's girls would.

Of course, through her, I might have been getting a little of Mr. President of the Bank's money early. You never can tell, can you?

Jeff and I continued to have a wonderful life together—almost boringly so, in the context of this book. Jeff liked the Elks Club, so we began spending many weekend evenings there. They brought in bands from around the state—and we danced till our feet were swollen. One of my favorite memories is of a luau party at the Elks Club. They have one every year—Hawaiian music, Hawaiian food,

Hawaiian drinks. And one time Jeff designed our outfits so that his belt and tie would match my dress. We had as much fun getting ready as we did at the party.

But the night that best captures what I think of as the magic of my time with Jeff was out at a restaurant called Seven Hills. It was Christmas, I remember, and they had these little tiny twinkling white lights all through the room. I had never seen anything so mesmerizing in my life. Then it started to snow—just floated down. Watching from inside, we felt lighter than air. Jeff and I held hands and enjoyed how much in love we were.

He was a good man who didn't look down on anybody. I remember he befriended a little boy in the neighborhood, one who was smaller than the other kids his age. Jeff took this child under his wing and began to teach him about woodworking and other things. Then he started giving him little chores to do around the house. Once the boy earned some money, Jeff taught him about saving. "You must save ten percent of everything you earn," I remember Jeff saying to him. The child had never heard of saving money.

And Jeff would arrange for this boy to be in the games with the bigger boys without this boy's knowing what Jeff was doing—without the bigger boys' even knowing. It was amazing to watch. And I thought then, *No wonder Jeff and Bill get along so well. They both have a knack for bringing opposing factions together.*

But there were no better pals than Jeff and Roger. Jeff loved to take Roger fishing. It was a wonderful, wholesome antidote to the atmosphere of downtown Hot Springs—an atmosphere Roger hadn't yet discovered, but Jeff knew it was just a matter of time. He wanted Roger to know about another side of life.

I recently came across a letter Jeff wrote to Reverend Miles in 1971. "Dear John," he wrote. "I did the hardest job in my life Father's Day—telling Roger what had happened to me and that I was applying for a Pardon. It has only drawn us closer, if that was possible." Jeff went on to ask John for a letter of recommendation to accompany his pardon request.

This was the unseen turbulence underneath Jeff Dwire's smooth surface. The fact of his having gone to prison was torture to him, and it had affected him in profound ways. Here was a man who seemed to have everything—looks, talent, charm, intelligence, boundless ability. Bill Clinton developed a warm relationship with Jeff. In fact, Bill also wrote a letter on behalf of Jeff's pardon request. Here's what Bill said about him:

> . . . Besides that [family] relationship there is our close friendship. When I am able to go home, we talk for hours on end, and I am continually amazed at the breadth of his knowledge, especially in the fields of my primary interest, politics and law. Few citizens are more conscientious students of public affairs; few have a better grasp of the great issues that face the nation today. If ever a man deserved to have his vote returned to him, this one does. There are, then, the following statements I can make without reservation about Jeff Dwire. He has worked hard and been successful. He has overcome the initial reservations many people had about him and is much respected by the members of our community, including the chief of police. And he has made a family life that is a truly wonderful thing to observe and to be a part of. I have known great and famous men who have not done better. I doubt very much that I will be able to do better. If Jeff Dwire is not worthy of pardon, then I do not see how any of the rest of us are worthy to be citizens.

Bill got so he would seek out Jeff's opinion on questions about law and politics. "Jeff," he would say in some late-night phone call from law school, "I wonder if you could save me a trip to the library." Then he would pose his question, and Jeff almost always knew the answer. Turns out Jeff had used his time in prison to study law. I've always believed that law is basically common sense anyway, and Jeff had an abundance of common sense.

Hillary loved Jeff from the very beginning, just as he loved her. He would phone her occasionally, just to check in, and they would chat for a while. "Jeff was very smart," Hillary says. "Not well educated necessarily, but very intelligent, and very interested in current events and what's going on in the world. He loved to talk to us about all that. But he was kind of self-conscious, or maybe a little bit self-effacing at times. You know, he'd say, 'Well, you know, I'm not really sure about that.' He would kind of withdraw a little after asserting himself."

It really pains me to think about how hurt Jeff was, because he made me so happy. For different reasons, each of us was enjoying making a home together, being part of a family that worked. But Jeff was always struggling with his private war—to get back his rights as a citizen. To clear his name.

In early September of 1970 he had written to the Department of Justice, applying for a pardon. Later that month he got word that his request had been received—but that there was a large backlog, and it might be up to three years before a decision was reached.

I tried to lift Jeff's spirits by reminding him of the great work he was doing. I told him that most people weren't artists, as he was; that most people couldn't draw and design and build, as he could. He would cheer up for a while, and then maybe he would stare out into space and I could tell it was more than deep thinking.

Of course, I still had *my* war, too. I had even enlisted some of my own troops into it by now—business had been so good that I had hired a nurse-anesthetist couple, Bill and Grace Seaveno, to work with me. We operated out of our houses still, but we were a team. I bought their gas machines, and I paid an independent agency to do our bills and collections. Grace and Bill were wonderful family people, with young daughters, and though I was glad to have them on my side, I hated for them to have to endure the poisonous atmosphere in Hot Springs. Poison: That's the image that comes to mind when I think of the Hot Springs medical profession in those days.

I'll tell you how nasty it had gotten. One night Jeff and I were at the Vapors with some friends for dinner and a show. The Kim Sisters, I believe, was the act. Suddenly I got a phone call: Bill Clinton had been in a wreck. My Lord, we got up and rushed out of there so fast the Kim Sisters didn't know what had hit them.

It wasn't much of a wreck, fortunately. In fact, Bill had fallen into a situation that was pretty prevalent in Hot Springs for a while. As I've told you, this is a town in which the con job is considered an art form, and during a period in the late sixties, early seventies, there was a rash of people slamming on their brakes so someone behind them couldn't possibly miss ramming into their backsides. If the "injured" driver was lucky enough to get taken to the right hospital and hooked up with the right doctor, why, there's no telling how serious an injury that little whiplash could turn out to be.

Now, I'm not going to name the principals in this scheme, but I had suspected for years that something like this was happening. My good friend Dr. Bennett, who had helped my husband Roger so much, had had *such* a difficult time getting his practice going, and I'd told him, "Something's going on." Dr. Bennett was too brilliant a doctor to be having so much trouble.

Jeff and I arrived at the scene of the accident in time for me to hear the state trooper instructing someone to call X ambulance service, take the patient to Y hospital, and tell them to call Dr. Z. "Dr. Z," incidentally, was the doctor I told you about who wouldn't postpone surgery for thirty minutes back when I was working round the clock.

"Whoa," I said. "I might be the one paying for this, since my son is involved. Call A ambulance service, take the patient to B hospital, and call Dr. C." In case you can't figure it out, C was Dr. Bennett.

The next day I called the state trooper and said I wanted to see him at my house. When he got there, I told him I knew about the conspiracy—knew that it had been going on for years. I said, "If you don't correct this, I'll report you to your superiors." I don't know how many other troopers were involved, but this particular one was in a responsible position, so I don't doubt that he had told others to do the same thing. There was obviously lots of money in it for everybody.

He didn't say a word, he just listened. What could he say? He knew I had nailed him—and he knew I would do exactly what I told him I would do.

He put his hat back on and walked out and got into his patrol car.
A week later he resigned from the force.

ta

Bill came home to teach law at the University of Arkansas in Fayetteville, way up in the northwest corner of the state, and to launch
his political career. He had been away nine years, had traveled much
of the globe, and had met thousands of people. He had studied and
done well and prepared himself for the job ahead of him. I had known
ever since he got back from Boys' Nation in 1963 that government
service had won out over music in his dreams. Just shaking the hand
of his hero, President John F. Kennedy, had seemed to cinch it for
him. He'd been bubbling over with idealism when he got home from
Washington that summer.

And no matter what opportunities might've been presented to him
after Yale, Bill had always told Hillary he would come back to
Arkansas someday. He wanted her to come here with him. When
graduation was over, however, she had landed a position on the committee that was trying to impeach Richard Nixon for the Watergate
conspiracy. Bill had been offered a spot on that committee, too, but
he had his own agenda. So he came home without her.

I brooded about that for him. Oh, how I brooded. And more than
once, I thought about a day a year or so earlier, when he had been
leaving to go back to school and had stopped in to see Jeff and me
at the beauty shop. After he had said his good-byes, I walked him
out to his car and sat with him for a while. "Mother," he said, when
it was time for him to go, "I want you to pray for me. Pray that it's
Hillary. Because I'll tell you this: For me it's Hillary or it's nobody."

I couldn't stand it. Here was this woman I didn't understand,
didn't feel comfortable with. And she was all he wanted. I worried
so, because I knew Hillary had so much going for her. She could
write her own ticket, and that ticket just might not include a stop
in Arkansas. If I had been in her shoes, I sure might not've come.

So I did pray, prayed night and day. If my sons want something,
then I want to get it for them. Of course, once I got through praying,

I would grind my teeth and wish I could sit Hillary on the edge of my tub and give her some makeup lessons. Show her how to bring out all that natural beauty she was covering up by going natural. None of that mattered to her, though. She was too busy getting educated and doing good things like starting youth-advocate programs. Makeup didn't mean a whit to her.

I laugh today when I hear the news media remark about Bill Clinton's willingness to surround himself with "strong women." The man is my son; he was partially raised by my mother; he was adored by Mama Clinton; he was like a son to such people as Virginia Crawford and Marge Mitchell: Heck, Bill was weaned on grit. No wonder it was "Hillary or nobody." A shrinking violet would've lasted no time with him.

My conversion came on the road to Arkadelphia. I know that sounds almost biblical, and I actually felt that it was. Arkadelphia is a little town between Hot Springs and Hope, and I had been in Hope to see my relatives. As I was driving home, I was just turning this situation around and around in my mind. Bill was home by now, teaching in Fayetteville. Not long before this, he had said something to me about my attitude toward Hillary. He said he thought I hadn't displayed the warmth toward her that was my nature. He said he thought I wasn't treating her with the respect she deserved.

And I said, "Me? What have I done?" Well, hell, I knew what I had done. The Miss Innocent act didn't play with Bill or me.

So on the road to Arkadelphia I was thinking about all that, and suddenly tears started streaming down my cheeks. Right before I got to Arkadelphia, it finally dawned on me: *What kind of fool can you be? You are about to sacrifice one of the sweetest, greatest things in this world to you.* I realized that if I didn't do something to mend that fence, I was about to put Bill in the position of having to choose between the two of us. And I thought, *God, if you'll let me get back to Hot Springs, I'll spend the rest of my life correcting this, if I can.*

The minute I got home, I sat down and wrote Hillary a letter. I poured out my heart to her. I asked for her forgiveness. In my mind, I had made peace with her.

We have never discussed that letter, but I'd stake my life on the fact that she still has it. At least I don't remember our discussing it, or her answering it, and I think I would remember something like that. But that's okay. Once I mailed that letter, I began to live again.

❧

Jeff's request for a pardon was denied. After that, he was often moody, the way Roger had been—though not with the mean edge to the moods that Roger had. Jeff was just sad, sometimes even at work.

To make matters worse, he was beginning to have health problems. He continued to take his diabetes medicine faithfully, but he started having difficulty breathing. I always thought it had to do with his having inhaled so much hair spray over the years, but I don't know for sure. In any case, he got tired easily, had to rest more than he had before. He was also vain, like Roger, and I would catch him looking at himself in the mirror, studying himself to see if he detected a diminishing of his looks. He was in his midforties—three years younger than I was. I thought he looked wonderful still, and I repeatedly told him so.

But his condition was real. One of the results was that he could no longer go with me to the nightclubs where Roger had begun singing professionally, because the smoke bothered him so. I guess the year was 1972, because that's when Roger turned sixteen, and that's the age he was when he began his professional career. Jeff urged me to go with my girlfriends, because he believed we ought to support Roger every way we could. Most parents of teenagers have a hard time seeing their child's side, but Jeff was always able to put himself in Roger's place. For Roger's sixteenth birthday, we gave him a 1967 Mustang convertible. And it was thanks to Jeff that Roger got his own telephone.

I had to have a phone line free for the hospital to call me. One day Jeff said, "You know, that's not really fair to Roger. He dates over the phone." I had never thought of it that way, but Roger did "date" by phone. Girls would call him day and night, and he might spend forty-five minutes to an hour on the phone, instead of going out. I couldn't believe those girls would be calling a boy. Mothers of sons have to learn to live with ambivalence in this contemporary world—we're females, but when push comes to shove, we'll support our sons over any female who walks the earth. In my case, I believe I've learned a thing or two about men and women, and I think females are much more conniving than men. Men don't really scheme, like when I used to go to Janet Clinton's and we would sit there at the window watching poor Roger driving up and down the street looking for me. I don't think a man would take his time to do something like that.

But even though I had misgivings about the girls' phoning Roger, his having his own phone did solve one of our household problems. I believe the telephone was one of Jeff's first gifts to him.

One of the lounges Roger played was a little spot called the Club Car, down on Central Avenue. I would go hear him as often as I could, usually corralling Nancy or Ann Tyler or Marge, and we would be Roger's cheering section. We were silly and loud, but Roger loved having us there. I remember he used to sing "Gentle on My Mind" a lot, and later "The Green, Green Grass of Home." Oh, how I loved that song. Bill loved it, too. Another favorite of mine was Elvis's "Wise men saayyy, only fools rush iinnn." I was mesmerized watching Roger up there in the spotlight singing those songs that he knew were so dear to me. This was the little boy who had crooned to me about "red roses for a blue lady" so many years before, when life was so hard back on Park Avenue. This was the sweet child who had once called me Dado, and who didn't anymore. Where had all the years gone?

Even though Bill was back in Arkansas, we didn't see as much of him as we would've liked. He was busy teaching, but occasionally he would come spend a weekend with us. In late 1973, he decided that the time was right for him to begin his political career. Congressman John Paul Hammerschmidt, a Republican, had represented the third district of Arkansas—which included Fayetteville and Hot Springs—for years, and Bill decided to challenge him for the office. There would be a primary in May 1974, with the general election that November.

This was an exhilarating time in my life—a time when I was beginning to get a glimmer of my sons' futures, of the results of their educations and their upbringings. I was no longer just a mother and a protector; I was now a partner in their lives. I wanted to help each one realize his goals.

As they had through all my ups and downs, my friends wanted to help, too. When Bill told me he was running, I asked Leonard Ellis, Raymond Clinton, and Gabe Crawford to come over to Scully Street to talk with him—to give him the benefit of their years of experience in politics. Together they had an impressive, hands-on body of knowledge on the subject. They told Bill how tough it was going to be, and that he had chosen a formidable opponent to kick off his political career against. Pretty soon, of course, the subject got around to finances. Gabe offered Bill his airplane for the campaign and Gabe and Raymond cosigned a note for $10,000 to help Bill get started. Raymond opted to remain behind the scenes in the campaign. Through all his years in politics, he had picked up a lot of enemies, and he wanted Bill to begin with a clean slate. He provided an old house in Hot Springs that became Bill's campaign headquarters for Garland and Montgomery counties. Leonard Ellis has actively worked for Bill in all his races, offering his building for later campaigns and drumming up support, both financial and otherwise. It was wonderful seeing Leonard at the presidential inauguration—he had plugged as hard as anybody to get Bill to that day.

But there on Scully Street, as I watched those men talk, my mind drifted back to the day twenty-seven years before when I had taken that little baby boy over to Roger Clinton's Hope apartment to meet Virginia and Gabe Crawford. I thought of how Leonard Ellis had taken Bill hunting for the first time. I thought of the night little Roger was born, and how Raymond Clinton had gone to Park Avenue to pick Bill up and keep him safe until morning. They had all been involved in his raising, and now they were helping him become the man he wanted to be.

Of course, this meant I would now be doubly busy, because I wasn't about to let everybody else have all the fun of the campaign. One of the first things I did was call our former little-girl-next-door, Rose Crane—who had moved down from Little Rock to be Bill's coordinator for Garland and Montgomery counties—and tell her we were going shopping. We went to a men's store and bought Bill a blue-and-white seersucker suit, so he wouldn't have to wear the same thing all the time. Besides, who ever heard of a Southern politician worth his salt who didn't own a seersucker suit?

This campaign was truly grassroots, and it was a learning process for all of us. As winter gave way to spring, Rose and another of Bill's Hot Springs friends, Patty Howe, would come over to my house, and the three of us would sit at the dining room table dividing up Bill's card file of contacts and phoning volunteers and asking for contributions. And then we took every opportunity we could to let people know the name of our candidate. Whatever little dignity I had before, I gave up on behalf of my son's career—I covered myself with buttons and put on red-white-and-blue hats. Everybody agreed, it was *me*. Good thing: I was going to look like that the rest of my life. We also decorated our cars. I was driving a chocolate brown Buick Riviera that year, and you could hardly see the brown for all the posters, decals, and bunting. We drafted Jeff, too. He used his artistic skills to help with the hundreds of stenciled CLINTON FOR CONGRESS signs that we plastered everywhere.

I kept up my schedule at the hospital, but every chance I got I would be over at the campaign headquarters, doing whatever I could to help. Sometimes my natural take-charge spirit got out of control. Rose still laughs about the morning I woke her up with a phone call at seven A.M. "Why aren't you over here at the campaign?" I demanded. "Somebody might come in and want some information."

Bill won the primary, and then there was a short breathing spell. Then on July 4, he spoke at the traditional picnic at a place called

Mount Nebo; if you're going to run in Arkansas, you better be ready to give a sermon on the Mount. Bill was, and Rose and I drove up to hear him. It was the first time in years I had missed the Mitchells' Fourth of July party, but they made up for it the next month by inviting a huge throng to their house for a party to kick off the general election.

That may've been where Bill told Jeff he wanted him to come to Fayetteville. By this time, Jeff was having difficulty standing up in the beauty shop, but Bill admired Jeff's organizational skills and thought he could certainly sit at a desk and help direct the campaign by phone. Jeff was pleased, of course. So was I. Even though I hated to be apart from Jeff for a while, this was worth the sacrifice.

❧

Jeff had been gone two weeks when Bill called and told me he was concerned about him. Not that Jeff was complaining, mind you. But Bill had been watching him, and he could see that the work was taking its toll. Bill was shocked one night when Jeff spent the night with him: Jeff couldn't breathe lying down, so he literally had to kneel on the floor and rest his upper body on the bed in order to keep his lungs functioning so he could sleep.

When we talked with Jeff, he admitted that he just wasn't up to the job physically. He hated that, but there it was. So he came home.

We took Jeff to the VA hospital in Little Rock, where they diagnosed something called cardiomegaly—enlargement and deterioration of the heart muscle. It was a complication of Jeff's diabetes. To this day, there's nothing that can be done about cardiomegaly short of a heart transplant, and we didn't know anything about heart transplants then. I couldn't believe it: Here was this good, young man, bound to die. And I confess that I wondered why I was being tried like this again, too. For six too-short years, this man had made me happier than I had been since Bill Blythe. What was it about me? Years later, when Dick Kelley asked me to marry him, I would tell him—only half-joking—that maybe he should take a harder look at my track record.

One August afternoon, I was getting to the end of an unusually difficult day at the hospital. At least, I kept thinking I was getting to the end of it—and then another case would get thrown at me. Jeff needed to eat, and I was anxious to go home and fix dinner for him. Finally, late in the afternoon, I got a forty-five-minute break. I dashed over to the Club Cafe, where they had wonderful meals—as close as you could find to home cooking in a restaurant. I had them fix a tray for Jeff and for Roger, too.

When I pulled up in the driveway, I noticed Roger's car was gone. It was twilight. Lights were coming on in houses around the neighborhood, but you could still see outside. When I opened the door, the house was quiet—eerily so, as I think back on it now, though that's probably just a scene I've painted in hindsight. I walked down the hall toward our bedroom, but Jeff wasn't there.

Then I looked in the bedroom across from the bathroom, and there he was, lying peacefully on the bed. This was a bedroom he never slept in. I can only guess that he knew he was dying—that he came to this neutral room in order to die. I placed my hand on his shoulder, and I knew immediately that he was gone. He hadn't thrown back the cover, there wasn't a wrinkle in the sheet. I might've known that Jeff would die impeccably.

Even though I had seen it coming, I wasn't ready. I probably went into shock, but my instincts took over. The first thing I did was call for an ambulance; the second was to call Bill. Then I flew out of the house and into the street—just ran out into the middle of Scully Street. I was dazed, sobbing, flailing my arms. A beer distributor lived two doors down, and he happened to be coming home from work when he saw me. "What's the matter, Virginia?" he said. "What in the world's wrong?"

"I don't think Jeff is living," I shrieked. "I think he died." News like that is wildfire; I had a houseful of people there before I knew it.

Rose Crane was one of them, and she stayed after the others had gone, until Bill got there. Rose has a wonderful, calming way about her, and it was just what I needed. She calmed Roger, too. He was torn up by Jeff's death—not just by the fact of it, but by his having left Jeff alone in the house. Roger had decided to go bowling, and before he left he opened the door to where Jeff was sleeping. He was going to tell him where he was headed, and to say good-bye. But Jeff seemed to be sleeping so soundly that Roger didn't want to disturb him. Jeff may've been dead even then. Roger remembers wondering why Jeff was in that particular bedroom—and then he shut the door and left.

Roger wanted to go out driving by himself, but Rose insisted on going with him. She took the wheel while Roger sobbed and said, over and over, "It's just not fair. I'm hardly eighteen years old, and I've lost two fathers."

Rose and I talked for hours that night, before she finally persuaded me to get some rest. When she was a little girl, living behind us on Park Avenue, she had once found her mother comatose, and she had called me. Now it was our turn to call Rose. We talked about her mother, about Jeff, about Bill, about Roger, about life in general. Rose remembers that that was one of about five times in her life that she's seen me without makeup—it had long since been smeared off, but for once I didn't care.

She saw me that way the next day, too, and the next. I just couldn't pull myself together. I had never bounced back so slowly before, but I was feeling a bit like Roger was feeling: It just wasn't fair. Marge Mitchell came over and stayed with me—hardly left my side until the funeral was over. While I was wrestling with myself, Bill and others handled the arrangements. Jeff had wanted to be cremated. At that time, there was no crematorium in the entire state of Arkansas, so we had to ship the body to Texas to have it done. Rose remembers Bill telling her later, "I never had a sense of the effectiveness of cremation until I compared the cost of the freight to Texas and back."

Bill gave the eulogy at the memorial service. He wrote it himself, of course, and it was a beautiful statement not just of who Jeff was, but of how Bill felt about him:

Jeff Dwire was an extremely personal man, and so we thought it appropriate that someone who knew and loved him personally, intimately, should offer a few remembrances of him. Many will recall how debonair, sometimes even flamboyant, he was in his wonderfully bright-colored clothes. Others will remember how he loved to go places and party and enjoy life with his family and friends. Still others will note that he was one of the most intelligent, versatile men—one of those who seemed to know something about everything—that they ever knew. But what was really important about his life is that he worked so hard at it and that his real joy came from giving to others. You can see it in the little children whose lives he touched with so much tenderness. You can see it in the old, the poor, the unschooled to whom he gave work and whom he treated with such dignity. You can see it in those who worked for him and those who called him friend, in their grief at losing a man whose like they will not see again. Most of all you can see it in his family, who knew him best—the bad with the good, the torment of his past, the frustrations, the unfulfilled hopes—they above all know how worthy of love and respect he was, because he truly graced our lives and he helped us when we needed it sorely, because—as my brother has said over and over since Jeff went to sleep Monday—"he tried so hard." To the rest of his family—his brothers and sisters, his daughters, his son, my dear mother—I can honestly say I never knew a better man. To all of you, let me urge that your most lasting memories of him be on what Wordsworth called "that last best hope of a good man's life—the little unremembered acts of kindness and love." May God have mercy on all of us who loved him and on his own precious, finally resting soul.

I saw Marge standing by the dock as the airplane began to descend toward the place at the end of her pier where Jeff had spent so much time alone—and with me. This was his favorite fishing spot, but it was more than that: This was the place he could go and forget his troubles. When he told me he wanted to be cremated, he said this was where he wanted his ashes scattered.

As the plane neared its target, I opened the small urn. Soon we were almost over the spot, and I reached out and began letting Jeff's ashes float on the wind.

A few days later, I received a letter that meant the world to me:

Dear Virginia:

Here are copies of the eulogy Bill delivered for Jeff and the original Bill wrote and spoke from. He made a few minor changes that show up in the typed version. I think every day about you and Jeff. With Bill, I can honestly say I never knew a better man than Jeff. I also have never known a more generous and stronger woman than you. You're an inspiration to me and so many others. In addition, you're just as good a politician as your son. After he wins, we'll have to decide what position you'll seek. If there's anything I can do for you, please let me know.

Be well.

Love,
Hillary

Twelve

NEVER AGAIN: THAT'S what I promised myself. Here I was, fifty-one years old and widowed for the third time. Maybe I wasn't meant to be married. Maybe I wasn't supposed to be happy.

If it sounds as though I was feeling sorry for myself, I was. You bet I was. I was wallowing in my misfortune—was up to my false eyebrows in it, in fact. But part of my well-developed "defense mechanism," as Rose Crane calls it, is a built-in Pitiful Pearl Detector. It would be years before Al-Anon would acquaint me with the actual name Pitiful Pearl, but my mother had drilled the concept into me decades earlier. Whenever anybody would be going, "Oh, woe is me," Mother would look at them with such disdain that I would feel uncomfortable, too.

So I grew up knowing that it was a despicable thing to feel sorry for yourself. It's an indulgence nobody can afford. You always have two choices: You can give up, or you can plug ahead. I've never been willing to give up. I had climbed hills before, and I could climb another one.

The morning after Jeff's funeral, I appeared at campaign headquarters dressed for work, with a smile on my face, my makeup as impeccable as it had ever been. But before a soul had seen me that day, I had sat at my dressing table and steeled myself to deal with life again. I went through my ritual carefully and deliberately, choosing my paints for their boldness. When I was finally ready, I looked myself in the eye and said, "Well done." Then I picked up my purse and went to face a world without Jeff.

Bill lost his election that fall. No, let me rephrase that: He didn't emerge victorious. The margin was just six thousand votes, and the closeness of the race was all the more frustrating because of the circumstances. That was the first year we had ever used voting machines in Garland County, and most of them broke down. No one had had the foresight to print up enough paper ballots. Also, we suspected election irregularities in various places.

I was fit to be tied. Bill had worked so hard and had come so close. He had walked all over the state during that campaign, meeting people and shaking their hands and telling them what he wanted to do for them. I still have the big old black size-13 shoes whose soles he wore out that year; maybe one of these days I'll bronze them like mothers used to do with baby shoes, though that much bronze would likely break me. But those shoes are a testament to Bill Clinton's determination.

Hillary had helped in the campaign that fall. Once President Nixon resigned, her committee job was finished, and she was offered a teaching position at the University of Arkansas Law School. She had missed Bill and was glad to be with him again. But though she seemed devoted, somewhere along the way I began wondering how she really felt. I don't recall what it was that made me wonder that, but in hindsight I've decided it had as much to do with geography as anything. Through the years, I've observed that people from the North and the Midwest are less demonstrative than Southerners are—especially a touching, hugging, bubbling-over Southerner like me. Dick Kelley is another example of that: He was born in Kansas and spent his early years in Minnesota, and he's more reserved about his expressions of love than I am. But he loves just as much, I know he does. And I'm sure now that Hillary does, too. Back then I wondered, though. I watched her that fall and wondered.

Campaigning had been a time-filler for me. After it was over, the real letdown began. Roger had left for college in the fall of 1974, soon after Jeff's death. I had dreaded his leaving even while Jeff was alive. Every fall when my boys were growing up, I would inevitably hear other mothers breathe a collective sigh of relief. "Thank God they're out from underfoot," they'd say. I never felt that way—I always loved having them right there, underfoot. In the weeks before band camp and band tryouts, there were sometimes five different friends of Bill's playing five different songs on five different musical instruments at the same time in my five bedrooms at 1011 Park Avenue. Later, at Scully Street, Bill and Roger both had bands, and they would practice in our garage. I had twenty years of all that, and I loved every minute of it.

Well, not every minute. I won't try to pretend I'm a candidate for sainthood. There were times when I prayed to God that the hospital would call me with an emergency. But, in general, I made up my mind: You might grow to like it if you listen, and if you don't like it, it's not going to last forever in your house. And you're darn sure going to miss it when it's gone. Roger was at Hendrix College, an excellent school in Conway, Arkansas, eighty miles away. To me, it might as well have been a thousand miles.

Bill came to see me quite often during the year or so after Jeff died. We would go out together, something we'd never done before. Just go out and listen to music and talk. I had never had any trouble thinking of Bill as a grown-up, but this period put our relationship in a new place. We were friends. He remembers thinking that I seemed to be "on automatic," seemed to be trying to just keep going.

After a while I dated some, if you want to call it that; mostly, my dates consisted of going to the racetrack or dinner with old friends who happened to be male. I went alone, or as a third wheel with the Sebas, to the Mitchells' twice-a-year parties—but of course I'm never alone for very long. Never have been. I got to know Dick Kelley better at those parties. Sometimes his wife would be with him, but most of the time not. Dick, as usual, seemed to genuinely enjoy being in the middle of such throngs—and people obviously liked being around Dick, too. He's a big bear of a man with an engaging smile, which he uses often. But besides being a laugher and a kidder, he struck me as a genuinely interesting person, one who had seen much more of the world than I had. He lived in Hot Springs, but he and his brother owned a successful food-brokerage business—Dick described it as "making sure Kroger's doesn't run out of Star Kist tuna"—in Little Rock. He loved to travel, he told me, and through his business he was often awarded wonderful trips. He also came across as a man's man—a golfer, a hunter, a man who liked adventure. It was fun to see Dick at those parties, and I looked forward to the next one so I could kid with him again.

For the vast majority of my time after Jeff, however, my girlfriends again came to my rescue. I saw Dixie all the time, of course; Nancy, too, who had separated from Gabe a year or so before. But what I remember most about the period immediately following Jeff's death was being out at Marge Mitchell's. Marge had retired by then to the luxurious life of a lawyer's wife—except for her weekends in the nurses' station at Oaklawn. I spent hours and hours sitting out on her deck with her, talking, crying, and seeing just how brown I could get. Sometimes we would go out on the dock, the dock Jeff loved, and fish for crappie. On the radio around that time was a song that tore me up—"The Way We Were" by Barbra Streisand. Every time I heard it, I thought of Jeff. That song helped me get a lot of my tears out. Little did I know that Barbra and I would one day become friends, too.

Of course, I went to the track as much as possible, which is to say every day Oaklawn was open. Until Bill started running for office, the racetrack took up at least a third of my life—my boys and my work making up the rest. Racing has always relaxed me, and I look back on my days in the box with Dixie and Joe as among my happiest. I remember one day—I've still got the program somewhere—when I picked the winner on every race, until the last one. That probably happened twenty-five years ago, but I still think about that glorious day. Another time, the three of us started with $5 apiece, and we invested it in the show parlay. We just kept letting it ride, betting it again and again, until we had close to $275. We bet it all on the feature race—on an even-money horse to show. Now, you'd think an even-money horse would have a pretty good chance to show, wouldn't you? Well, he flipped in the gate or something—never even finished in the money. At moments like that you have to look at racing philosophically: It's not the finish, it's the joy of the running. Of course, it's easier to say that when you've only got $2 bet on the outcome.

Besides going to the races, I traveled to see Elvis a few times in the midseventies. During most of the 1960s, Elvis hadn't performed in concerts, but now he was back, and I was ready. I saw Elvis three, maybe four times in all. Once was in Texas, once was in Omaha, and once was in Pine Bluff, Arkansas. Seems to me there was another time, but I can't place it, if you can believe that.

I particularly remember the Pine Bluff concert. A bunch of us women piled into somebody's car and drove over there. I forgot my binoculars, and our seats were so far away that I could hardly see Elvis. But I could see enough so that, as we were driving home late that night, I told the others, "If something doesn't happen to Elvis, he's not going to live long." He was bloated and pasty looking; he sweated like a Hope watermelon. But, God knows, there was nothing wrong with his performance. Dressed in his white Las Vegas jumpsuit, a powerful orchestra behind him, he sang all my old favorites and then some. And he was still sexy. Somewhere inside all that excess was the same man who had thrilled me for twenty years.

&.

In the midseventies, the medical profession in Hot Springs really took off. The reason was Medicare and Medicaid, which had started in the 1960s but were now booming. Suddenly there were hundreds of new patients, and more business than we had ever seen before. For many reasons then, both personal and professional, it was the perfect time for me to throw myself into my work.

After having worked out of my home my entire career, I decided to go for broke and establish my own office. I rented a building right across the street from the Vapors, which for the past few years had been struggling along with the other remnants of Hot Springs' glory days. I felt at home near the Vapors, scene of so many good times. Now, I felt, good times were on their way again.

I'm making it sound as though I just decided to open my own office and went out one day and did it. By now, though, you ought to know my life doesn't work that way. I had to have an ordeal first.

I can't remember exactly what prompted my suspicions, but in early 1975 I decided my collection agency was cheating me. Collection problems had dogged me my entire career, it seemed. I've told you about how, early on, I wasn't able to get my money myself and was saved by that woman at Clinton Buick. That worked for a long time, though there were still people who didn't want to pay. Incidentally, I draw a big distinction between people who can't pay and those who don't *want* to pay. I'll work with the can't-pays all day long. But the others—well, it's five in the mouth if I ever run face-to-face with them.

I remember once when we were living at 1011 Park Avenue. Back then, a nurse anesthetist might work several hours on a case and the bill would never be over $35. And there was a man in town who owed me $15—had owed me for the longest time. One day I was sitting outside sunbathing and listening to the radio, and little Roger was playing in his little rubber pool. Suddenly, I heard that man's business being advertised on the radio. *If he can afford that,* I thought, *he can sure afford to pay me.*

I went into the house and changed Roger's and my clothes, then put him in the car and drove to the man's place of business. He had a filling station, and he also sold a few groceries and fishing supplies. I pulled my car up crossways, blocking his gas pumps. No way any customer could fill up as long as I was there. I got Roger out of the car and locked it. Then, taking Roger by the hand, I went inside to see the owner.

He wasn't there, but his wife was. "I've come to collect my fifteen dollars," I said. "I won't leave without it."

"Well," she said, "you may have a long wait. He's out fishing. And he's the only one who can pay the bills."

"Fine," I said. "I've got the rest of the day. We'll wait."

Pretty soon all these horns started honking. People were yelling, getting out of their cars, and gesturing toward mine.

"You'll have to move your car," said the woman.

"It'll cost you fifteen dollars to have that car moved," I said.

We stood in stony silence for a minute. Outside, people continued to honk and yell. Some of them had started driving away, looking for accessible gas pumps elsewhere.

"Okay," the woman sighed, opening the cash drawer. "Here's your money."

Contrary to what some might think, I don't enjoy those kinds of encounters. Which is why, once my business got big enough, I hired a billing service and a collection agency—the collection agency I began to question.

They were supposed to get a certain percentage of what they collected during the first three months; after that, they got a higher percentage. I guess I started feeling cash-flow problems, and when I looked into it, I found that they weren't even billing until after three months. In other words, they weren't trying to get me my money early; they just waited until they would get paid more to do the work. I figured they had profited $29,000 by not billing on time.

I called Bill in Fayetteville and told him to come to Hot Springs immediately. Then I called Sam Anderson, my lawyer friend. As soon as Bill got there, we borrowed a truck and all three of us went to the collection agency at once, swooping in like G-men and removing all my records from their office. Doing business in Hot Springs has never been for the faint of heart.

What now? I thought. If I couldn't do the billing myself and I couldn't trust an outside agency, then what on earth could I do? Sam Anderson had an answer: his wife, Shirley. She hadn't done this kind of work, but she had been a legal secretary and an office manager. We got together and hit it off immediately. She was smart, she was curious—and she was from Chicago. I'd met a Chicagoan or two in my day, and I preferred to have them on my side.

So with Shirley as the office manager and the Seavenos and me as the anesthetists, we began doing business as Hot Springs Anesthesiology. To learn the ropes, Shirley worked in a doctor's clinic for a few days to see how they did it. Then she sat in at the hospital, and then with the Medicare people. Pretty soon, she knew the system cold. The system inside our own office was something else again. We were used to being independent contractors; none of us had ever run a real business before.

Even though we were making it all up as we went, I remember that time as extraordinarily happy. It was a good office. The Seavenos were wonderful people—talented, diligent, dependable. Not only that, but there wasn't a thing about a gas machine that Bill Seaveno couldn't fix; I think he could've built one if he had had the parts. And Shirley Anderson ran a first-class operation. I never liked worrying about money, I just wanted to do my work. Shirley allowed me to do that. She even took care of my personal money and expenses, including Roger's tuition bills. If I wanted to buy something, I would just say, "Shirley, do I have enough money?" and she would tell me. I had lost a lot in my personal life, but here was something to fill the void. Here, finally, was the payoff on that gamble I had taken when I left my son and went to New Orleans to better myself.

There was a snag, however. Medicine was changing, and with change came bitter new truths. A Medicare regulation stipulated that nurse anesthetists had to be supervised by an MD; otherwise, the operating physician would bear responsibility. That regulation had all the impact of handwriting on the wall: For me to keep working for myself, it said, I would have to hire someone with an MD after his name. It was going to be an interesting trick to pull off. Essentially, I would be looking for an MD who, for record-keeping purposes, would supervise all our nurse anesthetists, even me. It was a practice I didn't believe in, but that's what the profession had evolved to. The nurse anesthetists would actually administer the anesthesia, but the MD had to sign all the papers.

So I set out to hire myself a doctor. The deal I was offering was that the MD would be paid exactly what I was paid—no more, no less. As owner, I had been getting a portion of the other anesthetists' fees, and the MD would, too. I had decided to split my percentage with whomever I hired; it didn't seem fair to make the other nurse anesthetists kick in more of their paychecks so the doctor could get his share.

Finally, I would still be the boss. It would still be my group, even though the MD would have to "supervise" me. As I say, it was going to be a trick. On the other hand, I had built up quite a practice by this time. Seemed to me it would benefit any MD to get into this group.

After much interviewing, I found an anesthesiologist who seemed exactly right. I couldn't believe my good fortune. Having confronted the inevitable and bent it to my purposes, I felt pretty proud of myself. Plus, I was working smart: I had involved the administrator of Ouachita, a man named Wendell Burns, in every stage of these changes, and he was very supportive of the direction my group was headed. To both of us, this change seemed to provide Ouachita with essentially the same service Dr. Klugh's group provided St. Joseph's. *Maybe,* I thought, *this'll put a stop to all the undermining and backstabbing.*

Looking back, it's hard to believe I could've been that naïve.

One day along in here Roger called and wanted to have a family meeting. This was the way we had started doing things, Bill, Roger, and I. If we had some important piece of family business to discuss or decide, we would have a family meeting and put it to the vote. All votes were equal, now that my sons were grown. And with the three of us, we always had a tiebreaker.

Roger wanted us to meet at my house; he had already called his brother in Fayetteville. The first thing I thought was, *This baby wants to get married.* That shows how much I knew.

What Roger wanted was to drop out of school. That's not the term he used, however—he called it "laying out a year," during which he would concentrate on his music. We would relive this scene several times over the course of Roger's college career. He laid out a year after his freshman year, two years after his sophomore year, and three or four years after his junior year. Roger always made good grades without even trying. Some of his high school teachers used to say he was every bit as smart as—and maybe smarter than—his older brother. But the truth, I think, is that he never really wanted to be in college; he wanted to play his music.

Part of Roger's spiel was inevitably an ironclad promise that he would go back and finish his education. "I'm not a quitter," he said during that first meeting, and I knew it was true. Still, though I had all the faith in the world in Roger, and though I knew he would someday be a fine musician, I wanted him to get his degree first.

When the vote came, Bill voted with Roger. I don't know for sure what Bill's thinking was—maybe he felt Roger wasn't applying himself anyway, so he might as well go with what he loved. I know Bill Clinton well enough, though, to believe he was influenced by his brother's promise to go back and get his degree.

Time would tell.

&

When Hillary was in Arkansas helping with Bill's congressional campaign, a friend of mine confided to her that if she ever expected to marry Bill, she was going to have to bite the bullet and move to Arkansas.

"Thanks," Hillary said dryly. "You're not the first person who's told me that."

Bill and Hillary were married in October 1975 in Fayetteville. The announcement came as no more news to me than Bill's Arkansas bias did to Hillary. She had been in the picture for years now, and though we had circled around each other quite a bit at first, we had made our peace. Still, I was a little uneasy; I've always had trouble turning loose of things, and maybe I was just a mother brooding over her son's final break for independence.

I drove to Fayetteville with Marge and Bill Mitchell and Patty

Howe. Bill and Hillary had bought a house that they were fixing up—and I mean right up to the time of the wedding, which was supposed to take place in the house. When we got there, they had paint buckets out and light fixtures to put in and all this mess everywhere. Now, I'm one of those people, if I'm supposed to be somewhere, I get there an hour early. And yet neither one of my sons has any concept of time. Roger Clinton inevitably gets to an airplane as they're shutting the door—and the irony is, he seldom misses a flight. Bill, when he was governor, would delay and delay and delay, and then when he would finally get to his airplane, it would make him angry when his regular pilot insisted on going through his normal preflight checklist. "Come on, come on, let's go," Bill would tell him.

And this pilot, bless him, would look at Bill in that John Wayne way pilots have, and he would say, "You should've left a little earlier, Governor." I loved it.

The Mitchells and Patty and I were staying at the Holiday Inn. The morning of the wedding, Bill came over to have breakfast with us. He was late, of course, so we were all in the restaurant eating and laughing and cutting up as usual, and finally Bill strolled in. He pulled up a chair and got coffee and all that, and after a few minutes of small talk, he said, "Mother, I need to tell you something."

I hadn't been a mother for twenty-nine years without learning that those words mean trouble. I steeled myself for whatever was coming. "Well?" I said. "Go ahead." The others stopped chewing so they wouldn't miss anything.

"Hillary's keeping her own name," Bill said. He went on to explain that that was perfectly fine with him, but he'd wanted to prepare me before the ceremony. It was just something everybody needed to know was going to happen. While he was talking, his actual words began to fade and all I could focus on was the roar that filled my head. My tears started to flow. Marge later told me she almost cried, too.

Almost twenty years after the fact, my response probably seems laughable, but it sure didn't to me then. During interviews for this book, Hillary described me as "a feminist who would never describe herself that way." She went on to say that I never allowed myself "to be demeaned or victimized or subordinated in any fashion." Coming from Hillary, that's high praise. And there's a lot of truth in it.

But I go back to that old song I loved when I was a girl, "Don't Fence Me In." I don't like labels. I'm just me, and that's all I can be. I've never met the world with the kind of anger so many women seem to have, especially toward men. I like men. I've found them to be trustworthy friends and companions. Yes, I fight back when someone does something to hurt me. But I'm open and loving and trusting until that happens. I'm only half-tough—and proud of it.

If you're who you want to be inside, names don't matter. Bill knew that as far back as 1962, which I guess is why he didn't have any conflicts of pride about Hillary's keeping her own name. "It's not the name, Mother, it's the man," he had told me years before. And the woman, too, I suppose. Bill and Hillary being the lawyers they were, they could argue that question from either side.

But on that October morning in Fayetteville two decades ago, the way I stayed clear about the world was by seeing it in black and white. And I'll be honest with you: Part of the reason for my reaction to this news was pure shock—I had never even conceived of such a thing. This had to be some new import from Chicago.

I think Roger's feelings about the name change went in the general direction mine did, though he probably dredged up anger from other sources as well. Hillary puts a lot of stock in self-discipline, and in those "laying out" days Roger may've been feeling—and reacting to—what he saw as her disapproval of him. As Dick Kelley now says, "Hillary realized early on that Roger was Virginia's 'baby boy.'" Just as big Roger was Mama Clinton's.

Shortly after the wedding, Bill decided to make the run for attorney general. He wasn't about to let any grass grow under his feet. I was delighted, of course; campaigning had gotten into my blood. It also gave me another way to stay busy. We used the same headquarters as in the congressional race, that old rickety house owned by Raymond Clinton. In general, the local headquarters was manned by the same cast of characters that had worked there before, except that Rose had gone back to Little Rock and Nancy Crawford had taken her place as coordinator. I still drove everybody crazy.

In November 1976, Bill was elected attorney general. Besides getting his political career off the ground, this also meant he and Hillary would move to Little Rock, an hour from Hot Springs. This would be the closest Bill had lived to me in twelve and a half years. I looked forward to burning up the road between here and there and hoped my attorney general son wouldn't have to throw me in jail for too many speeding tickets.

。

About a year into my arrangement with the MD, I began to feel uncomfortable about him. So I began looking for somebody else. The doctor I found was named Raymond Peeples. He was working for Dr. Klugh.

I went to Dr. Klugh and asked permission to speak with Dr. Peeples. If Peeples would come work with me, I said, I'd be willing to forget St. Joseph's and focus instead on Ouachita. The truth is, I was weary of the stress of seeing Dr. Klugh all the time—had been for years. Besides, St. Joseph's had already chosen him, and Ouachita was a county hospital that really seemed to need me. Dr. Klugh was gracious about all of this, agreeing that such an arrangement would probably be an improvement over our present one.

When Dr. Peeples came to our group, I felt a load lifted off my shoulders. A few short years later, I would find out that I had made a crucial mistake in this particular transaction. In putting my eggs all in one basket, I had neglected to secure a contract with Ouachita. I had trusted that they would always need *me* the way I needed them.

At first, Dr. Peeples seemed perfectly fine with our setup. But as the months passed, he and I began to spar about everything under the sun. It was an old-fashioned power struggle—two headstrong people each with his back up—and it wasn't a pretty sight for the people in the office to have to watch. Nor was it, in the politicized climate of Hot Springs' medical circles, a situation I would've wanted known beyond our walls.

We had hired some other anesthetists by this time, two young women who had once worked for Dr. Klugh's group. Supposedly, they had gotten on the outs with Dr. Klugh and had sought refuge with us. Some of our people worried about having them—worried, essentially, that they were spies for the other side. There was never any evidence to that effect, and I was just glad to have them on our team, glad to have help with all the work that needed to be done.

In my opinion, Dr. Peeples got greedy. (Plus, of course, he appeared to have that God complex most doctors seem to have.) He and I were the only two in the office who got a monthly report showing all the business that had been done, and it must have begun to burn him up that I—a mere nurse anesthetist—was getting a percentage of the other people's billing. Today he denies having been bothered by that, but to me his attitude seemed to be, well, who is she? *I'm* the doctor.

And he *was* the doctor. That fact alone gave him privileges I didn't have, such as the right to attend any hospital meetings. He played that to the hilt—Shirley recalls that he didn't want me consulted about anything at the hospital, because he was the doctor.

You can imagine how all that set with me. Today, Shirley laughs about the meetings we used to have in the office, though they weren't funny at the time. She recalls that I would come in with my happy-go-lucky act fully in place, obviously determined—once again—to stop contributing to this dysfunctional situation. Shirley says I looked like I was psyching myself up: *This is going to be a normal meeting, a good meeting, and I'm going to be calm. I am I am I am.* Once we all gathered, everything would be going along all right—and then Dr. Peeples would disagree with me, or I would disagree with him, and that was it. We lived in an impasse. If I hadn't needed him so much, I'd have sent him packing.

This situation lasted for years, and the situation outside the office wasn't any better. Instead of decreasing, as I had hoped, the backstabbing seemed to increase. Remember, the stakes were higher now, since Medicare and Medicaid. To someone who wanted to monopolize the anesthesia business in Hot Springs, Ouachita now represented a respectable share of the market.

At one point in the late seventies, some of the doctors in town began pressuring the Ouachita board to oust Wendell Burns, the Ouachita administrator—and, not so incidentally, my patron at the hospital. As I recall, two board members were really out to get him. I'll do anything to help a friend, and I considered Wendell my friend. Besides, I thought he was a good administrator. I can't remember the ostensible reason for their wanting him out—probably some little trivial something or other. But I fought for Wendell. He didn't ask me to, I just hated what I saw happening to him. They had already accepted his resignation, but I got busy and made a lot of noise. I stood up in the face of the board and everybody else. In the end, that was enough. They hired Wendell back. And all over town, doctors began sticking a few more pins into their Virginia dolls.

My group's internal problems became common knowledge in the medical community, and that added fuel to the fire. I began quietly trying to find a replacement for Dr. Peeples—as though there were such thing as quiet in that incestuous little world. Pretty soon Peeples heard I was looking, and the vicious circle just got wider and wider.

I countered all this nastiness by concentrating on my beloved patients. With them, I felt needed. I felt appreciated. I felt indispensable. With them, I could block out the rest of the world.

And, thankfully, I had Bill's campaigns.

He hadn't been attorney general much more than a year when he announced he was a candidate for governor. After two races, we were beginning to feel comfortable with the process. Plus, Bill was known now, a definite boon when it came to attracting money and workers. Again, Nancy ran the campaign in Garland and Montgomery counties. And me? I put on my buttons and my funny hat and hit the road. After the hardball politics of Hot Springs medicine, real politics felt like pure sport.

What I remember most from that campaign are the hilarious days

I spent with Nancy driving all over God's own boondocks nailing CLINTON FOR GOVERNOR signs to posts and trees and anything else we could find that would hold a nail. Hammering signs into the Arkansas ground was a different story entirely. An inch under the surface here, there's nothing but roots and rocks. I guess that's what they mean by hardscrabble. Here we were, a bunch of hundred-pound ladies—I use the term loosely—armed with sledgehammers, and we were supposed to pound these campaign signs through ground you couldn't have tilled with a jackhammer. Finally, somebody got the bright idea to carry gallon jugs of water in the car with us; we found that if we poured water on the earth and let it soak in, the ground would soften just enough to allow our signs to penetrate. I came to think of the process as planting the seeds of Bill's success.

With so many anesthetists in my group by then, I could take more time for this campaign than I had for any of the others. I especially wanted to be involved in the door-to-door politicking. I hope I can say this without sounding immodest, but I am one crackerjack of a cold-call campaigner. I loved knocking on those doors and telling those good people about what a wonderful governor my son was going to make. Nancy and I balanced each other pretty well: I was generally stronger in the morning, and she rallied in the afternoon—just about the time I was ready to go have a couple of Scotch and waters.

In November 1978, Bill was elected; two months later he was sworn in, at age thirty-two, as the youngest governor in the United States.

I won't bore you by telling you how proud I was; I'm sure you can imagine.

Much less obvious was how Bill's elevation to the governorship changed all our lives—increased the stakes, if you will. Roger, who had been trying to get his music career started, was suddenly thrust into a different kind of spotlight. *Everything* was now illuminated. I was suddenly Virginia Dwire, the governor's mother. What I did or didn't do wasn't just fodder for the gossip mill. Now it might even be news.

As it happened, the year Bill was elected governor was the year a young mother died under my care. In twenty-nine years of nurse-anesthetist work, I had never lost a patient. This woman's name was Laura Slayton. She was twenty-two years old. She had had a cesarean section, and for some reason she wouldn't heal. She'd been opened and closed several times, and each time she would develop an infection and break open again. It was obvious each time that she was getting weaker and weaker. She'd just been through so much.

It could've been any anesthetist there the day she didn't come out of it, but it happened to be me. She died in the recovery room. I was shocked. I hated it for her family, of course. Life isn't fair. But I believed I had done all I, or anybody, could have done for her. Even Dr. Klugh says you can't save them all.

Nevertheless, you could almost hear the drumbeats starting. All over town, my enemies had caught the scent of blood.

Thirteen

I ASKED NANCY to meet me at the Sawmill, one of my favorite gathering places. It's a converted railroad station in downtown Hot Springs. During lunch and after work, the place is packed, and of course I know just about anybody who walks in the door.

Nancy and I took a table in the lounge and ordered our drinks. We hadn't been sipping them more than a couple of minutes when the door opened and Dick Kelley walked in. I waved, and he came over to the table. I introduced him to Nancy and asked if he'd like to have a drink with us, which he did.

Now let me give you Nancy's recollection of this event. "You were very cutesy about this," she says, laughing. "I remember you called me one day—out of the blue, I thought—and said, 'Do you want to go to the Sawmill for a drink?' I said, sure. So we went down there, and we hadn't been seated five minutes before this big, tall man comes over. I looked at him look at you, and I thought, *Well, you little sneak.* You hadn't told me a thing."

She's right. We women are funny about introducing a new man to our friends. No matter how they react to him, it changes the balance of things. Of course, I knew this wouldn't be like when I had introduced Jeff around; my friends would approve of Dick Kelley immediately. Dick just has an aura of solidness about him, if that's a word. Part of that is due to his six-foot-three frame, but beyond that is his business success, his travel experience, his strong sense of family, his wide circle of friends. As Bill Clinton told somebody, "Every man Mother's ever fallen for has been good-looking, smart, aggressive, and had a little bit of trouble." Unless you count the separation from his wife, Dick Kelley had all the qualities but the trouble.

In fact, Dick did represent a change in the kind of men my friends had seen me with. Dick wasn't part of the "racetrack crowd," a phrase I speak lovingly but still understand when others use it with less warmth. He was *in* it but not *of* it, if you understand the distinction. Bill Clinton was elated when I started seeing Dick. "I thought he was the most stable man you'd ever been with," Bill says today. Bill says he sometimes thinks of Dick as one of those strapping, gung ho heroes you expect to see stepping out of a World War II movie. "He's an anchor," Bill says, "a rock."

But not, thank God, a sanctimonious rock. He drinks vodka and water, light on the water. He's perfectly happy to go to the races, to get together with other couples for a poker party. He likes to eat and laugh and go and do.

So Dick and I had started seeing each other, and now I was letting my friends know. This was the late 1970s. Dick was sixty-three, though he didn't look or act it. I enjoyed his company and was happy to have someone to go places with. We even went to Louisiana Downs, taking Nancy along as our chaperone. I still had no interest in getting married, however; I was convinced I was snakebit. Besides, *I* was fifty-five years old. In addition to "Don't Fence Me In," I now included one other theme song in my personal repertoire: "My Way."

I preferred the Elvis version.

❦

Rush Limbaugh, when this book was announced, said I would probably include a weepy chapter about how those twelve awful years of Reagan-Bush had been so hard for my family.

I wish I could blame Ronald Reagan for my misfortunes in the 1980s, but even he couldn't have created the mess I found myself in. And the decade had started off so beautifully.

On February 27, 1980, Hillary gave birth to Chelsea. Oh, what a day that was. I had always wanted a daughter, and now I had one, in a way.

Bill and Carolyn Huber, the administrator of the Governor's Mansion, had just walked in the door from a governors conference in Washington when Hillary's water broke. Bill called me and said they were heading for Baptist Hospital. Have I ever told you how far it is from Hot Springs to Little Rock? The map says fifty-three miles, but that's deceptive. That's city limits to city limits, and neither my house nor Baptist Hospital is on the city-limits line.

I made the trip in forty-eight minutes. Where's a state trooper when you really need one? I was hoping I'd get stopped so I could explain and they'd let me drive even faster.

I got to the hospital at eight P.M., and Carolyn was already tapping her foot in the waiting room. We waited. And we waited. Nobody would tell us a thing.

Finally, at eleven-thirty-four, we got word that the baby had been born, but nobody would tell us what it was, how it was—nothing. Several times I grabbed the administrator, and all he would say was, "Everything's fine."

"Well, tell us what it *is*," I said.

"Everything's fine," he repeated.

By this time it must've been one A.M. I'd had just about all the suspense I could stand. I grabbed the administrator. "*Why* won't you tell us anything?" I said, and he could tell my patience was at an end.

He looked at me and smiled serenely. "They're *bonding*," he said. At one-thirty A.M., Bill came out in scrubs and introduced me to my granddaughter.

There's nothing like a newborn baby to renew your spirit—and to buttress your resolve to make the world a better place. Just before she was born, I had found a wonderful brass cradle that I thought would be perfect for my first grandchild. I tore back to my office. "Shirley," I said, "do I have enough money to buy this cradle?" Shirley looked at my books and gave me my balance. "Oh, good," I said, and went back to the store and got it. I loved rocking Chelsea in that brass cradle. Silently I prayed that life would always treat her so gently.

From the very beginning, I could see her parents reflected in her. As a baby she looked like Bill, and even now she has his hands—those long, long fingers. As she got older, I thought she began to resemble Hillary more, in looks and in attitude. Even if she hadn't looked a thing like Hillary, you would've known they were mother and daughter. The way she walked, the way she talked—the way she balked. Chelsea is strong willed—another in a long line of strong-willed women in Bill Clinton's life, I'm happy to say. There's nothing namby-pamby about Chelsea Clinton.

I remember one time when she was visiting me in Hot Springs. It was in the Lake Hamilton house I'm in now. She couldn't have been older than three or four, and she had just gotten some new shoes. Beautiful patent leather. She was crazy about them, as well she should've been. The problem was, she didn't want to take them off.

I was getting ready to wash the car. "Can I help, Ginger?" she said.

"Why, sure," I told her—adding that she would have to take off those patent leather shoes first, though.

"I don't want to." She had a head about like I do.

"Well, Chelsea," I said, "you can't wash a car in those shoes. You'll ruin them."

Next thing I knew, she was stomping off toward the house. Slammed the door and everything. I let her go, but, living on the lake, you don't take your eyes off a child for a minute. Pretty soon I went inside to check on her.

I heard a small voice coming from my bedroom. Very quietly I stuck my head through the doorway. She didn't hear me at all. I almost died laughing at what I saw. There she was, sitting on the floor in the worst funk you've ever seen in your life, and she was saying, over and over, "That is the meanest woman. That is the meanest woman."

Chelsea's birth was definitely the high point of 1980 for me. After that, it was as though the ground beneath me gave way to some seismic shift.

Dick Kelley—the "rock"—began showing disturbing signs of possessiveness. He wanted my undivided attention, something no one can have. I couldn't take it, and I broke up with him. I declared a one-year moratorium on our relationship.

Also that year, Bill lost his bid for reelection. It was a crushing blow, certainly to Bill, but to the rest of us as well. I had even come close to getting eaten by dogs in an effort to put Bill back in office. Nancy and I had gotten permission to put up a CLINTON sign in this outlying area of Hot Springs, and we had driven out there to do it. It was a big sign, and a lot of people who came in from the country would see it. Just as we were unfurling the thing, a man came fuming out of his house. "You can't put that up here," he said.

"Why, we sure can," I said. "We've got permission."

"I'll tell you what," he said. "You put up that sign and I'm going to turn my dogs loose on you." We could hear them barking in the distance. They sounded like they hadn't eaten for weeks.

"Well, I'll tell *you* what," I said to the man. "You hide and watch, because we're going to put this sign up."

So we proceeded to go about our business as the man stormed back to his house. We just about had the sign up when suddenly these yapping, gnashing, snarling animals came bounding around the house toward us. "Virginia!" Nancy yelled, and we made a beeline for our car, maybe twenty yards away. We slammed the doors just as the beasts skidded to a stop, running into the car, flapping saliva all over the windows, furious at being denied a taste of our juicy flesh.

Bill wasn't so lucky. His loss has been chewed to death, so I won't take the space to do it again here. Everybody said he had irritated the voters by raising their car tags and by not fighting harder to keep Cuban refugees from being shipped in to be housed at Fort Chaffee. Arkansans don't like anything crammed down their throats, even if it's right. So they decided to send him a message.

Incidentally, they also didn't like the fact that Bill's wife's name was Rodham instead of Clinton.

The final blow of the year came totally from left field: One day I was asked to come to a meeting at the Burton-Eisele Clinic. When I got there, lawyers were present: The parents of Laura Slayton, the young mother who had died after surgery in 1978, were suing me for the death of their daughter.

I couldn't believe it. I had always thought that if you did the best you could, that was enough. I preached that to my sons. And I had done the best I could for Laura Slayton; not only that, I had done the best *anybody* could've done. I don't know for sure what made her family decide, after two years, to sue. But what I believe is that the lawsuit was a result not just of that one case, but of the poisoned atmosphere in the Hot Springs medical community.

Only later would I see that it was a poison I had helped to inject.

⅋

One June morning in 1981, I was awakened by a phone call from the hospital. They wanted me down there right away. As I drove in, I wondered what calamity, what human drama, I would find waiting for me. Having been a nurse anesthetist for more than three decades, I thought I had seen pretty much everything. But nothing had prepared me for Susie Deer.

As I later understood the story, Deer, a seventeen-year-old who lived in the small southwest Arkansas community of Dierks, population two thousand, had asked her aunt to take her for a night on the town in the big city of Hot Springs. Deer had never been anyplace larger than Dierks, and said she wanted to go to Hot Springs "if it's the last thing I do." The aunt agreed.

After a night of dancing and drinking, Deer, her aunt, and three others were cruising along a questionable section of Grand Avenue about four A.M. when they got into a shouting match with two people walking along the street. Someone in the car apparently threw a beer can out. The next thing they knew, one of the people on the street had picked up a large rock and hurled it at the moving car. It was one of those scenes that, if this had been a movie, they would've shown in slow motion: the rock leaving the thrower's hand, rotating slowly, the car hurtling ever toward it—until finally the two reached the same precise point in space at the same precise time. The rock could've missed, but it didn't. Instead, it went through the open front window on the passenger side of the car and smashed into the right side of Susie Deer's face. The velocity of the car combined with the velocity of the rock made the blow even more devastating.

We worked desperately to repair her broken jaw, nose, and sinus cavity, but Susie Deer died on the operating table. During emergency surgery, the doctors and nurses and anesthetist and everybody operate like a machine, just working furiously, going on instinct. But when the patient dies right there in front of you, it's like the air has been sucked out of everybody. No longer a machine, they become individual human beings again. Everybody is quiet, the pain and frustration evident in their eyes.

I didn't realize I had been blamed for Susie Deer's death until later. Not by the girl's family, but by members of the Hot Springs medical community who pointed the finger at me—saying that I'd had trouble moving the air tube from the nose to the mouth. The fixing of blame was a gradual thing, gathering steam over the next couple of months in doctors' offices all over Hot Springs. There had been an autopsy by the state medical examiner, of course; however, it stated that Deer had died of "blunt trauma" to the head.

But one of the surgeons later told the newspaper that Deer's death was "the last straw" for some doctors who had become uncomfortable working with me. (The next-to-the-last straw was apparently Laura Slayton's death, for which I was still being sued.) The surgeon admitted that several doctors had begun pressuring Ouachita to stop using my anesthesia service.

The rumors were nasty. One I particularly abhorred was that I had been shining my shoes during surgery. Can you believe that? Before the crisis occurred, I'd noticed that a little blood had splattered onto my shoe, and I had leaned over for a second to wipe it off. The patient was breathing fine at that point, everything was under control. But the rumor mill made it sound like I'd been blithely shining my shoes while Susie Deer lay dying.

The truth, I believe, is that they weren't trying to get rid of me because of those two deaths. They wanted me out because I was a nurse anesthetist and anesthesiologists were determined to take over anesthesia in Hot Springs the way they had in a jillion other cities. But since I wouldn't go quietly, they were seizing on these two cases to discredit me.

To make matters worse, Ray Peeples chose then to decide to leave our group. He didn't give me any reason. Of course this left me with no supervising MD, and in the current climate I was going to have a hard time finding one. Twenty-five years after the start of my war with Klugh, it was finally all coming to a head. My thirty-three years of work as a nurse anesthetist was on the line. It was more than work, though; it was my life. With all the grief I had endured over Roger's alcoholism and the loss of husbands, I had sometimes thought that God had allowed me anesthesia as a gift. The minute I stepped foot in the hospital, my personal problems never crossed my mind. Anesthesia had anesthetized me.

I went looking for another doctor. Several seemed interested—until they'd spent a few days in Hot Springs. They insisted on talking with Dr. Peeples, of course, and they wanted to meet with others in the community, too. After that, it was inevitably, "Thanks, but no thanks." According to Medicare regulations, during this period the physicians performing surgery were legally responsible for the anesthetic my nurse anesthetists and I administered. I was in a race against time, since I knew this situation couldn't last long. Increasingly nervous about malpractice, the doctors would soon lay down the law to the Ouachita board, and the hospital would have to make other arrangements.

While I frantically shopped for an MD, I called everybody I knew, everybody I could think of who might help me buy time—might, in the final analysis, come to my defense. Oh, what a sad lesson in human nature that was. Here were people who had for years told me privately they believed I was in the right, but now that I needed them to go public, they were backpedaling.

I would say, "Please, So-and-so, I need your help on this one." And So-and-so would hem and haw, "Well, now, Virginia . . ." They were wishy-washy, lukewarm. I could tell they were abandoning me. But what hurt most of all was that nobody had the courage to come out and say, "Virginia, your time is up. The handwriting is on the wall." I believe I would've gotten over this whole mess a lot quicker had they been that honest. But, no. It was too easy to work behind the scenes and under the table. That was the Hot Springs way.

My ace in the hole was Wendell Burns, Ouachita administrator, the man whose job I had helped save a few years before. I met with him, told him what they were trying to do to me—as though he didn't know. Wendell assured me he could hold it all together.

That's my recollection. I consider it a sign of maturity that I'm now willing to admit rational people might've seen it another way. Bill Clinton worked years to teach me that. "Mother," he'd say, "there are two sides to every story." And I would say, "Yeah. My side and the wrong side."

In a hospital, says Wendell Burns, "the power structure emanates from the physicians." In other words, there was nothing he could do. He recalls that during this period when I was without an MD, Dr. Robert Humphreys, an anesthesiologist with Dr. Klugh's group, expressed interest in taking over the anesthesia program at Ouachita. "He hadn't expressed interest—and then he did," says Wendell. "Probably through the encouragement of some members of the medical staff. Who, I couldn't say."

By that time, so many doctors were against me that it would've been easier to name those who *didn't* encourage the change, instead of those who did. In any case, my anger, my frustration, my suspicions, all now zeroed in on a new nemesis: Dr. Humphreys. The irony was, I had known Robert Humphreys for years—since he had been an orderly in our operating room. I even encouraged him to become an anesthesiologist.

&

Dick Kelley hated seeing what was happening to me. He was worried, calling all my friends. They kept me informed, of course. And he would just happen to show up at places where I would be—at the Sawmill, at parties. In some respects, love isn't much different whether you're fifteen or sixty. I was touched. I really did love Dick, but I was still worried about that possessiveness business.

Dick's love for me was obvious, too. Nancy, who cares for him as she would her own father, told me she had fixed him up a couple of times during our time off, but that he couldn't work up even a passing interest in anyone but me.

When I thought back on our relationship, which I found myself doing more and more during these troubled days, I had to laugh out loud at some of the fun we'd had. For example, during racing season, Dick and I had a ritual we followed every single day. We would go to the track, but leave before the final race. Before we left, we would make a bet on that last race—a bet between the two of us.

Nancy lived just a few blocks from the track in those days, and we'd drive directly from the track to her house. Nancy didn't go to the races much herself; she says she learned the hard way that the track would only get her in trouble. So she'd be at home, and maybe a gentleman friend would be there, too. We would all fix drinks and then we'd see who won the bet. I couldn't stand it—Dick Kelley seemed to beat me every time. Of course I would fork over the dollar or two. The money wasn't the point; my pride was.

That happened two or three times. It was getting positively tiresome. So the next day I was ready: When Dick won, instead of handing him the dollars, I told him there was no law saying I had to pay in bills—and that I preferred to pay in dimes and pennies. Not only that, I was going to hide them and he'd have to find them. He was good-natured about it, laughing along with everybody else.

I hid the coins all over the house—under pillows, behind chair legs, inside the refrigerator. Unfortunately, my mean streak came out while I was salting Nancy's house with money: one of my most inspired hiding places was in the commode.

"Virginia!" Nancy said. "That is the meanest thing I've ever seen you do. Dick isn't going to go sticking his hands into some commode to get that money."

"Want to bet?" I said. And I was right—he did it.

The next day Nancy brought him some rolls of pennies so he could get me back, but Dick declined. He allowed me to play that trick on him, but he was above doing it to me. Nearly a year later, I decided you could read a lot about Dick Kelley's character in a gesture like that.

If I didn't have Dick, though, at least I had Roger. He had come to stay with me for a while. It's hard to say where Roger actually lived in those days. "I don't think I lived anywhere," he says today. Occasionally, though, he would come home, and I was always glad to have the company. Unfortunately, he never seemed to be at home for long. He was always "going out, Mother." I never knew exactly where.

I was out of town the day the bottom dropped out. It was September 1981, I think, though Shirley recalls that it was on her birthday—October 19. It doesn't matter, really. Shirley got a call at the office from Wendell Burns. The medical staff at Ouachita was going to have a meeting at which Dr. Humphreys would present his plan for anesthesiology. Wendell just wanted to let us know. As Shirley recalls it, she told him I was away, and he said he didn't think it would be any big deal, that I didn't need to rush back.

Later I called in and Shirley told me about the impending meeting. She urged me to come home and be available. I didn't see any need. "It'll be okay," I told her. I trusted that Wendell would be able to do as he had told me he would—to hold it all together.

But it didn't happen that way. Shirley recalls that Wendell phoned the next day with the news that, effective immediately, Ouachita Hospital would no longer be using our anesthesia services. Dr. Humphreys was taking over. Wendell's recollection is that the doctors liked Dr. Humphreys's proposal and studied it for several days before accepting it.

One of the things they liked best about it was that Dr. Humphreys said he wouldn't be responsible for any nurse anesthetist who wasn't directly under his supervision.

That was it for me. There was no way in the world I was going to work for Dr. Humphreys. I don't remember exactly when I heard the news, though I do think I was out of town and Shirley called to tell me. I remember vividly, however, how stunned I was. Have you ever had something happen in your life—the death of a loved one, a house fire, the loss of something irreplaceable—that was just too big to comprehend? That's the way this was. This was the end of my career. There was no place left in Hot Springs for me to work. *The end of my career.* I could say it over and over again and it still didn't sink in. Out on the street other people were going about their business, as though nothing had changed.

When I got home and Roger heard what had happened, he was livid—shrieking, yelling, crying, ready to hurt someone. And the person he wanted most in the world to hurt was Wendell Burns.

"I'm going over there!" he screamed.

"No, Roger," I said. "That won't solve anything. Please don't go." Roger inherited the temper I inherited from my mother, but sometimes he doesn't control it the way I have.

"Mother," he said, "you're going to have to trust me on this one. I've always listened to you, but this time I'm not going to. This time I'm going to do what I need to do."

He got his car keys and headed for the door. "Roger," I said. "At least don't hurt him." He didn't even look back.

The story was all over town in a flash. Roger burst through the front door of the hospital and stormed past the receptionist. "Roger," she said. They all knew him there, of course. "Roger. Where are you going? What on earth's wrong?"

Roger didn't slow down. "I'm going to see Wendell Burns."

"No, Roger!" the receptionist said. "You can't—"

But he could. Wendell probably heard him coming—it's hard not to hear Roger Clinton when he's that upset—although, not surprisingly, Wendell doesn't want to discuss this particular episode. Roger says Wendell's door was locked. Roger stood out in the hall screaming his head off: "Wendell! Wendell! You better let me in!" Other people had gathered around, of course, and they were phoning security—as they certainly should have. But none of that stopped Roger. Finally, he broke the door in.

Wendell was in his office, behind his desk—"shaking like a leaf," as Roger says. Roger still gets upset remembering that day. My sons have always been protective of me—sometimes even when I might wish otherwise.

"I grabbed him by his throat," Roger says, "and I pulled him up in his chair. He was backing up, shaking, and I remember calling him yellow. I kept saying that awful word: 'You're yellow, yellow, yellow! My mother saved your job and you turned your back on her! How can a person as low and cowardly as you affect the outcome of a person as good and strong and wonderful as my mother? It's not fair! You took my mother's life away. I ought to take yours away!'"

Thank God he didn't. Roger threw Wendell back down in his chair. As I heard it, Wendell was crying, Roger was crying, people were outside the door gasping. It was an awful scene.

I was as low as I'd ever remembered being. Hearing the news while I was away was easier somehow; now that I was home, I actually had to face the reality of it. Sometime in the middle of my tears, there was a knock at the door. When I answered it, who should be standing there but Dick Kelley—like Bill says, a hero right out of a World War II movie.

I was never so glad to see anybody in all my life.

&.

Shirley and I decided to keep the office going for three months. Cases already scheduled would be kept, of course, and the billing cycle for such cases would take that long or longer. But we kept the entire office open because of the human factor, too: We wanted to give our people as much time as possible to find another job. Some of our anesthetists went to work for Dr. Humphreys, and I held no grudge against them. Others, such as the Seavenos, moved on to look for jobs in other towns. Me, I had always prided myself on my independence—and maybe the word *prided* is key. I wanted to work for myself, but this was the end of an era. Unfortunately, it was an era that I personified.

Years later, someone asked me what I had learned from all this. "When they make their first move, go along with them," I said. "If you want to keep working." That's what I learned. I can't do it, but I did learn it.

I tried my hardest to stay upbeat around my staff, but this had bruised me badly. One day I picked up the phone and called Buddy Klugh. I asked if I could come over and talk with him. He was nice enough to say he could see me that very afternoon.

It was an amazing meeting, considering all the bad blood there had been between us. I had hated this man, had felt that his one purpose in life had been to do me in. But on that remarkable afternoon in 1981, he and I sat in his office and talked about everything that had happened over the years. Both of us were tired of it—I know I was, anyway. Hatred and bitterness isn't my nature, and this war had taken a toll on me. That day, Dr. Klugh and I agreed: no more fighting. He even told me, "It would be good if we could work together—" I was happy to hear that, because at that point I probably would've gone to work for him.

Then he continued: "—but the people in my group would never hold still for that." He had done the same thing I had done. Everybody in my group knew how I felt about him. Everybody in his group knew how he felt about me. We had both poisoned minds so much that the others couldn't possibly be comfortable with us working together, even if he and I could. I think he later even checked with his people, who were probably flabbergasted at such a notion. The answer that came back was, "Fine—as long as *Klugh* supervises her."

It was clearly too late. But at least he and I had buried the hatchet. I felt relieved—cleansed, somehow—about that.

With nowhere left to go, I had no choice but to retire from anesthesia. I'll never forget the day I went to Ouachita to get my gas machine. I'm sure I looked like Pitiful Pearl, and I guess I felt like her, too. I was rolling my gas machine down the hall toward the door when a doctor named Bill Mashburn saw me. He's coroner now, but at the time he was a general practitioner who performed circumcision, tonsillectomies, things like that.

"What are you doing?" he said. I couldn't believe he didn't know, but he had been out of town. This was the first he'd heard.

"I'm moving my equipment out of here. They've curtailed my privileges. Yesterday was my last day."

He was speechless. Today, Dr. Mashburn says the memory of that day still brings tears to his eyes. It does to mine, too, because he was one of the few doctors in town willing to show support for me at the end. "Well," he said, "after all you've done for this hospital, I refuse to let you roll your gas machine out of here. I'll do it for you."

Fourteen

DICK AND I were married January 17, 1982. My only condition was that I would get to keep sitting with Dixie in her box at the track instead of sitting with Dick in his. The ceremony was held in the very spot where we first met—before the blazing fireplace of Marge Mitchell's lake house. To show us how special we were, Marge even allowed us to stand on her antique oriental prayer rug.

It's a good thing—we were going to need all the help we could get. Roger's reaction to our marriage was, "Fine—as long as nobody expects me to think he's my father."

Oh, Roger. He seemed to be at such loose ends in those days, and I didn't know what to do about it. Dick didn't appear to like Roger any more than Roger liked Dick, which was no surprise to anybody. Dick Kelley is a get-up-early-and-get-busy sort of guy; Roger would happily sleep until noon and then go out for a long, leisurely lunch— all a prelude to staying out most of yet another night. He called himself a musician, though he wasn't working much that I could tell.

After we married, Dick moved into 213 Scully Street with Roger and me. That was a short-term arrangement if I'd ever seen one: Dick is a proud man, and there was no way he was going to be happy living in the house I had lived in with Roger Clinton and Jeff Dwire. And yet I agonized over saying good-bye to that place. Home is important to me. I enjoy traveling, and Dick and I have been fortunate to be able to go practically all over the world since we've been married, but I seem to have about a three-day clock built into me. After three days, four at the outside, I'm ready to come home and slip into my robe and curl up with a drink on my very own couch. Even when I go to the White House, that three-day clock is ticking.

Dick had a little farm he'd been living on since his separation from Jane, but that didn't seem to be the solution. He had lived on Lake Hamilton before and had loved it; I had always wanted to live on the lake, too. As a matter of fact, Bill and I had gone in together on a lake house, mainly as a retreat for him when he was governor. Actually, calling it a "lake house" is giving it more credit than it deserved. It was a small piece of property with what amounted to a cabin on it, just around the bend from Marge's sprawling lot. Across the road from our property were several mobile homes. Dick wasn't exactly impressed.

But once we started thinking about expanding it—knocking out that wall there, enlarging this room here (especially the master bath, to make space for my makeup table)—why, the place seemed to have real promise. Bill, who never had spent much time there, asked Dick if he'd like to buy his share. Dick jumped at the opportunity. We built a big bedroom for Roger on the other side of the house from our room. I didn't want Dick having to watch Roger sleep any more than necessary.

I decided to sell 213 Scully by auction. If I was going to have to sell that house, the one I had bought and my sons had grown up in, then I didn't want any slow, agonizing process: I wanted the place to move. On the day of the auction, Dick took charge. After a last look around, I left for my aerobics class—something I had taken up since my forced retirement. Even if I hadn't been exercising, I'd have had to find somewhere to go. I just couldn't stand there and watch the place change hands.

About twenty minutes later, Dick showed up at my class with the papers in hand. The house had sold for twice what I had paid for it.

I took to retirement approximately the way I had taken to Dr. Klugh. Dick was only semiretired at that point, so every Monday he would go to Little Rock for the day. The rest of the week he would be buzzing around here lopping off tree limbs, mowing grass, installing a pump so we could water the lawn with lake water, and so on. And here I was, facing this void. Oh, I made myself get up and go exercise or walk at the mall with the girls, and I would generally have lunch with one of my friends. But it was busywork. I felt empty inside.

I'm sure I was hard to get along with. On those days when Dick was gone, I would think about rolling up my sleeves and plunging into . . . cleaning out a drawer. Cleaning out drawers is a woman thing, and I liked being alone to do it. Then he would come back Monday night and for the rest of the week I would think, *Oh, I can't clean out that drawer with Dick around.* It was an excuse, but it worked. I didn't clean out the drawer—and I was angry at Dick about it. In truth, I was just angry and I was taking it out on him. He told a friend about life with me during this time: "When I go inside, she goes outside; when I go outside, she goes inside." What a sweet man to've put up with me.

I gave up cooking, too. In fact, I'm so well known for not cooking that my friends recently gave me a package of paper napkins that said "The Queen Doesn't Cook." Even giving up cooking wasn't as simple as you might think, though. All those years of working day and night and then coming home and preparing a meal for your family—it gets in your blood. Working women often punish themselves needlessly, I think. When it's convenient they should cook, but it's a mistake for working mothers to have the same idea that our grandparents had about cooking. Our grandmothers didn't have jobs—they were right there at home. That's not true today. Today, I believe the one who's home all the time should cook. And if nobody's at home all the time, eat out. I wouldn't be surprised if it isn't cheaper these days to eat out than to prepare meals at home.

I say all that now, but when Dick and I got married, I still had some of that old guilt percolating inside me. I would make my list and start out for the grocery store, and Dick would stop me. "Let me do that," he'd say. "I've spent my life in grocery stores. I can do it faster than you can." Then when it came to cooking, I'd start to fix a meal and Dick would say, "Let me do that." He loves to cook fish and grill meats, and he makes the best gumbo you ever put in your mouth.

Still, I wasn't used to this, and I felt funny about it. Maybe even resentful. Dick is from the old school: A woman is on a pedestal. I'd enjoyed being perched on a pedestal when I was married to Jeff, but back then I got to have my career, too. With Dick, I was feeling a little useless.

One day when I was at lunch with the girls, I was bemoaning the fact that Dick wouldn't let me cook or do the grocery shopping. "Are you crazy?" they said. Before that meal was over, they'd convinced me I didn't know a good thing when it was staring me in the face.

After that, I made do with my plants and my flower beds. But all too often, as I knelt by my roses with a spade in my hand, I would find myself obsessing about Dr. Humphreys. He was over there at Ouachita, tending to patients. I was here at home, tending to my plants. More than once the phrase *out to pasture* crossed my mind.

I was in New Orleans when I decided to sue. I had gone to a nurse anesthetists convention, and while I was there, I met a lawyer from Washington, D.C. Her name was Susan Jenkins. I told her my story, and she said, "You've got a case." I was ecstatic. I had paid my dues, had worked myself up to where I was earning about $80,000 a year, and then here Dr. Humphreys and Ouachita get together and take my career away from me: I couldn't wait to tangle with them.

Susan called in a Little Rock attorney named Steve Engstrom to be her cocounsel. After questioning me about all that had transpired over the years, the lawyers felt sure we had a good case. They saw it as a kind of antitrust suit, on behalf of the nurse anesthetists against the anesthesiologists. Because of that, they had one caveat: "You've got to name Dr. Klugh, too."

I couldn't believe it. I had buried the hatchet with Dr. Klugh. At that point, I was convinced that it wasn't Dr. Klugh who had finally done me in. I firmly believed that he was no longer my enemy. Many people tell me I was wrong about that, but that's how I felt.

No Klugh, no sue, the lawyers said. I argued and argued and argued. It seemed wrong from the outset. In my black-or-white world, this was as solid black as anything ever came.

The attorneys were adamant, and finally I gave in. The year was 1983—the same year my insurance company would settle out of court with the parents of Laura Slayton. The price tag for that settlement was $90,000. And now I was suing Robert P. Humphreys, MD, et al., for monopolizing the anesthesia business in Hot Springs.

❧

I had mothered Roger too much: That notion somehow made its way—finally—through my elaborate defense system. Roger was living here, he was living there, he seemed to be living everywhere and nowhere. Sometimes he had no money at all; other times he was rolling in it.

Dick never said much about Roger to me, but he didn't have to. Everybody who knows him knows when Dick Kelley is angry or displeased about something. It's a look, an attitude. Dick says today that he hated seeing me being taken advantage of by Roger. Roger is shrewd. When he was living in Little Rock, he would make sure he called me at least once a week just to check in. It never occurred to me that he would lie to me—but, as Dick says, "he would tell you one thing and do two others." Dick saw things more clearly than I did, and yet, as a stepfather to a grown man, he didn't feel it was his place to interfere. Especially when I would inevitably take Roger's side.

Looking back, I see that I made it easy for Roger to get away with the lie that had become his life. Do you know, I never once asked him how he was making a living? When he was in Little Rock, supposedly playing music but not really seeming to have many engagements, I didn't say, "Roger, how are you getting money?" I guess I didn't really want to know.

Today I even wonder if my decision to stop mothering Roger, to let him stand or fall on his own, was just one more way of denying what I knew deep in my heart—that there was a problem of some kind. After his drug bust, I would learn about something called "tough love," though I would have to be dragged, kicking and screaming, into it.

On the other hand, I've talked with people in the business of treating alcohol and drug abuse, and the words they use to describe such conditions are *cunning* and *baffling*. You can be sitting there having a conversation with your child, your spouse, your best friend, and you might not have any idea anything was wrong. As I've told you, Roger's father could be drunk as Cooter Brown and still straighten up when Mama Clinton called on the telephone. It's hard to know, after the fact, whether you could've done anything to make the situation different. I'm sure, however, that my decision to stop mothering Roger was a case of too little, too late.

I was certainly preoccupied with my own problems. Even Bill's 1982 reelection—thanks to his listening to the voters and having a more focused program, and a wife now officially called Hillary Clinton—was but a momentary joyous diversion. I had a lawsuit to pursue, and I was impatient to get it to court.

It's interesting, all these years later, to hear how the other side was feeling. Dr. Klugh says he was absolutely shocked when he received notice of the lawsuit: "I was hurt and devastated. Here I was at St. Joseph, not having anything to do with what went on on the other side of town, and I'm sued for five million dollars. I had never been sued in my life. For a while it was difficult for me to do anything other than my work at the hospital. I didn't feel like associating with anybody. I felt like it tainted my career—to be sued for anything."

Dr. Klugh says he had no choice but to fight fire with fire. The way the defendants intended to do that was by showing that I wasn't as well trained as a physician. One of Dr. Klugh's points was that I hadn't kept up with my education the way physicians have to. In discussions for this book, he was asked, "Did you ever feel that Virginia resisted keeping up with the times?"

And his answer was, "I think Virginia thought she was keeping up with the times."

He's darned sure right about that. I went to conventions, I read, I studied. I admit that today they have all these computerized machines that take special training. I don't think they're worth a damn, but they have them.

The other side hired the Jaworski law firm from Houston. I'll never forget my deposition as long as I live. It was like a movie—like *High Noon*, maybe—except, to my mind, the good guy didn't win. I sat on one side of this huge table, just me, accompanied by my two attorneys. On the other side were all these doctors and a bevy of puffed-up pin-striped lawyers from that hotshot big-name firm. There should be a law against that much arrogance being in one room at the same time. One of their attorneys asked me if I had been shining my shoes during Susie Deer's surgery. It went downhill from there.

Dr. Klugh says their strategy was to humiliate me, and they did. Their attorney began asking me medical questions that I would have no way of knowing the answer to. It was like he was speaking a foreign language. And while I was stammering, or sitting there dumbfounded and silent, I could see the doctors across the table leaning over and whispering other questions to the attorney—questions that would leave me twisting just that much more.

In the end, I dropped the suit. I guess the year was 1984—early 1984. We all agreed to pay our own legal fees and walk away. For me it was a disaster, a total defeat. They hadn't been able to intimidate me, so they humiliated me instead.

But if I thought for a second that that was going to be the hardest blow of 1984, I had forgotten that this was my life, not somebody else's. Unbeknown to me, the worst was yet to come. And the wheels were already in motion.

Maybe I should've had an inkling the night Roger came home with a knife hole in the canvas top of his Mustang convertible. I'm downplaying it when I call it a knife hole; it was a tear, a rip, a gash, down the middle. I was furious—this was a brand-new top I had bought for him. Roger was going to be twenty-eight years old soon; when was this kind of nonsense going to end?

"Roger, what in the world happened here?" I said.

He gave me that innocent-little-boy look that's always been able to melt me. "I don't know, Mother. I had it parked at some club and when I came out . . ."

"Well," I said, "I've got to call the police and the insurance company right away." Those convertible tops are darned expensive.

"No, Mother, you can't do that." That's what Roger said. And do you know what my response was? I said okay. I didn't call the police or the insurance company.

Where was my mind? Later I would learn that Roger had been carrying in his car some cocaine he was supposed to deliver, and somebody had slit the top and stolen it. Not only that, now he owed $8,000 to the people who'd given him the cocaine. Imagine the fear he was living with, and I had no idea. Part of it was my trusting nature, my disinclination to question things—not to mention my absolute, unshakable trust in my sons. But, too, drugs had never been part of my world. As crazy as we all had been back in my early days with Roger, the idea of something like cocaine was just alien to me.

Not for long, however.

Back then Bill had to run for governor every two years, and I was happy to have another campaign to fall back on after my crushing defeat in the deposition room. There was something comforting about putting on my silly hat and my buttons and my CLINTON FOR GOVERNOR T-shirt and going out among the people to tell them about my son. Besides, this campaign was going well. Bill was far ahead in the polls, and I thought for once we might have a halfway easy campaign and not have to work day and night. Nancy was campaign manager again, and I was happy to be back among all my other political friends.

One afternoon in the late spring I was working at campaign headquarters and got a phone call from Steve Engstrom, my former attorney. Steve is a nice man and a fine lawyer, and a good friend of Bill's. I had no ill feelings toward him about the lawsuit. "Virginia," Steve said, "I'm just calling to tell you how sorry I am about Roger."

I had no idea what in the world was he talking about.

He was incredulous. "You mean you don't know?" he said. There was a deafening pause, then he said, "Well, I've never been so sorry to call anybody in my life. I just assumed you knew. Roger is going to be charged."

There's no way to tell you what those words did to me. I thought I would die. *Thought I would die.* That's not just a figure of speech. It was really in my head that I didn't think I could live through this. I hung up the phone and sat there in shock, the tears welling up in my eyes. I didn't go to pieces because people were around, especially a man who worked back in that room near me. He didn't seem to have noticed a thing.

A few seconds after I got off the phone, Nancy came in. She took one look at me and knew something was wrong. "Please get him out of here," I whispered to her. She asked the man to go do something in the other room. As soon as he did, I let the tears come.

Nancy has a vivid recollection of that day: "I had seen you when Roger died. I had seen you when Jeff died. I had seen you go through all that stuff at the hospital. But never once had I seen you devastated until that day. I had never seen you hurt that much."

Nancy and I hadn't been talking but a minute or two when the phone rang again. She answered it, and it was Bill. "She's already heard about it," Nancy said, but Bill wanted to tell me himself. "Mother," he said, "I've called a press conference for three o'clock and I'll be right there as soon as I finish that." The press conference was about Roger. Then Bill got Nancy on the phone again. "Find Roger," he said, "and tell him to meet us at the house."

Find Roger: Bill never has minded asking you to do the hard things. Who knew where Roger might be? Nancy hadn't a clue. She started in on the phones, calling Sam Anderson, Jr., and some of Roger's other cronies. While she did that, I called Dick. He was playing golf at the country club, and I asked that they send someone out to get him in a golf cart. When he got to the phone, I said, "I didn't want you to hear this from someone else." Then I told him the news.

"I'll be right there," he said.

"No," I told him, "I'm okay. I want you to finish your golf game."

He didn't sound convinced, but finally he said, "Okay. I'll be home in an hour and a half."

Nancy's attempts to find Roger had come up empty. Then I thought about a little girl he had been going with. Her parents had a house out on Lake Ouachita, the other lake in Hot Springs, and Roger had been spending much of his time out there. He would just come home to shower and change clothes. I had known it wasn't a good situation, but he was a grown man; what could I say about it?

I called out there and the girl put Roger on the phone. He was crying. "Mother," he said, "I am so sorry. I can't tell you how sorry I am."

"Your brother wants you to meet us at home," I told him. "He'll be here shortly."

I have no idea how Bill got to Hot Springs so fast. It seemed like no time before he wheeled into the parking lot. I could tell he was hurting, too. As we were driving to the house, he told me, "Mother, we just have to hang tough."

Roger was driving in from the other side of town, tears streaming down his cheeks. "I had already decided I was going to commit suicide," he remembers. "I just didn't know the means. The reason was, so my mother and brother wouldn't have to go through this pain and embarrassment. That's how sick I was."

Bill and I hadn't been in the house five minutes before we heard Roger's car pull into the driveway. Later I would find out that Bill had known for weeks that this moment was coming. It had been inevitable since the day state police, investigating a drug ring, had found evidence that Roger was involved. They had taken the evidence to Bill. Bill had been torn up about it, but he'd had no choice: He had told the state police to keep going with the operation and to treat Roger the way they would anyone else.

We sat at the dining room table waiting. When Roger walked through the door, his eyes were swollen and red. "I need help," he said, sobbing again, and I don't think he was talking just about his drug problem. He was babbling a mile a minute. "I'm going to end it if I can't get help. I'm not about to let you go through all this embarrassment and pain. I caused it, I'm going to end it. I created it, I can end it."

I've never seen Bill so angry in all my life. He jumped up and grabbed Roger by the shirt and shook him till I thought Roger's head was going to come off. "How dare you!" Bill screamed. "How dare you be so selfish as to think that way!"

Those words seemed to reach Roger. After that, we all began to pull together. We sat down around the table. We were all crying, but we were calm. Dick came home soon after that, but he didn't sit with us. He seemed to feel that this was a matter for the three of us and that he shouldn't intrude unless asked. Occasionally, though, he would walk through the room and pat me on the shoulder with that big old hand as he went by. He just wanted to make sure I was all right.

"I can handle this," Roger told Bill and me, "unless you all start blaming yourselves. That I cannot handle. Believe me, there's nothing in the world you could've done to stop this. I don't even know how it happened myself."

We must've sat there for three hours or more. As the shadows grew long across the lake, we held hands, we hugged, we laughed, we prayed, we cried. "We've climbed other mountains," I told my boys. "We can climb this one, too."

&.

I went back to the campaign that fall because I knew how important hard work is in taking your mind off your worries. Bill was elected. A few days later, Roger was arraigned.

I was there with my head held high. And I'll tell you another thing: Whenever he testified in the trials of others charged along with him, my friends were there with me. Every single day. Not that I was surprised—that's what I expected, because that's what I would've done for them. Not all of Roger's friends came to support him, and I've never forgiven them for that.

Roger pleaded guilty—he just wanted to go take his punishment so he could get on with his life. He'd had a difficult few months. For a while, Bill and Roger and I had gone to see a counselor in Little Rock. Karen Ballard is her name, and I want to thank her from the bottom of my heart. She had her hands full getting Roger straightened out, because he didn't want to admit that he was addicted. She had just as hard a time with me. She would say something about Roger, and I would defend him with every fiber in my body. That was the last thing Roger needed, and Karen knew she was going to have to be tough with me if she could ever hope to help Roger. She never let up on me. This was the tough love I was talking about earlier.

Not too long ago I saw Karen, and I said, "Do you remember the times you sent me out of your office crying?"

"Yeah," she said. "Do you remember the times I called you later to see if you got home all right?"

During those sessions Roger was feeling so good about finally getting his life straightened out that he decided to go back to college. He only needed one year. I was proud of him—but dubious. He was under indictment and the whole world knew it. I thought he might have trouble getting in. But Roger wouldn't be deterred. He reapplied to Hendrix, and Hendrix accepted him—no problem. We all breathed a sigh of long-awaited relief. Maybe our lives were going to go smoothly for a change.

Roger was living in Little Rock and was commuting daily to college in Conway. One day a short while after Roger started school, somebody called me from Little Rock, I can't even remember who. "Virginia!" this person said. "You better get here quick. Roger's a sick man. He can't keep a thing down!"

Dick and I rushed over there as fast as we could, and I never saw anybody so sick in all my life. Roger had thrown up everything he had tried to put into his stomach. He was pale and weak and couldn't stand up. "Mother," he said, "I went to the man and begged him." I didn't know what he was talking about, but begging anybody was completely against Roger's nature. "'Please tell me what I've done,'" he said he told the man—whoever the man was. "'I've obeyed every rule. Please tell me why.'"

The man Roger was talking about was one of the deans at Hendrix, who that day had called Roger into his office and told him he couldn't stay at the school. Roger was doing well in his classes, but apparently that wasn't the problem. I've been around long enough to guess what the problem was—the dean had felt pressure from the parents of other students. I can just hear those mothers: "My precious daughter, she's not safe on that campus." And the dean had caved in.

It was a cruel thing to do to Roger, at a particularly sensitive time in his recovery. I could've understood Hendrix not accepting him in the first place—saying, Roger, maybe we ought to wait awhile. But that's not what they did. They accepted him, and then they booted him out. I will never forgive Hendrix College for that. Years later, after Roger started receiving Hendrix alumni mailings at my house— with requests for donations, of course—he went back to see that dean. "Don't you *ever* send another one of those to me or to my mother," he said. The mailings abruptly stopped.

Bill and Hillary came down the January day Roger was to be sentenced and leave for prison. He didn't have to report to the Federal Building until afternoon, so we all had brunch together at the house. We tried to laugh and talk like normal. We tried to keep one another's spirits up.

I didn't cry on the drive downtown. I was out of tears by then. I just thought about all that my poor Roger had faced in his young life. I remembered when he had first called me Dado. That was the sweetest thing. Here this child was, no more than nine months old, and he could say "Daddy" and "Dado" to distinguish between big Roger and me whenever one of us would walk into the room. And I thought, *I've got a child prodigy on my hands.*

I hated it the day he stopped calling me Dado. It was during his first year at Oaklawn School, over near Scully Street. We're huggers and kissers in our family, and I always dropped him off at school and he kissed me good-bye. To this day, the first thing Bill or Roger will do when they see me is kiss me and give me a big hug. I love that, need that—always have.

But one morning as Roger and I were in the carport getting ready to leave for school, he said, "Dado?"

And I said, "Yes, Roger?"

"Do you mind if I don't call you Dado anymore?"

It nearly broke my heart, of course. But I said, "Well, Roger, I knew this day would come. But you have a reason for everything you do, so let's talk about it."

"Well," he said, "the kids say it sounds like I'm calling my dog."

"Okay," I said, "that's reason enough. But I don't like 'Mama.'"

"Oh, no," he said, "I wanted to call you 'Mother.'"

I told him that would be perfect.

"One more thing, Mother," he said. "Does it make any difference to you where I kiss you good-bye?"

"No," I said, "I guess it really doesn't."

"Well, then," he said, "I think I'll do it right here, before we get to school."

When we got to the Federal Building, Steve Engstrom, Roger's attorney, met us. The authorities were waiting. Roger was sentenced to two years at a prison in Fort Worth—more time than we expected. I bit my lip as the lawmen slipped the handcuffs on him. I listened carefully as they talked to him—listened not just to the words, but to the tones of voice. You work your entire life trying to do and get and be—and then a tiny thing like some man speaking kindly to your son ends up meaning all the world to you.

We watched till they drove Roger away. Then Bill and Hillary said their good-byes and left for Little Rock. Dick and I went home in silence. It felt to me like I had just experienced the death of a child.

❧

I began 1985 in mourning—there's no other way to describe it. By the time the year was over, I had come to believe that this whole episode had probably saved Roger's life. Had he not been caught, he would've surely destroyed himself.

Roger called every single day for a while—collect, which was the only way he could do it. I thought we were going to have to sell the house to pay for those phone calls, and it would've been well worth it to me. I drove over to see him as often as possible—every couple of weeks, at least. And, of course, I got to see him during the trials of the two other men involved in this same drug business. One defendant was a Colombian national from New York; the other was Sam Anderson, Jr., son of my old friend and attorney. Our family wasn't the only one that was hurting.

By May, I was able to note in my calendar diary, in the box for the twenty-eighth: "This ends the 4th month for Rog. What a change. He's beginning to be a man." He was getting in shape again physically, but it was the emotional and spiritual change in him that was most remarkable. I had been so blind I hadn't even noticed how immature Roger was. He was a fourteen-year-old in a twenty-eight-year-old's body. Alcohol and drug addiction keeps you from maturing—that's something I learned during the year Roger was in prison. Nancy and I spent a week in Fayetteville taking a workshop on alcohol and drug abuse. I learned that because the abuse keeps you from maturing, you have to be hurt very badly before you're ready to be helped. Only after "hitting bottom" can you start growing. But I had helped Roger avoid hitting bottom by rationalizing away his childishness. As Dick says, I had pinned diapers on him all his life.

We mothers—maybe especially when there's no father at home—want *so* for our children. We want to give them the good things and protect them from the bad things. There's nothing wrong with that—until it's carried to such an extreme that it keeps the children from growing up. That's what I did with Roger, and that's what I was trying to change when I decided to "stop mothering" him. By then, though, the damage was done. All this became clear to me one day in the spring of 1985. I was working in the yard and I heard a chirping noise. I looked around and saw a baby bird on the ground under our big elm tree. He couldn't fly yet, but he was hopping and ruffling his wings. The noise, though, wasn't coming from him—it was coming from up above. There in the nest was the mother bird, just making an awful racket. Suddenly it dawned on me what had happened: She had kicked her baby out of the nest and was now lecturing him about getting busy and learning to fly. And I thought, *Who's the birdbrain here? That mother bird is smarter than I am.*

In the mideighties, parole was still allowed in federal cases, and Roger was supposed to get out early and be released to a halfway house. His scheduled release date was December 2, and I starred that box on my calendar. But when December 2 finally came, Roger didn't. Because of an infraction of the rules—he ate his lunch at a time other than his assigned one—they told him he would have to stay in prison another thirty days. He was packed, dressed, and everything—and the guard said, "You're not going anywhere." My calendar notation for December 3 reads: "God help me—Roger didn't get out—How can I stand more?" This meant he wouldn't be home for Christmas. The idea of my son spending that holiday in that place almost killed me, and I knew I had to be there with him. I told Dick what I was going to do, and he offered to go with me. No, I told him, he should spend the holiday with his own children.

Nancy and I drove to Texas together on December 24. You've never appreciated the concept of "home" until you've spent Christmas Eve in Fort Worth in a truckers motel. I don't remember the name of the place, and even it was almost empty. Maybe there were a couple of lonely rigs parked way out in the lot under a solitary light pole. Talk about not a creature stirring. Even the bar was closed. Fortunately, I had brought a bottle of Scotch, and Nancy had some rum.

Getting something to eat was a more difficult matter. We drove and drove. Even the fast-food signs were dark. Finally, way out in some Podunk section full of rusted cars and derelict filling stations, we found a chicken place open. Obviously, this place was so bad and hard up that it needed to stay open on Christmas Eve just to make one more pathetic sale. We bought some fried chicken and took it back to our room. While Nancy laid out the dinner, I fixed me a Scotch and water and her a rum and Coke.

We turned on the TV and sat on the beds and took a bite. The chicken was inedible. It dripped grease every time you bit into it. We were hungry, but we weren't desperate. "I saw a candy machine in the lobby," Nancy said, so we pooled our change and she made a run. In a few minutes she came back with bags of Fritos and about six Snickers bars. Both of us love Snickers bars.

So that's how we spent Christmas Eve, 1985. Pretty soon the drinks took hold and we were giggling like girls again. We talked about everything under the sun—Gabe, Roger, the good old bad old days we had shared. And now we were sharing another one. Once we really started thinking about our situation, we were rolling all over the floor laughing. Here we were, alone in a truckers motel in Texas on the night before Christmas, eating Snickers bars and drinking whiskey and getting ready to go see my son in prison. That night I finally realized why I had never liked country music: My life was too much like a country song.

Fifteen

AFTER SPENDING JUST over a year in prison, Roger landed a construction job building bridges. Even I recognized the symbolism in that.

For a while after he got home, Roger was living in a wonderful halfway house called Serenity House, run by members of Alcoholics Anonymous in Little Rock. I remember that on Roger's last day there, Dick and I were scheduled to leave for San Francisco to attend a food-broker's convention. The courts had decreed that Roger had to get a job and support himself. I was a nervous wreck because I had no idea where he was going to live or what he was going to do. By then, though, I had been indoctrinated in tough love, so I kept repeating to myself, *It's Roger's life, he's got to do it, it's Roger's life.* Still, I was as miserable on that trip as I had been nearly thirty years before when big Roger and I had left our baby for that turnaround visit to Las Vegas.

When Dick and I got back, though, Roger was fine. He was more than fine. In fact, he was living in a mansion with the owner of the construction company and his family. I breathed a sigh of relief. From then on, my only worry was that the construction company owner happened to be a Republican.

Some of the bridges Roger was helping to build were on the winding old Benton highway, the one Bill and I had taken years before on those horrible Sundays when we had gone to visit my mother in the state mental hospital. I had hated the highway then, but now I loved it. I was so glad to have Roger home that I would drive out to where he was working and spend his lunch hour with him. Soon the other young men got used to my coming, and I started picking up sandwiches for them, too. As I approached, I would see them working high up on the bridge with the hot summer sun beating down on their bare backs. I could tell when they saw me, because somebody would point and before long they would be bounding down the grassy slope toward the road.

We would sit in a field next to the highway, and I would pass out sandwiches to those hungry boys. I felt like that mother bird. There was a lot of laughing and kidding among them, and I was right in the middle of it. Those were golden days. After we finished our lunch, sometimes Roger and I would lie back and I would smoke a cigarette and we would look at the sky until he had to go back to work. Sometimes we wouldn't even say anything. The big, open sky said it all.

To my mind, Roger's bridges led to a new life for both of us. I had probably been clinically depressed for all of 1985, but I never once thought of going to a psychiatrist. Instead, my friends and I started the Birthday Club. In the beginning, clusters of us girls would run into one another on Fridays at one of our favorite restaurants, such as the Sawmill or Rocky's Corner. We would pull up a few chairs and hoot and laugh and have a couple of drinks to wash our cares away. After a while, we all decided to *plan* to meet on Fridays—why leave such fun to happenstance?

Eventually somebody got the bright idea of meeting on each of our birthdays, too. I say *too* because even though there were a dozen of us, one for each month of the year, the birthdays weren't spread that neatly over the calendar. Anyway, we needed one another too much to meet only twelve times a year. I've always said that the Birthday Club is more than a bunch of rowdy old ladies who like to drink at noon; it's a life-support system, and I don't know what I would have done these past few years without it.

Various members have come and gone since the beginning, but in the recent past the membership has held pretty steady. There's Nancy Adkins, formerly Nancy Crawford, my friend and confidante for decades; Estelle Blair, a sweet woman who once worked for Mayor Leo P. McLaughlin, and who knows the skeletons in half the closets in town; Clover Gibson, an aspiring poet who makes us laugh like hyenas; Edith Irons, who was high school counselor to both Bill and Roger—she pointed Bill toward Georgetown—and who rivals me for the loudest clothing; Virginia Livingston, a former Miss Hot Springs who knows the skeletons in the *other* half of the closets; Berenice Lyon, who'll snatch the cake off your plate if you don't watch her; Marge Mitchell, my old pal, who keeps herself busy working now that she's a widow and consequently misses much of the fun; Elizabeth Ross, a brave lady whose battle with cancer has been an inspiration to us all; Dixie Seba, my sounding board and soul mate from day one; Johnette Taylor, my loyal friend and helper in so many things; and Edie West, the newest member, a neighbor of Nancy's who has become as dear to us as any.

Beginning in 1986, it seemed that my life might finally smooth out a bit. Roger was doing well, and all of us were getting along. Dick, I think, has always been willing to try to feel better about Roger—he just wanted Roger to grow up some. Roger had even exchanged letters with Hillary when he was in prison. I, of course, was still fighting the mothering instinct—but I was doing better, too.

The one real problem on the horizon was my health. I had gained fifteen pounds while Roger was in prison—depression is hell on a diet. The worst thing about it was, I knew I would have to quit drinking in order to lose weight. What's that old line—"My doctor told me to quit drinking, so I changed doctors?" But I'm convinced it's true. I've counted the calories in alcohol, and it's not the calories that kill you; alcohol does something to slow down the metabolism, and *that's* where the weight gain comes from.

So that year I turned to healing myself. The past two years had nearly crushed me. In addition to coping with Roger's situation, I still pined for my career. Losing my work had broken my heart. For two long years, every time I would hear a siren wail in the middle of the night, I would feel a pang. How many times in my life had I heard an ambulance and jumped out of bed and started putting on my clothes—*knowing* the phone would ring in a few minutes? The one and only time in thirty years that I refused a call from the hospital was when I was waiting for Bill to call with the outcome of the Rhodes scholarship. "You'll have to get somebody else," I had told them. "I'm not leaving the phone today." And I didn't. Late that afternoon the phone rang and it was Bill. "How do you think I'll look in British tweeds?" he'd said.

But I had loved being needed, and for three decades I had slept with an ear cocked for the siren call. What cured me, finally, was a snowstorm. It was late 1986, I believe. We were snowed in for about ten days, which is unusual for Arkansas—couldn't even get the cars out of the driveway. One night I heard an ambulance, it must've been two o'clock in the morning. I looked at the glowing face of the clock, then at the ghostly snowfall in the moonlight outside. I smiled and turned over and covered up my head. That's when I realized I had finally gotten over the pain of not working.

Dixie and I started meeting at the mall every morning at eight, and we would walk two miles of laps inside. After that, we would go have coffee and usually end up having lunch. I was off alcohol, so I would just stick to water. I drank thirty-two ounces a day, and the pounds just melted off. When we got bored with walking at the mall, we started our aerobics classes again. You should've seen us, two old sisters prancing around like we were getting ready for the Miss America pageant. We did that for about a year and a half—until we realized we weren't ever going to win any prizes. Then we went back to the mall.

In 1988 I stopped smoking. I had smoked for forty-eight years, and I mean smoked like a steam engine—a couple of packs of Pall Malls a day, never a moment when there wasn't a cigarette in my mouth, my hand, or in an ashtray nearby. With that came holes in my clothes and smoke in my hair. It wouldn't surprise me a bit to find that my gray streak was nothing but cigarette smoke.

Chelsea is the one who made me quit. Whenever I went to her house—which is to say the Governor's Mansion—I wasn't allowed to smoke inside. Hillary had strict rules against that. So I would step outside and light up, and when I would come back inside, Chelsea would look at me with eyes so sad she reminded me of those big-eyed-waif pictures you used to see all over the place. "Ginger," she would say, "why do you smoke? Don't you love me enough to quit?" What a manipulative little so-and-so. Naturally, it worked. On Chelsea's eighth birthday I declared myself officially smoke free. I quit cold turkey and never lit up again.

I did begin to chew an awful lot of gum, however.

&

It was during the campaign of 1990 that my doctor found the lump in my breast.

Bill's career had reached a new level. There was talk, serious talk, about his someday being a candidate for President. Of course, I wasn't the least bit surprised. For the moment, however, we had to get him reelected governor. I had been doing my usual press-the-flesh and pass-the-word politicking, but I had made time for my annual checkup. Ever since I'd turned forty-five I'd made sure to go. Besides, Dr. John Haggard was an old friend, and I was always glad to see him. I usually scheduled my appointment for June, the month of my birthday, because then it was easy to remember. But I had been so busy that summer that I hadn't gotten around to it until August.

I was lying on the examining table looking straight up at Dr. Haggard when I noticed his expression change. He had already checked my left breast and was concentrating on the right. I could tell by his face he had found something he didn't like. "Virginia," he said, "have you not felt this?" And I hadn't—even though I checked myself regularly, the way we're told to.

To say that Dr. Haggard looked worried is an understatement, though he turned his face to try to keep me from noticing. He checked his watch. It was late afternoon, but the sun was still high. "I don't want you to leave until we have a surgeon look at you," he said.

I nodded and he left the room. I lay there staring at the ceiling.

The lump was such that all they had to do was touch it, and they knew. They would've operated the next morning, but I told them I needed forty-eight hours. I called Roger and Bill, both of whom were stunned. Here I had worked around sick people all my life, and none of us had ever given a thought to anything like this happening to one of us.

Two days later, Dick, Bill, Roger, and my friends were all in the hospital waiting for the outcome. Me, I wasn't at all surprised to wake up and find my breast gone. I had seen this too often. I knew.

I also knew I had to pull myself together one more time. It's interesting—I can be stronger when something happens to me than when it happens to my sons. That's why I nearly fell apart watching Roger go through his ordeal. My cancer was my problem, and I could handle it.

I almost scared Nancy to death, though. The day after my surgery she came to my hospital room and I wasn't there. *My God, something's happened,* she thought, and she tore out looking for the nurse. Nancy found me walking the halls in my robe (but with my makeup on), rolling my IV along. I had been visiting with the nurses, the doctors, people I hadn't seen for a while, and getting my strength back. I may've even been politicking for Bill a little bit. "Don't ever do that to me again," Nancy said.

They say that living with cancer is attitude, so I felt from the beginning that I had a good chance. Besides, surviving cancer runs in my family. My uncle Buddy had a lung removed—I bet it's been twenty years now. That was cancer, and he's lived long enough to become a philosopher. His sister, Opal, the one I called Otie, had cancer of the colon. I would go to see her thinking it would be the very last time—but she would just keep on living. She lived for years after they told her she was terminal. Whenever a cloud of doubt crossed my mind, I thought of Buddy and Otie.

Dick has been a pillar of strength, as usual. Early on in our marriage, he and I settled into a routine at night. We sit in the same room, but we don't talk much. When Linda Ellerbee came to interview us for a TV special on breast cancer, she talked with Dick out in the yard. I didn't hear what he said, and he didn't tell me. A month later, as he and I sat in the living room together watching the show, I was so touched I cried. He had told her how strong I had been, and how he didn't care a whit that I was missing a breast, he loved me anyway. That meant the world to me. Another time, I was worried about a bone scan I was going to have the next morning. Dick and I had sat reading and watching TV all night, and I finally told him I was going to bed. Obviously, he had known how worried I was, because he got up from his chair and walked over to me and cupped my chin in his hand. "It's going to be okay," he said, and he kissed me on the forehead.

Dixie became my regular cancer companion. That was only natural, because she and I had a history with cancer. Besides all the other crises we've shared over the years, I was with her when she had a breast removed. That was twenty years ago. She recalls it to the day, because Jeff and I came to visit her in the hospital the night before, and we were all dressed up to go partying on New Year's Eve. Actually, Dixie hadn't known she was going to have surgery the next morning. They had done the biopsy, but hadn't yet told her the results. I knew, though. As I held her hand, she talked about everything being fine, about going home and getting back to normal. She remembers that I squeezed her hand and told her, "You're not out of the woods yet." That night she prepared herself.

After her operation, I went with her to be fitted for a prosthesis. Now, two decades later, she insisted on being with me every step of the way. She wanted to be the one to take me to the doctor, and after my first session of chemotherapy had gone so well, we both started looking on Dixie as my good-luck charm. I'm not generally a superstitious person, but I do stick with what works. For example, when I go to the track, I always make sure I have on one piece of jewelry from each of my sons. Roger gave me a gold racehorse that I wear around my neck most of the time. And years ago, Bill gave me a ring—a horse's head with a horseshoe around the neck. In the horseshoe are little diamonds. I remember when he gave me that ring I looked at it closely—it was a beautiful ring, but there was something wrong. I counted the diamonds. There were thirteen. *What does Bill Clinton know about gambling?* I thought, and I took the ring to the jewelry store and had a fourteenth diamond put in, right smack in the horse's eye. You can't hope to win at the track wearing a thirteen-diamond ring.

By the same token, I came to think that I couldn't hope to win at the doctor's office without Dixie. She once begged me to postpone a doctor's appointment for a day because she had to be out of town with her husband. I didn't give it a second thought—I called and told the doctor I'd have to make it later.

And when it came time for me to shop for a prosthesis, Dixie was right by my side. I'd rather lose a breast than a friend any day.

&

The older you get, the more you see life in relative terms. For example, once I had been diagnosed as having cancer, any little ache or pain stopped me in my tracks: *Oh, Lord,* I would think, *it's back.* I strained my shoulder one day, and I just knew it was cancer. That night, Dick rubbed some Icy-Hot on it, and the pain went away. I slept like a baby. Later, a technician told me it was probably just a touch of arthritis. That's what I mean by seeing life in relative terms: Suddenly I was thrilled to think I had developed arthritis.

I was trying my best to stay positive, not just for me but for my friends and family. Roger was working in California for Harry and Linda Bloodworth-Thomason—he started as a gofer on their TV shows, and then they began letting him and his band entertain the studio audience between sets—and he would call me all the time, just worried sick. Bill was trying to decide whether to run for President. I assured them both that I was fine. Say it enough and there's a chance you'll start to believe it.

One day at the Birthday Club, Elizabeth Ross gave me a beautiful gift. Elizabeth, as I've told you, has had a terrible time with cancer—and still she battles on. She's had it show up just about everywhere and has had so many operations you can't believe it. Whenever I started feeling like Pitiful Pearl, I just took a look at Elizabeth and that set me straight.

The gift was one she had made herself—a sampler that read, "Lord, help me to remember that nothing is going to happen to me today that You and I can't handle." Coming from her, it meant as much as any gift could mean. I told her I would find the perfect place in my house for it, and I did. I finally settled on the bathroom, where I start my day. I can't tell you how much that little framed saying has done for me. If I have any advice for cancer sufferers, it's to get up and go as long as you can. It's amazing what you can do once you make up your mind.

In June 1991, about four months after my chemo was over, my Hot Springs doctor, Timothy Webb, told me he thought it would be good for me to visit with specialists in Little Rock, who might have better access to investigational therapy. One of the doctors was Kent Westbrook, and after he examined me he sat me down and we had a little talk. Dick was with me. I had known what the doctor was going to tell me. My cancer, while there was no sign of it at the moment, was a particularly bad kind. Dr. Webb had already told me that. It wasn't just in my breast, it was down the nodes of my arm. There are thirty nodes in your arm, and when doctors see someone with more than six or seven nodes positive, they figure it's just a matter of time. I had twenty-seven nodes positive.

What Dr. Westbrook was trying to tell me, I guess, was that I was going to die of breast cancer. I listened to him, and I smiled, and I thanked him. He didn't actually say the word *die,* as I recall, but even if he'd said it, I just couldn't have allowed myself to hear it. One of my sons was about to run for President of the United States, and the other was busy rebuilding his life. I looked the doctor straight in the eye. "If they ask," I said, "you tell my boys I'm fine."

Bill announced his candidacy in October, and from then on we were traveling a mile a minute. I made it my business to go to the

Little Rock campaign headquarters and meet everyone from James Carville on down. To me, everybody was important—and it was important for everybody to be doing his job. Johnette Taylor laughs at me. "They all thought you were up there socializing," she says, "but you were really assessing their work." She's right, too, I guess, though the tendency is so ingrained that sometimes I don't even know I'm doing it. But Bill can't be everywhere. I try to be his eyes and ears whenever I can.

Through that first fall and into the winter I did what I could to make sure we turned out for all his rallies. Nancy, who had run so many of his Garland and Montgomery county campaigns, had a job this time around, so she couldn't be as involved as she'd have liked. At my urging, Johnette organized caravans to wherever Bill was speaking. We had come up with the caravan idea years before, but it had taken a bit of tinkering to work the bugs out. One of our first successful ones, during Bill's second gubernatorial campaign, had been to a town called Kirby, Arkansas; we only turned out about seven cars, but what we lacked in number we made up for in color and noise. We looked like a homecoming parade for a high school football team. After that, people seemed to get the idea, and we never again launched fewer than fifteen or twenty cars decorated with signs and crepe paper and packed with very vocal Clinton supporters.

❧

Nobody ever talks about what cancer does to your good-looking legs.

I had always prided myself on having legs that others took a second glance at. In my younger days I wore hose with seams, of course, and I was a late convert to the seamless kind. I just thought the ones with seams were sexier. For the first year after other women wore seamless, I kept my seamed hose. Then one day I noticed I was the only woman left in the world who was constantly looking around to see if her stockings were straight. I gave the seamless hose a try and I liked them.

Panty hose are something else again. I've got a drawer full of them that I've never had on my legs—life's too short to be bound up like that. If you ask me, thigh hose are the perfect answer. Today they've even come out with thigh hose that stay up without garters. You live long enough and miracles *do* happen.

Starting in 1991, though, I developed a condition called lymphedema. Women who've had breast surgery often develop lymphedema in their arms, especially on the side where the breast was removed. In my case, it's in my legs and mostly on my left side, opposite the breast that was removed. It makes my feet and ankles swell. It's really ugly. I used to paint my toenails and wear pretty sandals in the summer, but I can't anymore. Now I pray for winter when I can wear boots to cover up the swelling. That's just one of the unsung laments of cancer.

Another is, you might as well forget dieting and exercise. The poison they pump into your system makes you queasy around food, so you need to eat as much as you can manage to keep from withering away. And the treatments sap your strength, making what used to be a whirl around the mall seem like a trek around the world. Now I think all my friends are using me as an excuse not to exercise.

In May 1992, almost two years after the surgery, my cancer came back. I had been taking hormone treatments and checking in regularly with Dr. Webb in Hot Springs. That May, however, he told me I needed to go to Little Rock and see Dr. Westbrook again.

The word wasn't good. The cancer had spread to my spine. When they took bone X rays, they found it was also in my skull, my pelvic bones, and down into my leg bones. Dr. Westbrook stopped short of giving me a time frame—he could tell I didn't want to hear one. What difference would it make? Certainly no positive difference—I already intended to live life to the fullest. Plus, I knew I would do that better by keeping this distressing news at arm's length for as long as possible. Bill had taken an awful beating in the media that winter, and right then I had some politicking to do.

Dr. Westbrook told me I needed radiation therapy to keep the bones from crumbling and possibly causing paralysis. "I understand," I said. "But you can't tell my sons my condition."

His mouth dropped open. "What are you going to tell them about these radiation treatments?"

"I'm going to tell them it's a new treatment for a herniated disk." He just shook his head. I smiled—I liked that answer.

After that, I began what has been a constant, never-ending combination of radiation and chemotherapy treatments. Two months after those started, I sat at the Democratic Convention in New York watching my son become his party's candidate for President. During that trip, I also went to see "The Will Rogers Follies" on Broadway, and that was the very first time I noticed any change in my own status. Mac Davis, the star, announced from the stage that "there's a celebrity in the audience." I craned my neck to look, until I realized he was talking about me. Then I half-expected some attention-starved girl to run up and hog the spotlight, the way a girl I used to know had so many years ago.

If I thought I was busy before, I hadn't seen anything. I had made a deal with Johnette—she would run the Garland and Montgomery county headquarters, and I would get out and shake hands and pound the pavement. My friends laugh at me still, because my car was just about as well stocked as the national headquarters in Little Rock. I would be driving along and people would wave me down wanting buttons, pins, flags, bumper stickers. I'd screech to a stop and get out my wares. And just in case they had a notion of sticking a bumper sticker in some scrapbook somewhere, I would put it on their car myself. I'd plaster a second one on, too, when I could get away with it. After that, I asked if they wanted anything else. I carried copies of Bill's speeches on education, AIDS, health care, the economy. They wanted it? I had it.

I met more people in that one year than I had in all my other years put together. Every major newsperson in the country came and sat at my dining room table to interview me. I went on the talk shows. I remember the morning I did the "Today" show—I had thought of Katie Couric as flippant before I actually met her and was prepared to pounce if I detected the slightest sign of that with me. I don't recall what had given me that impression, but I couldn't abide anybody being flippant—especially about something as important as electing my son President. The moment I sat down for the interview, though, I fell in love with her. She was so nice, she treated me with such respect, that I just couldn't help it. And I thought, *I wish some of these media people who're prejudging Bill and Hillary could just get to know them. They would change their minds, just like I did with Katie Couric.*

I did meet some bona fide jerks, of course. Once I was in Las Vegas with Lynda Dixon, who was Bill's secretary when he was governor and now helps run his Arkansas office. When you're campaigning in Las Vegas, you need to take a little time to rest and rejuvenate, and that's how I happened to be placing a little wager one day at the Sportsbook in the Mirage Hotel. The man taking bets asked where I was from. When I told him, he cackled. "Home of Slick Willie," he said. I won't repeat what I said to the man, but here's one bet you can take to the bank: In the future, whenever he hears the words *Slick Willie,* chills will run down his spine.

Along with Dick, Lynda Dixon became my constant traveling companion during the campaign—afterwards, too, for that matter—and I knew right away that she and I were well matched. One of her jobs was to keep an eye on me, to keep me from wandering off and getting into fights with rude casino employees. Slot machines are mighty attractive, however. One night Lynda and I were playing slots a few feet away from each other. She recalls that she looked over at me and there I was, pouring money into the machine. Then her machine started paying off—every time she pulled the lever, quarters flowed into the tray and washed over onto the floor at her feet. She looked up to see if I had noticed . . . and I was nowhere to be found. *Oh, my God,* she thought, *Virginia's disappeared.* Suddenly she had a moral dilemma on her hands.

In a flash, Lynda says, the answer came to her: *Virginia wouldn't want me to leave a winning slot.* She was absolutely right. She told others to look for me while she stayed and played until the machine stopped paying. When she finally came upstairs, I was fast asleep in my bed.

You have to celebrate life, not brood about death. Life isn't neat, life isn't orderly. Too many people seem to think life is the tablecloth, instead of the messy feast that's spread out on it. They want to keep the cloth clean and pressed and tucked safely in a drawer. That's not life. Done right, life leaves stains. That's why I don't judge Bill Blythe for the things I found out about him. That's why I feel sorrow, not hatred, for Roger Clinton. That's why I love my mother, even though many a day she made me feel like murdering her. Heck, that's why I even feel warmth for Buddy Klugh. He may've set out to do me harm, or maybe that was all in my mind. But I *know* I did him harm. Suing him is probably my biggest regret in life.

Why focus on regrets, though?

I've always gotten a chuckle out of people thinking there's something heroic about my ability to find some joy in every day. What's heroic about that? There's plenty to find joy in—my sons, my work, my friends. If there's nothing else to laugh about, then I'll laugh at how miserable I am. My friends are that way, too. They all have stains on their tablecloths, but that doesn't keep them from coming back to the table. I like that. It's called resilience.

Bill told a friend recently that he's always been more obsessive than I—than his brother, too, for that matter—but that during the presidential campaign he consciously thought of my life and tried to draw strength from it. That makes me very proud. "She knew," he said, "that almost no matter what happened, the sun would come up the next morning. During those really tough days in the campaign I would think about how so many of Mother's difficulties had gone on for years and years. In my case, the voters would simply make up their minds and everything would be resolved with the election, so I might as well get up each day and do my best and do what I believed in and try to have a good time."

I didn't let Bill know exactly how serious my cancer was until months after the election was over, and even then I was reluctant. Linda Bloodworth-Thomason had been calling me and talking about an experimental treatment in Colorado that she and Harry had heard about. They had met a woman in California whose breast cancer had responded remarkably well to this treatment, and they wanted me to go investigate it. Harry had also called Bill and urged him to try to get me to go. The treatment involved removing and freezing your white blood cells and then keeping you in a clean room for a month—during which time they bombarded you with chemotherapy. Once your red blood was up to par, they reinjected the white cells. The whole process took six weeks.

Harry Thomason's mother had died of cancer, so he and Linda were acutely aware of the nuances of the disease, and they were concerned about me. Plus, of course, since Roger worked for them, they lived with his worry every day. Linda had called the doctor in Colorado—a woman named Elizabeth Shpall—and asked to bring someone for an interview. She didn't say who it was. I talked with Dr. Westbrook, and he knew Dr. Shpall's work. He thought it was worth a trip. So did Bill. I told Linda and Harry I would do it—providing that neither of my sons would be told the seriousness of my cancer.

It was March 1993. Harry flew his plane to Little Rock and picked up Dick and me. Lynda Dixon went with us, as did Harry's brother Danny, and Dick's brother and sister-in-law, Al and Nancy. When we got there, we all took a tour of the facility. Then Harry, Lynda, Dick, and I sat down with the doctor. She said things like, "You should do this soon." We all knew what she meant by that.

During a break, Harry and I happened to be standing together in a corridor. Nobody else was around. "You heard her," Harry said. "I want you to do this."

Harry Thomason is a wonderful man. He and Linda care so much, and have done so much, for my family. Because they care, they want me to explore every last possibility for staying alive. To my mind, though, living and staying alive are two different things. At my age, with my cancer as bad as it was, I didn't want to leave my home and friends and go sit in a pristine room in Colorado for six weeks.

I smiled at Harry to let him know how much I appreciate him. "You tell my boys I'm doing fine," I said.

I'm convinced that that's exactly what he did. Still, soon after the Colorado trip, Bill got suspicious that maybe I wasn't as healthy as I'd been saying, and I finally decided it was time for him to know. I suggested that he call Dr. Webb and Dr. Westbrook for a heart-to-heart talk. To them, I said, "It's all right. Go ahead and tell him."

There was nothing duplicitous about my not telling Bill and Roger this news earlier—news they couldn't do a thing in the world about. Roger would be devastated, I knew. And I had wanted Bill to focus on getting elected. Once he *was* elected, I wanted him to focus on getting his administration off on the right foot.

To be honest, there was also a bit of selfishness involved in my determination to keep my condition secret. Once Bill and Roger found out, all my friends would hear, and then the media would get wind of it, and then *everybody* would know. Next thing I knew, I wouldn't be able to walk into a room without people blubbering all over me, dropping tears on my clothes, smudging my makeup. Who needs it? I prefer to laugh, not cry. I prefer to celebrate life, not stand around waiting for the grim reaper to show up. That's how I've lived for nearly seventy years, and I don't intend to stop now.

As a matter of fact, soon after Bill was elected, I did something that gave me as much joy as anything I've done in my entire life. Most of us in the Birthday Club had made our reservations for the inaugural as far back as August. I don't mean we'd just phoned Washington and held a hotel room with a credit card; we had paid cash money. Not only that, we had persuaded others to do it, too. Three months before the election, we had more than one hundred people signed and paid so they'd be *sure* to be there when Bill became President of the United States.

Seven of the Birthday Club girls were going, but five weren't. Age, not money, was the main problem. You probably wouldn't notice, but we Birthday Clubbers have logged quite a few birthdays among us—which only means we've had an awful lot of good times. But the prospect of getting on an airplane, making connections, arranging transportation to the hotel, then fighting through crowds of people for *days*—well, it just seemed like too much for some of my friends.

I hated it, though. Oh, how I hated it. I knew they wanted to be there. How many times had I heard Estelle Blair say, "All I want out of life now is to see Bill Clinton President."

I decided I had to do everything I could to make that happen. I called Johnette and told her my plan, and we started working. We called the Inaugural Committee to get invitations. We talked with United Airlines to get tickets. We arranged cars, hotel rooms, and people to help smooth the way everywhere we'd be going.

The Birthday Club had planned a bon voyage luncheon at the Sawmill, and it promised to be some kind of party. This group had seen many a lively luncheon in its day, but this was a once-in-a-life-time occasion. But even though everyone was laughing and talking, and drinking, I sensed that a handful of the girls—the five who weren't going to be at the inaugural—were feeling a little left out.

I called for silence. I looked at all those women, those dear, dear friends who had seen me through so many hard times. There wasn't a subject that hadn't been discussed among us. Every one of us knew the intimate details of every other one's life. If they had all been there to share my pain, how could they not all be there to share my joy? I passed out the invitations and tickets to the other five, and the room burst into laughter and tears. It was a moment I cherish. *The Birthday Club was going to Washington.*

Sixteen

INAUGURAL NIGHT, January 20, 1993. Actually, it was January 21 by the time we got home. Home meaning the White House.

What a night it had been—a magical evening. Bill and Hillary had danced at the Arkansas Ball. Roger had performed at the MTV Ball. Dick and I had met Barbra Streisand, and she and I hit it off like we were old friends. At the Arkansas Ball I said I was going to go next door and hear Roger sing. "I'll go with you," she said, and we walked off hand in hand.

Valets had moved our things into the White House during the afternoon, but this was our first look at the place. To be honest with you, I was too tired to pay much attention. Dick and I were staying in the Queen's Bedroom, which is right across the hall from the Lincoln Bedroom. Harry and Linda Bloodworth-Thomason were in there that night. It's a beautiful room, all right, with a huge, ornate bed that Mary Todd Lincoln paid a piddling amount for, but it still caused a stink because the cost of the bed and a few other odds and ends ran her over the government's budget. Too bad she didn't have a Shirley Anderson to balance *her* checkbook.

The Queen's Bedroom was where Winston Churchill always stayed, and they say he used to terrorize the help by appearing at the door and walking into the hall naked. I didn't know all that on the first night, of course. That night Dick and I were ready to hit the hay. Our bed was big and canopied, and that's all I can tell you about it. Bill Clinton, on the other hand, probably knows the history of every stick of furniture in the White House. I remember one time I visited him in Texas when he was working on the McGovern campaign. He got me a room at this antique hotel right across from the Alamo. I've forgotten the name of the hotel, but it was where Teddy Roosevelt and the Rough Riders had stayed. Oh, Bill was so pleased with himself. And do you know, the room had no TV, no radio, no nothing. The mattress *had* to be the same one Teddy Roosevelt used. I knew then why they called them the Rough Riders.

While Dick was finishing in the bathroom, I lay back on the bed. Even for an old girl who's pretty much seen everything that goes on after dark, sleeping in the White House for the first time is quite a feeling. I wished my daddy could've been there to watch his grandson become President—or even to see his daughter stretched out on the Queen's bed. What a journey it had been. Lord, the hills we had climbed.

Recently, in doing this book, I've wondered why there were so many hills. Is there something about our family, some built-in need to live life as though it were a StairMaster? Then I thought, *Oh, I'm giving us too much credit for eccentricity. Maybe, behind the scenes, every family is like ours.* But Dick's family wasn't. And Hillary says her family wasn't, either—the Rodhams didn't have crises every four minutes. What, then, explains all our turbulence? I keep coming back to what my friend said about leading with my heart.

By now, you've seen ample evidence that that's true for me, and you've seen the results. It's also true for my boys. Roger leads with his heart so much that he makes me look as deliberate as a Supreme Court justice. And Bill tends to trust people until they prove untrustworthy, instead of the other way around. That's part of leading with your heart. But in Washington, where people tend to climb the ladder by stepping on other people's hands, such a trusting attitude is considered naïve. My response to that is, "If you know so much, why aren't you President?"

In Bill's line of work, however, he's had to learn—more than Roger or I—to keep his heart in check, or it would've destroyed him. Bill says he thinks that was basically the problem he had in his first term as governor—believing he knew better than anyone what Arkansas needed, and pushing ahead without consulting the voters. So he's tempered his heart, and I have to say, it doesn't seem to have hurt him career-wise. Incidentally, Bill says he's noticed, since my surgery and his campaign, that I've learned to rein in *my* heart a bit—to be able to listen to people who have a completely different viewpoint and not blast them out of the room. Lord, I've tried—for his sake, not mine. I've tried to learn to laugh at Bob Dole, instead of wasting my anger on him. But I'm *still* not there with those media people who treated Bill so shabbily during the campaign.

Roger, whom everyone in the world thinks needs to grow up—and who *has* grown up in many ways—recently told me, "Mother, I never want to lose part of the child in me. As much trouble as we had, I had a wonderful childhood, and I want to hold on to that. That makes me happy." I agree with him one hundred percent—you have to try in this life to do what makes you happy. Other people are going to try to stand in your way, but you can't let them.

Ultimately, I believe, you can't negotiate with your heart. You can agree, as Bill has, that you'll allow your head some play in order to attain what your heart seeks. And, of course, you have to have enough sense not to allow your heart to destroy you. But for all the turbulence in my life, I don't regret, not for a second, any of where my heart has led me. I've gotten to the point that you could tell me I might've handled my career differently, and I might agree with you. But actually doing anything differently if I had it to do over? I doubt it.

Heart is a word I like a lot. It's the word they use to describe racehorses who never give up, who come from behind to lead the field. Regarding heart and racehorses, somebody recently said something very nice about me. They called me "the Ruffian of First Mothers." Ruffian was a racehorse, a filly, who died in 1975 after a match race with the colt Foolish Pleasure. During the race, Ruffian snapped her leg. Even then, she kept running—*insisted* on running—until finally the jockey managed to pull her up. She didn't want to quit the race. Coming out of the anesthesia after surgery, she began to flail her legs again, as if she were trying to throw off the cast or as if she were still trying to run. Finally they had no choice but to destroy her. Today she's buried in the infield at Belmont Park, her head toward the finish line.

❧

Once, after Bill had rescued his brother and me from one of big Roger's drunken rages, he told us, "We will not live our lives in fear." We all three agreed. That night at the White House I gave a thought to the future, and I remembered that pact. I wondered what Bill's election would mean for all of us. From the relatively tame experience of his having been governor, I knew one thing for sure: None of us would ever be the same again.

Among the many things I didn't know: The very next morning, Bill would take me out and show me the *exact spot* in the Rose Garden where he had shaken hands with President John F. Kennedy.

In a matter of weeks I would have a port implanted in my chest so my chemo could be administered easier. Besides Dixie, who was with me and knew the seriousness of it, the only others I would tell would be Nancy and Johnette. Choosing public places to give them the news, I would explain that this was only for insurance, to make sure my cancer wouldn't come back. Later, when I would start needing regular transfusions of blood and platelets, Dr. Webb would do it in the privacy of his office, instead of sending me to the hospital.

Hillary and I would talk about how hard Bill was working, and I would urge her to get him to take time to enjoy all he had accomplished. One night in the middle of summer, he would call me late, crying, and tell me about Vince Foster's death. Of course, I would cry, too, about Vince. What a waste. What a brilliant man. And I would tell Bill that night, "Every man has his breaking point. We just don't know where it is." Later, when Bill would take a long vacation—something he hadn't done in years—he would make his mother happier than I'd been in a long time.

Roger's music and acting career would begin to take off, and he would meet a wonderful girl, Molly Martin, and plan to get married. Thank the Lord! For years, he hadn't been ready, and I had shuddered to think what it would be like to be married to him. Now he's ready, and he's going to be a fine husband and father. He has *so* much love in him—so much heart. Someone once said to me they guessed Bill's becoming President was about as good as it gets for a mother. "No," I said. "Hearing that Roger's getting married is every bit as sweet."

Dick and I would continue to travel, and to meet wonderful people everywhere we went. We would have drinks with Col. Tom Parker, Elvis's manager, at his Nevada home. We would get to know Dr. Elias Ghanem, Elvis's best friend, who would treat me to a spin in Elvis's Stutz automobile. Ralph Wilson, owner of the Buffalo Bills, would become dear to us both and would send his plane to fetch us to the Super Bowl and the races at Saratoga. I would pretend I didn't know women wore hats up there—I no longer owned any good ones and, at this stage of the game, didn't want to fool with buying one.

In September, just before I made another visit to the White House, Dixie would take me on an ultrasecret mission to the Little Rock airport. My doctor had told me the chemo might begin to take its toll on my hair, so Dixie and I had come to meet Christophe, the California hairdresser, who was flying in to make me a wig. We would check into a motel room near the airport where he would work on me throughout the afternoon, shaping and dyeing the wig—and leaving a perfect gray streak. Lynda Dixon would later tell me, "At least you never have to worry about another bad hair day."

In November, and then again in December, I would wear that wig to Washington to share the holidays with my family. We would spend Thanksgiving amid the brooding mountains at Camp David, and then Christmas at the White House. All of us would be there together, and we would say, over and over, "Isn't it perfect? Could it be any more perfect?" Those would be precious days indeed.

Finally, to close out the year, Dick and I would fly to Las Vegas to hear Barbra Streisand sing at the MGM Grand Hotel.

❧

All of that was in the future, though, and you can't live in the future—or the past, for that matter. Life happens in the present, and you'd better make the best of it.

At the White House, in the Queen's Bedroom, Dick hung the order form on the door so they would bring us breakfast. I brushed my teeth, got into my gown, and turned off the light. I lay there a few minutes saying a prayer of thanks for all we had endured, and asking for guidance as the journey continued.

Then I plumped my pillow and tried to sleep. Morning comes early, and there's paint to put on.

Epilogue

VIRGINIA DIED IN her sleep on January 6, 1994, and was buried two days later, on Elvis's birthday.

She was laid to rest in Hope, in the plot with her mother and father and first husband. The story of her death was the story of her life. Just as you could never not notice her entrances, you couldn't miss her exit. No church was large enough for her funeral, and Reverend John Miles says he thought about having it at the racetrack. It was held at the civic center instead. There were so many roses, her favorite flower, that the air in the vast room was gently perfumed. In attendance were U.S. senators, governors, and numerous figures from the heady worlds of sports and entertainment, including Barbra Streisand. But Virginia's friends cut across all classes, and most of the three thousand people there were just folks, the kind of people Virginia herself had come from. "Virginia," Reverend Miles said, "was an American original."

A seemingly endless caravan of cars drove on a crisp, sunny winter day the eighty miles from Hot Springs to Rose Hill Cemetery. People parked on the overpasses to pay their respects as she passed. Some of them held American flags; others had their hands placed over their hearts. At the gravesite, as at the funeral, Reverend Miles evoked a relentlessly human Virginia, and he celebrated—as she chose to do—her life, not her passing. "Let me tell you what Virginia Clinton Kelley was like," he said. "She was like a rubber ball. The harder life put her down, the higher she bounced. She didn't know what the word *quit* meant." Roger buried with her cassettes of his new recordings. Bill held the family together, as always.

She left very little unfinished business. For weeks before she died, she'd been urging Johnette Taylor to vote a new member into the Birthday Club. The woman Virginia was championing was Ruth Heffernan, whose sense of humor matched her own.

"Virginia," Johnette said, time and again, "you know we can have only twelve members." And Virginia would back off.

In mid-December, at the Club's Christmas party, Virginia sidled up to Johnette in the kitchen. "I think we ought to vote on Ruth tonight," she said.

"Virginia, I've only got twelve place settings," Johnette said.

"Don't worry about that," Virginia told her. "I'll make sure you have enough."

So they cast their ballots, and Virginia sat smiling as she watched the proceedings. When Ruth was voted in, Virginia asked Johnette her china pattern. "You'll have another by next Christmas," Virginia promised, knowing full well she wouldn't need it.

Acknowledgments

BY NOW YOU know that Virginia Kelley's life brimmed with loving friends, bitter foes, and people at every station in between. I know she would thank them all for their part in shaping her remarkable story.

As part of the process of jogging her memory, she introduced me to many of those people, without whose help this book wouldn't have been as rich and as full as I like to think it is. Dale Drake and Oren "Buddy" Grisham helped me understand the Bodcaw and Hope that Virginia was born into and grew up in. John Wilson and Dick Moore told wonderful stories about Virginia's father, and John graciously pointed out the landmarks of a bygone time. Jack and Jimmy Hendricks recalled their irreverent classmate. Dot Fenwick good-naturedly allowed her husband, Richard, to reminisce with me about his high school sweetheart. Karen Lively gave me a tour of Virginia's childhood home, and Neva McClellan and Margaret Polk recalled their neighbor on Thirteenth Street. Helen Aldrich told me where the bullet hole is. Norma Truitt Howell spun hilarious tales of her nursing-school roommate. Dr. Jim McKenzie helped recreate Virginia's early work life. Mary Nell Turner provided last-minute fact checking help. Falba and George Lively and Elaine and Wayne Johnson consistently made me welcome and allowed me a place to hang my hat between interviews.

In Hot Springs, where Virginia lived for forty years, Leonard El-lis and Inez Cline gave me the benefit of their firsthand knowledge of that town's lively past. Clay Farrar, a walking history lesson, shared his interpretations of the town's quirky personality. Janet Clinton provided insights into the Clinton family, as did Virginia (Crawford) Heath—who also regaled me with irreverent stories of the old days. Charlie and Ann Tyler recalled a friendship that spanned decades. Toni Karber's eloquent assessment of her Scully Street neighbors was a valuable addition to the book, as well as a joy to hear. Carolyn Staley helped enormously with insights into the daily life in that neighborhood. Louise and Joe Crain illumi-nated some of Virginia's darker moments, and Shirley and Sam An-derson each spent hours with me going over critical parts of the story. Dr. Walter Klugh, Jr., and Wendell Burns graciously agreed to speak about times that weren't particularly pleasant for them to recall. John Wells and his staff at the Garland County Library pointed me in the right direction on many occasions.

Many others provided key facts and insights into Virginia's life, among them Rosalie Brown, Ola Mae (Blythe) Hall, Ann Grigsby, Elmer Greenlee, Shirleen Adcock, Reverend John Miles, Steve Eng-strom, Dr. Martin Eisele, Mauria Aspell, Dr. Timothy Webb, Dr. Kent Westbrook, Bill and Grace Seaveno, Harry and Linda Blood-worth-Thomason, Carolyn Huber, Dr. Robert Humphreys, Dr. Ray-mond Peeples, and, as a group, the Birthday Club—Nancy Adkins, Estelle Blair, Clover Gibson, Edith Irons, Virginia Livingston, Berenice Lyon, Marge Mitchell, Elizabeth Ross, Dixie Seba, Johnette Taylor, and Edie West—who welcomed me to their luncheons and clamored to have their pictures taken with me, giving me some small insight into what it must've felt like to be Elvis. With all due respect to the entire Club, however, I must single out the contributions of Dixie, who had a clubhouse seat for much of Virginia's race; of Nancy, who shared so many intimate moments with her; and of Johnette, who became her dear and trusted friend.

Beyond the realm of pure reporting, many others helped make this book a reality. Virginia's attorney, Robert Barnett, knew from the beginning what a compelling story this could be. So, fortunately, did my own agent, Joseph Vallely, who encouraged me all the way. Alice Mayhew and Becky Saletan of Simon & Schuster—the editors Virginia persisted in calling "the producers in New York"—took a chance on us, and during the day-to-day work Becky consistently demonstrated a cool head and a sure hand, two qualities every writer hopes to find in his editor. Lynda Dixon, of the Arkansas Clinton office, smoothed the way at every turn, and even snapped pictures of Virginia and me in the White House. Betty O'Pry, who transcribed scores of tapes, gave me enthusiastic feedback along the way. The Klein Shore Resort's Dave and Lu Richards, hosts during my stint in Hot Springs, put themselves out to make me comfortable. I hope they like the resulting book enough to place it on every bedside table, right next to the Gideon Bible.

I owe special thanks to Rose Crane, who was not only part of the story but was instrumental in my getting to tell it; and to Ann Tyler, who crystallized everything for me by saying, "Virginia leads with her heart."

My wife, Beth, who bore the brunt of my highs and lows, was a constant inspiration to someone writing about a strong woman. I'm grateful to her for believing in me and this story—and to Blair, Bret, David, and Matt for their encouragement, love, and understanding.

My regard for Virginia's family is boundless. I thank Dick Kelley for his patience when I monopolized his wife, and for his help in so many ways during the preparation of this book. First Lady Hillary Rodham Clinton graciously made time for me during one of her most hectic first weeks in the White House. Roger Clinton sat with me for hours, laughing, crying, revisiting even the most difficult chapters of his life. President Bill Clinton first sat for an interview, then took over the reviewing for Virginia after she died. I was astonished by the time and attention he gave to me while he ran the country, and touched by the love with which he dispatched this final duty as a son.

I told Virginia once, early on, how glad I was that we didn't have to go through chapter after chapter of dull stuff to get to the lively parts. She laughed. She loved the process of reliving her life almost as much as she loved living it. I'll be forever grateful that she chose me to tell her story to.

—J.M.